T0372958

"With this book, Joanne Lara and Susan Osborne present to prepare students with autism spectrum disorder to trar ment. This interactive resource is an essential guide for te with young people to develop the necessary skills for gettɩ.ɩ ɯ ɑʋ keeping a job."

—*Doreen Granpeesheh, CEO, Center for Autism & Related Disorders (C.A.R.D.)*

* * *

"Being part of Autism Works Now!® makes me feel more positive about the future and possibilities to help me reach my goals. That makes me happy."

—*Zachary Inkeles, author and artist, candidate, Autism Works Now!®, Los Angeles*

* * *

"With an estimated 50,000 kids with autism reaching adulthood in the U.S. each year, thank you Joanne Lara and Susan Osborne for creating an innovative program to prepare these young adults for employment. With the help of Autism Works Now!® they will reach their full potential and lead independent, productive, meaningful lives. Hallelujah!"

—*Yudi Bennett, Co-Founder, Foothill Autism Alliance & Exceptional Minds*

* * *

"This is a much-needed resource that fills the gap in this country's school-to-job programs!"

—*Areva Martin Esq., President, Special Needs Network, USA*

* * *

"This book develops the skill set that our youth need in order to compete in the job force with dignity!"

—*Matt Asner, parent, advocate, VP at the Autism Society of America*

* * *

"Joanne Lara and Susan Osborne have created a comprehensive work readiness program with Autism Works Now!® and their Workplace Readiness Workshop. With this valuable resource, many individuals with autism will gain the ability to get and keep meaningful employment so they can go on to become valued members of their communities."

—*Alex Plank, autism advocate and Founder, WrongPlanet.net*

* * *

"Joanne Lara and Susan Osborne raise thought-provoking questions and unpack ideas relating to how we are preparing our students on the autism spectrum for life after high school. With this book, they lay the groundwork for educators and families who are helping young people develop the tools they need to work and live in the 21st century."

—*Dan Phillips, Transition Specialist, Culver City Unified School District*

* * *

"This is the quintessential handbook for every teenager and young adult on the autism spectrum and their employers! It's a fabulous guide to making certain individuals with autism are successful in their careers and job search. Exactly what we need right now."

—*Susan Corwin, parent/advocate*

* * *

"Joanne Lara and Susan Osborne have created an innovative pre-employment program for young people with ASD that is like no other. My son, Christopher, had the good fortune to join Joanne and Susan's group Autism Works Now!® over a year ago and has gleaned extremely important and useful pre-employment skills and information that he was not privy to during his high school years. This book gives me hope that future generations of students leaving high school will be better prepared to meet the 'real world' of employment and social challenges that have previously been ignored by our educational system."

—*Pat Grayson-DeJong, M.Ed., parent and retired Autism Specialist, LAUSD*

Teaching Pre-Employment Skills
from Age 14 to Young Adulthood

of related interest

The Autism-Friendly Guide to Self-Employment
Robyn Steward
ISBN 978 1 78775 532 1
eISBN 978 1 78775 533 8

Just the Job!
A Light-Hearted Guide to Office Life for the Autistic Employee
Debby Elley and Maura Campbell, Tim Stringer
Illustrated by Tim Stringer
ISBN 978 1 80501 248 1
eISBN 978 1 80501 249 8

An Employer's Guide to Managing Professionals on the Autism Spectrum
Marcia Scheiner (Integrate Autism Employment Advisors) with Joan Bogden, Meron Philo
ISBN 978 1 78592 745 4
eISBN 978 1 78450 513 4

TEACHING PRE-EMPLOYMENT SKILLS FROM AGE 14 TO YOUNG ADULTHOOD

The Autism Works Now!® Method.
Revised and Expanded Second Edition

Susan Osborne and Joanne Lara

Foreword by Temple Grandin

Jessica Kingsley Publishers
London and Philadelphia

This edition first published in Great Britain in 2025 by Jessica Kingsley Publishers
An imprint of John Murray Press

First edition published in 2017 by Jessica Kingsley Publishers

2

Copyright © Susan Osborne and Joanne Lara 2025
Foreword copyright © Temple Grandin 2017

The right of Susan Osborne and Joanne Lara to be identified as the Author of the Work has
been asserted by them in accordance with the Copyright, Designs and Patents Act 1988.

All rights reserved. No part of this publication may be reproduced, stored in
a retrieval system, or transmitted, in any form or by any means without the
prior written permission of the publisher, nor be otherwise circulated in any
form of binding or cover other than that in which it is published and without
a similar condition being imposed on the subsequent purchaser.

A CIP catalogue record for this title is available from the
British Library and the Library of Congress

ISBN 978 1 80501 267 2
eISBN 978 1 80501 268 9

Printed and bound in Great Britain by CPI Group

Jessica Kingsley Publishers' policy is to use papers that are natural, renewable and recyclable
products and made from wood grown in sustainable forests. The logging and manufacturing
processes are expected to conform to the environmental regulations of the country of origin.

Jessica Kingsley Publishers
Carmelite House
50 Victoria Embankment
London EC4Y 0DZ

www.jkp.com

John Murray Press
Part of Hodder & Stoughton Ltd
An Hachette Company

The authorised representative in the EEA is Hachette Ireland, 8 Castlecourt Centre,
Castleknock Road, Castleknock, Dublin 15, D15 YF6A, Ireland.

To Joanne who was taken from us too soon. You were a beacon of light and a fierce advocate for everyone you supported, mentored and loved. You will be remembered by all for your warm essence, sharp wit, and brilliant intelligence. I miss you every day, but your memory will live on in my heart forever.

To my son Jacob, who has taught me more about love, patience, and hope than I ever thought possible, and my husband, Doug, who has always provided me with unconditional love and support. Susan Osborne

Contents

Part II: WORKSHOP STRUCTURE

Foreword (from First Edition)

TEMPLE GRANDIN

My sense of identity is based on my work. This is normal for lots of people. Many common surnames are also the names of occupations such as Cook, Mason, Carpenter, Smith, and Farmer. Being successful in my career has given my life purpose. I am what I do. When I was in my twenties, I wrote an article on how I made a slow transition from the world of school to the world of work. Too often, students with autism spectrum disorder (ASD) graduate from either high school or college and they have had no work experience. Work experiences should begin long before graduation. Students need to learn how to do tasks that are on a schedule. To be most effective, the tasks should be outside the immediate family. I want to emphasize that it is never too late to start. If you are working with either a high school or college graduate who has not learned basic skills, he or she needs to be gradually eased away from the couch or the video games.

Mother knew how to stretch me, to try new things that were just outside my comfort zone. When I was 13, she set up a sewing job with a freelance seamstress. Today, middle school-age children could walk dogs for the neighbors or do volunteer work at a church or community center. At age 15, after I had gone to a boarding school, they gave me the job of cleaning the horse stalls. I loved the responsibility of taking care of the horses. The following year I spent the summer at my aunt's ranch. Mother gave me a choice; I could go for a week or stay all summer. It is important to give the child some choices and I ended up loving the ranch and staying all summer. In college, I did two internships. One was at a research lab where I ran experiments. During this summer, I had to live in a rental house with another person. The other was at a summer program for children with autism and I lived in a rented room. These internships were set up through local contacts. Throughout both college and graduate school I was doing freelance sign painting and learning more work skills.

During my career as a designer of livestock facilities, I have worked with many skilled trades people who were either dyslexic, had attention deficit hyperactivity disorder (ADHD) or were mildly autistic. They got and kept their jobs because they had both paper routes as young children and vocational training in high school. Parents need to work to get vocational skills back into the schools. Today there is a huge shortage of mechanics, welders, electricians, and plumbers. I worked with skilled trades people when they were building big Cargill and Tyson beef plants. These were big complex projects that required lots of brains to build them. My job was to design the cattle-handling facilities. I have designed the front end of every Cargill beef plant in North America. A vocational career may be appropriate for about 25 percent of students with ASD or ADHD. Do not get hung up on labels. In fully verbal students, the diagnoses may switch back and forth between ASD and ADHD.

Parents and teachers must avoid the tendency to over protect and shelter students with ASD. I am seeing too many middle school and teenage students who have not learned basic skills such as shopping, because the parents always did it for them. This book has lots of advice on practical skills that students with ASD need to be taught. One basic skill that should be drilled in before graduation from high school is how to be on time. When I went to college, I had many social difficulties but being on time was not one of my problems. Once I had decided that I was going to study, I was on time. My science teacher gave me a reason to be motivated to study. Studying became important when I had the goal of becoming a scientist.

In conclusion, students must be willing to walk through the door of opportunity, when it opens. When I was asked to design the first dip vat (these are the projects that were shown in the HBO movie) I said yes because I wanted to prove that I was not stupid and that I could do it.

Sell yourself with a portfolio

I sold my design services by showing off a portfolio of drawings and photos of completed projects. The work must be neatly presented and you should always have it available on your phone or tablet. You never know where you might meet a person who can give you a job. Do not put too much stuff in your portfolio. You want a 30-second WOW when you show it to somebody. You need to target your audience. For example, do not show weird science fiction drawings when you are selling graphics to a client who has a car dealership. During interviews, I would open up my portfolio to sell freelance jobs. I learned to sell my work instead of myself. Having a career has given my life meaning. People a long time ago named their families after the names of occupations because it helped define who they were.

Preface

JOANNE LARA

Let's get out there and show people what people with autism can do!

Temple Grandin, Temple Grandin and Friends:
Autism Works Now! Event 2015 Los Angeles

Human resource interviewers should look beyond the resumes of individuals with autism spectrum disorder (ASD) when searching for qualified employees. With 50,000 autistic individuals each year graduating from United States high schools, with approximately an 80 percent unemployment rate, this population has proven to excel in "splintered skill sets," meaning they are often good at one job. For instance, they can excel in jobs such as computer graphics, computer science, coding, analytical calculations, patterns and inconsistencies, all highly regarded job qualifications that are specific to many employers' needs. The ASD population wants to work, to be self-sufficient, and to be contributing members of their communities.

If we begin to see job qualifications through different lenses, if we can reward individuals on the autism spectrum who have special talents in given areas, we can put these youths to work in detailed types of jobs (in which they excel), and it's a win-win for everyone. Their problem is they often can't get through an interview because of their social difficulties, so human resource interviewers need to ferret out their interests and the kinds of things they not only like to do but can do beyond most expectations.

Prior to 1975, very few people were even thinking about how students with autism could be brought into the workforce because they were not allowed to be educated in the public schools in most states in the United States before that time. The truth is that—after 19 years of the institution of the Individual Transition Plan (ITP) being enacted as part of the Individuals with Disabilities Education Act (IDEA) 1997 (with 2004 subsequent transition revisions)—only a small percentage of our autistic youth are transitioning into jobs in their communities, even though the primary goal of the ITP was and still is to assist our students in transitioning into the workforce after high school (WebAIM n.d.).

The IDEA 1997 and 2004 transition revisions were both well-meaning and direct descendants from the 1975 Public Law 94-142, but the program must be viewed skeptically because less than 20 percent of all graduating students on the autism spectrum have jobs—even inconsequential jobs after high school—and the percentages become worse over time. Most stay home and end up staying there, which is a human tragedy, however it's viewed. Sadly, this is known as the "school-to-couch" model.

While unemployment for our autistic youth hovers at 80 percent, it is time that educators present a truthful idea of what the student is capable of doing for a living, which means that we need to re-think the way that we are interpreting the ITP transitioning process, jobs, social opportunities in the community, and living accommodations after high school in this country. One of the reasons for these dismal statistics may be the lack of realism on the part of the Individualized Education Program (IEP) team members when they focus on the *person-centered planning* element, which concentrates on where the student's skill set in core reading and math actually lies and how this skill set can equate to a paying job. (A IEP is a legal document that is developed for each public-school child in special education).

IEP team members and parents often want to honor a student's dreams, but when the student's case history indicates that they will not be a scientist, an astronaut, a veterinarian, or have a three-picture deal at Warner Brothers Studio in Hollywood, we must ask ourselves if we are really serving the student by entertaining these fantasy dreams of improbable employment. In reality, the student may be able to work in a vet's office or neighborhood shelter, gain employment on the Warner Brothers' lot, or work in a hospital, but, to best serve the student, the IEP team needs to be addressing practical job options for students who are not going to transition into a four-year college or a two-year community college. The student should be directed down a path that will give them a realistic idea of job options when they transition out of the public-school setting.

The downfall of not entertaining realistic job options early in the student's academic years is that, often, the student becomes attached to the fantasy job and the impractical idea of where they might actually fit in the job market. In the case of their vision of becoming a scientist, a vet, or an astronaut, the student can often be reluctant to want to pursue or seek jobs outside these unlikely positions, even though other jobs could better meet their skill set and lifestyle—further contributing to the existing 80 percent unemployment statistic.

For the student who wants to be a scientist, why not have them research jobs that are available in a university science department? Or companies that do medical research? Or organizations where they can still be working in their area of interest?

It is in the IEP team meetings that we need to begin to present a more realistic approach to job options for the student and help them understand where they fit into the workforce. We stand a far better chance of getting the outside community employer's and stakeholder's support to help our youth be successful if we are realistic in how the student and the team view the student's potential, weighing in on their past success in the academic institution as a barometer for their future success. In addition, we all need to understand that there is a lack of vocational education in the middle and high school setting. Vocational education used to be prevalent across the United States in all public schools. Woodworking, metalworking, car repair, bakery skills, car detailing, horticulture, and animal husbandry were courses that could be found in any high school.

The Smith-Hughes Act of 1917 was the law that first authorized federal funding for vocational education in American schools and explicitly described vocational education as "preparation for careers not requiring a bachelor's degree." Vocational education was not designed to prepare students for college. It was created to prepare the student for a job force that required a certain specific skill set.

What happened to vocational training? In the late 1990s and early 2000s, the standards and accountability movement in the school systems was taking hold. States began to write academic standards or goals for what students should learn, what wasn't critical to the learning, and what was needed or not needed to obtain funding for the educational process. In 2001, Congress passed the No Child Left Behind Act. That law required states to test their students every year to ensure that all students would be proficient in math to federal education funding. This was the beginning of the end of vocational training in this country (American RadioWorks 2014).

A majority of vocational schools didn't meet the academic faculty "highly qualified educator" requirements of the No Child Left Behind criterion. While vocational educators had the skilled labor experts to teach the skills like metalworking, woodworking, horticulture, bakery, culinary arts, car detailing, and cosmetology, the instructors who taught these courses did not have the advanced degree in that discipline to fulfill the No Child Left Behind Act's standards. So, instruction in the very skill sets that could most benefit our youth on the autism spectrum—because what they would learn in vocational training could be turned into meaningful jobs—was no longer available in public schools in the United States. This is the paradox for students in the academic school setting with an IEP. The IEP team can assess the student to identify the student's skills that are suited for a job once they graduate from high school, but the school is unable to teach them that skill set because most schools no longer offer vocational training that would provide instruction in the skill set that would best serve the student.

In addition, the vocational programs for computer science, animation, art, home economics, shop, drafting, advertising/layout/design, photography, economics, banking, and budgeting that go hand in hand with teaching independent living skills currently only exist in the moderate/severe special day programs. These programs are typically not available for less-impacted students with autism who can also benefit from vocational training if they are to live self-determined lives after high school.

What can be done?

- The ITP must be started early in the school at 14 years of age, but parents need to have a vision for their child's future beginning in kindergarten and the early elementary school years. Everyone who is a member of the child's team, including the student, needs to be creating an idea of who that student is and what their capabilities are at home, in their community and their place in the world now and in the future. We do it for our neurotypical children. Why are we not doing it for our children with autism? Because we feel guilty? Because we ourselves are not certain that indeed there is a place for them in the community? In the job force? If this is the case, then we must work harder, yell louder, make our voices heard, that we want our youth with autism to have realistic choices for employment, options for social activities and outings in the community and alternatives to the "school-to-couch" living model.

- If there is an opportunity to bring back vocational programs into public schools—even if your child isn't oriented toward vocational education—support the effort, because it will benefit thousands of individuals, whether or not they are on the autism spectrum.

- At as early a time as possible while the child is still in high school, parents will need to evaluate and consider vocational schools for their post-high-school graduates, linking their child's interests and job skill sets to what is offered in vocational schools.

- Many of the subjects that provide great jobs and incomes are taught in junior colleges, such as agriculture/plant management, cosmetology, nursing assistant/ home healthcare, computer science, automobile mechanics, and restaurant/ food services. If they don't exist in your community, consider other programs, depending on their locations. Some of the best schools in cuisine/restaurant/ food services are in junior colleges in major metropolitan areas.

- Look at specialty schools like art institutes and design schools that offer pro-grams in retail training and management, accounting, electrical, plumbing, and a host of other high-end salary possibilities.

- If the student's goal is to transition into the workforce or college, consider pro-grams that teach independent living skills like budgeting, cooking, and basic home maintenance.

Why aren't our autistic students ultimately transitioning into jobs when the ITP should work?

In 2014, only 19.3 percent of people with disabilities in the U.S. were participating in the workforce which included those that were working or seeking employment. Of those, 12.9 percent were unemployed. By contrast, 69.3 percent of people without disabilities were in the labor force and 65 percent were employed (United States Department of Labor, Bureau of Labor Statistics 2017).

In light of these dismal statistics, we need to ask ourselves what is wrong with the current education picture. We spend an enormous amount of time assessing, teaching reading and math proficiencies, and making sure that the student is prepared for life after high school, only to find that the statistics are against them.

To summarize, the options after high school for our ASD youth fall into four categories:

1. Attend a special day program in the community where they generally develop life skills, go out into the community as a crowd, and often work either independently or as a group in a supported job environment.

2. Enroll in a community two-year or four-year college program with support provided by the regional center and the university or college disability support services center.

3. Transition into a part-time or full-time job.

4. Shift to a residential program where they can gain the additional job-readiness skill sets that they can take into the community and that will, it is hoped, equate to employment.

To be federally compliant, universities must have a disabilities support services center where students register when they enroll in the college. The disabilities support services center assesses the student, and the college and the student decide what accommodations are needed for the student to be successful in the college setting. The same modifications that were available to the student when they were in high school are available, as well as additional services like a sign language interpreter, a note-taker, extended time for assignments, extended due dates for tests, and extra time to get to classes.

Typically, by this time in the student's life they have reached the age of majority, when a young person is considered to be an adult. Depending on state laws, this can happen between 18 and 21 years of age.

At this juncture in a child's life, the state may transfer to that child all (or some of) the educational rights that the parents have had up to the moment. Not all states transfer rights at age of majority.

However, a state must establish procedures for appointing the parent of a child with a disability, or, if the parent is not available, another appropriate individual, to represent the educational interests of the child throughout the period of the child's eligibility. If under state law a child has reached the age of majority and not been determined to be incompetent and is determined not to have the ability to provide informed consent with respect to their educational program, then that representative will make the decisions.

Some programs are specifically transitional, meaning they teach life skills like budgeting, transportation, living with others outside the home, and college-level preparation coursework. Attending college requires students to develop self-determination skills, self-management, self-advocacy and social skills. Some basic planning strategies for college should include the following:

- Parents should register their child with the college of their choice and provide all the required documentation for registration. To receive special accommodation as mandated by the Americans with Disabilities Act (ADA), it is important to register with the college disability services.

- Families should be familiar with ADA, which mandates the laws as to how colleges must accommodate people with disabilities.

- Additionally, parents need to know if there is a special room in the dormitory or assigned location where their child can go during sensory overloads.

- Staff responsible for the dormitory should be trained and educated on the needs of students with special needs. They must be aware of the student's mandated accommodations to help make the college experience a pleasant one.

Paul Hippolitus, as Director Emeritus of Disabled Students Program, University of California Berkeley, developed a course called C2C+ or "Bridging the gap from college to careers"—a university/community 17-lesson model that includes internships, peer and career mentoring, and placement assistance for individuals with disabilities. The course is currently offered at San Diego State University, California State University Fullerton, and University of California Berkeley, Orange County Business Leadership Network, and San Diego Business Leadership Network. The College to Career (C2C) program at West Los Angeles College is another. It supports the learning needs and employment goals for individuals with developmental and intellectual disabilities, with a strong focus on building skills leading to employment and the ability to work in an independent, integrated placement following completion of the program. More and more of these types of programs are becoming available to our students with autism across the country, filling the void that is left when they leave public school at 18 or 22 years of age and transition into a secondary education or community setting and find that they are not prepared to compete in either arena.

Introduction

What is an Individualized Transition Plan (ITP)?
Should the student be attending?

The ITP process requires that the student must be invited to the ITP meeting, because the plan should be put together to prepare the child for life. The process takes place generally at the age of 16, but some states, like California, North Carolina and Texas, begin earlier at age 14. The secondary transition planning is a federal mandate, first authorized in IDEA 1997 and reauthorized in IDEA 2004, specifying that the transition services are to begin by 16 years of age instead of the 1997 mandate, which was 14. It also included a "coordinated set of activities designed within a result-oriented process" focused on improving both academic and functional achievement of the student with a disability to facilitate movement from school into post-school life (Individuals with Disabilities Education Act Amendments 1997).

The student should be a part of the process because the transition services should be based on the individual's needs, which should also consider the student's preferences and interests. The ITP must include appropriate, measurable, post-school goals based on age-appropriate transition assessments.

Transition services should include:

- instruction—academic or vocational instruction that will assist the student in obtaining a career path

- related services—occupational therapy, behavioral therapy, speech and language therapy, along with adaptive skills

- community experiences—outings in the community (community-based instruction, or CBI)

- the development of employment and other post-school adult living objectives

- the acquisition of daily living skills (when appropriate)

- functional vocational evaluation (when appropriate).

The ITP includes more accountability on the part of the school, and it also makes it clear that the ITP is not intended to be an activity that just occurs once a year at a student's IEP meeting. Transition planning should be ongoing throughout the student's academic years, thus making key players of the parent, the educators, the service providers, and the administration in assisting the student in making a smooth transition from school to the job force and community.

The ITP helps students develop independence. The student should not only be attending their IEP/ITP meetings; they should be playing an active role in the meeting. When the IEP/ITP process and the team are looked at as being proactive, this helps the student reach their career and adult-living goals faster. Transition planning should occur near the end of middle school, when the student begins planning their high school course of study. The goal should be for all our individuals to be independent and determined to obtain and keep a meaningful job. We want to move away from everyone doing everything for our individuals with disabilities to advocacy that is self-motivated and self-driven. As the saying goes, "Give an individual a fish and you feed them for a day. Teach them to fish, and you feed them for a lifetime."

Introduction addendum
Susan Osborne, 2023

Since the publication of the first edition of this book in 2017, the employment statistics for adults with autism in the United States have improved slightly. According to the 2022 U.S. Department of Labor, they now stand at 21.3 percent of people with disabilities in the U.S., up from 19.3 in 2017. This is still a very sad statistic, especially when compared to the percentage of people without a disability. For individuals without a disability, 65.4 percent were employed and participating in the workforce (United States Department of Labor, Bureau of Labor Statistics 2023).

Examining the data more closely, the statistics get even worse:

- Across all age groups, people with a disability were much less likely to be employed than those without a disability.

- Thirty percent of workers with a disability were employed part time, compared to 16 percent for those without a disability.

- Employed individuals with a disability were more likely to be self-employed than those without a disability.

- Individuals with a disability were less likely to have completed a bachelor's degree than those without a disability. (United States Department of Labor, Bureau of Statistics 2016b)

As Joanne Lara mentioned in her preface, vocational classes have been phased out in middle and high schools in the U.S., but in California, the Department of Education does provide funding to high schools and community colleges for Career and Technical Education (CTE) which consists of a multi-year sequence of courses that provide students with the academic and technical skills, knowledge and training necessary to succeed in future careers, and skills that they will use throughout their careers.

CTE programs are organized into 15 industry sectors, and the sequence of courses within the sector are called pathways. Pathways are designed to provide students who complete all required coursework with the knowledge and skills needed to be employed in the high wage, high skilled, and high demand jobs in the regional labor market. CTE instructors are typically professionals in the field, and the CTE curriculum is focused on teaching students the professional skills that are needed to be work ready on completion of a pathway.

The 15 pathways are:

1. Agriculture and natural resources

2. Arts, media, and entertainment

3. Building and construction trades

4. Business and finance

5. Education, child development, and family services

6. Energy, environment, and utilities

7. Engineering and architecture

8. Fashion and interior design

9. Health science and medical technology

10. Hospitality, tourism, and recreation

11. Information and communication technologies

12. Manufacturing and product development

13. Marketing, sales, and services

14. Public services

15. Transportation (California Department of Education n.d.a.)

In addition to CTE programs, many high schools offer dual enrollment in community courses where the student can earn college credits while still enrolled in high school. If a student is interested in a dual enrollment class, they should check with their school counselor for more information.

Attending a college class while still in high school is a great option if the student can keep pace with the social and academic demands of a college course. But not all high school students are ready for college. This can be especially true for high school students with autism. In addition to their challenges with social communication, sensory regulation, and executive functioning, as a high school student, they might be the youngest student in class and may not be mature enough to succeed in a college level course.

If the student has an IEP or 504 plan, many of the support and services that they are receiving in high school will most likely also be needed for their dual enrollment college course. The student's IEP team will also need to answer these questions to ensure the student's success:

- Can the student handle the academic, social, and executive functioning demands of a college class?

- Are they able to communicate with the instructor if they need help with an assignment?

- Do they have the social communication skills to make positive and appropriate connections with classmates?

- Do they have the skills to stay organized, complete assignments on time, and be on time to class?

- Can they regulate their emotions and remain calm if they become stressed or frustrated?

For any student enrolled in a college level course, it is important to consider all areas where the student requires support and make sure those supports are in place as soon as the student starts attending a college or university class. These must be specific to the student's area of need, including academics, social communication, and executive functioning. If the student falls behind in their studies and does not make meaningful connections with their fellow classmates, they can become discouraged and lose motivation to continue in their studies.

AUTHOR'S REFLECTION
My son's community college experience

I know from my son's experience how challenging it can be for a student with autism to be successful in a college class. After his graduation from high school, he enrolled in a class on career exploration in our local community college. I helped him register with the college's disabilities services office, but they didn't provide much support. He did receive priority seating in the front of the class and an in-class note-taker. My son was responsible for finding the note-taker, but the one student who volunteered quit after the first class. The only person I could find as a replacement was a family friend who had no prior experience of working with individuals with autism. He was good at helping with organizational support, but he didn't know how to help my son make any social connections with his fellow students.

Since the experience was not positive, my son lost interest in continuing his studies and he's not taken another college class since. I can't say for sure that things would have been different had his first college been more successful, but I do wish my son had received the support he needed so that his college experience was more fun and enjoyable.

Part I

UNDERSTANDING THE AUTISM WORKS NOW PROGRAM

CHAPTER 1

The Importance of Work

When you meet someone at a party, usually one of the first questions asked is, "What do you do?" For most of us, what we do is what we do for work. If we like our job, it's the essence of who we are. We'll say we are architects, accountants, and auto mechanics. We are the successful chief executive of a multinational corporation or the principal of the local high school.

If we don't like our job, we usually dream of doing something we like. Especially in Los Angeles, many waiters and waitresses aspire to work in the entertainment industry. When asked the question, "What do you do?" they'll say they are an actor, writer, or filmmaker. Their identity is not as an employee of the restaurant where they work. They see themselves as successful professionals in an industry where they want to be recognized and compensated for their talents and abilities.

Of course, making money is the primary reason why most of us get a job. It gives us the financial means to provide for ourselves and our families. Our well-being is greatly improved when we can afford to pay for all our basic needs like food, lodging, shelter, and transportation and still have money left over to enjoy the things we like. We can save up for a much-needed vacation, finance the car of our dreams, and enjoy a night out at the movies watching the latest blockbuster or indie thriller.

Another reason why we work is to provide a structure to our day. It's the reason why we get out of bed in the morning and go to sleep at night at a reasonable hour. If we work in an office, we arrive at nine, go to lunch at noon, and leave at five. We look forward to our time off. Wednesday is hump day and TGIF means that it's Friday and the weekend is almost here. We use our paid time off when work is slow, and we make plans on holiday weekends to get out of town and spend time with family and friends.

But does more money make us happier?

Researchers Daniel Kahneman and Angus Deaton analyzed over 450,000 responses from a daily survey of 1000 United States residents looking at their feelings of emotional well-being and levels of happiness. They concluded that respondents with incomes under $75,000 reported lower levels of well-being and more of life's misfortunes like divorce, ill health, and feelings of loneliness. Respondents with incomes over $75,000 reported higher levels of well-being but did not report greater levels of happiness. This means that once we have enough income to cover our basic living expenses, our jobs need to have meaning for us to be happy and fulfilled in our lives (Kahneman and Deaton 2010).

What is meaningful work?

While it is important to have a job that pays us enough money to cover our bills plus a little extra, it is equally important that we feel a connection to our work. Ideally, we land a job in our field of interest with people we like for a company that values what we do. Every person has interests and values that are specific to both their field of work and the people with whom they work, so the definition of meaningful work is specific to that individual.

The area of study around the concept of meaningful work is now being examined by psychologists. Michael Steger, Professor of Psychology at Colorado State University and founder and director of the Center of Meaning and Purpose, has done research on this topic, and he concluded that meaningful work has three central components.

1. Our work must make sense. We must understand what's being asked of us and be provided with the appropriate resources to do our job.

2. Our work must fit within a larger context. We must understand the purpose of our work and how our daily tasks are connected to the mission of our company.

3. Our work must benefit some greater good (Steger 2009, p.212). We must feel that our work is making a difference in the lives of others. This can be as grand as working to save the planet or as basic as volunteering to help shelter animals.

In other words, for our work to have meaning, we must:

•   understand what we must do and how to do it

•   know how the work we do fits into the larger picture

•   see that our work creates a benefit for someone outside ourselves.

Dr. Steven Wright takes this concept even further. He proposes that if people learn about the processes within their company or institution, they're more likely to do their jobs well, understand how their work fits with what other workers are doing, and how the product of their efforts creates value. This leads to a sense of meaning, which in turn makes people better at what they do (Wright 2009).

Patrick McKnight and Todd Kashdan apply meaningful work in a larger context, pointing out that "Living in accord with one's purpose offers a person the opportunity to find a self-sustaining source of meaning through goal pursuit and goal attainment. Meaning drives the development of purpose, and once a purpose becomes developed, purpose drives meaning" (McKnight and Kashdan 2009, p.242). In other words, once a person finds meaning in their work, they find their life's purpose.

What is Ikigai? How can it be used to find meaningful employment?

Ikigai is a Japanese concept meaning 'a reason for being' and roughly translates in English to 'a reason to get out of bed in the morning.' It evolved from the basic health and wellness principles of traditional Japanese medicine. Neuroscientist Ken Mogi says that ikigai can simply be translated as "a reason to get up in the morning" or "waking up to joy."

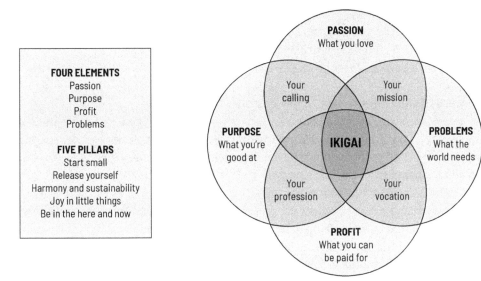

FOUR ELEMENTS
Passion
Purpose
Profit
Problems

FIVE PILLARS
Start small
Release yourself
Harmony and sustainability
Joy in little things
Be in the here and now

Figure 1.1: *Ikigai: A reason for being*

The concept of ikigai is divided into elements or "Ps":

- What you're good at: Purpose
- What can you get paid for: Profit
- What the world needs: Problems
- What you love: Passions.

Ken Mogi identifies the five central pillars of ikigai as:

- Starting small
- Releasing yourself
- Harmony and sustainability
- The joy of little things
- Being in the here and now.

Our own personal ikigai rests at the point in which our passions and talents converge with what others need and are willing to pay for. Finding our ikigai not only brings us more meaning and purpose, it also facilitates enhanced physical health and mental well-being.

Beyond a career, ikigai can also become the foundation for approaching life in a general sense. It is much like mindfulness. The key is to be present in the moment and to not get caught up in your thoughts, and looking forward to and savoring special moments as they occur. It teaches us simply to appreciate and consciously enjoy things once we have them. These can be small moments, like anticipating your morning coffee or tending to your garden, or large events, like starting a new job or planning a birthday party for your loved one (Hughes 2023).

Assessment 5a. 'Finding Your Ikigai' is included in the final chapter.

Why are friends important in a job search?

We are nowhere without friends. The essence of who we are as a civilization is based on the quality of our friendships. Without people in our lives whom we can depend on, we become separated from our communities, which leads to destructive feelings of isolation, loneliness, and depression.

School is the first place where most of us find friends. It provides us with a structured environment and a place to meet and see our friends every day. From preschool and through high school, we develop meaningful friendships through shared interests. In college, we find friends in classes based on our shared major and through campus activities. After we graduate, some of these friendships go on to last a lifetime. These friends become our colleagues, who often refer us to available jobs within our shared field.

After college, as adults, we spend most of our time at work, as the United States Bureau of Labor Statistics Time Use Graph indicates (United States Department of Labor, Bureau of Labor Statistics 2016b; see Figure 1.2). The graph tells us that work takes up the largest part of the day at 8.8 hours, followed by sleeping at 7.8 hours, then household activities, followed by leisure and sports at 2.6 hours.

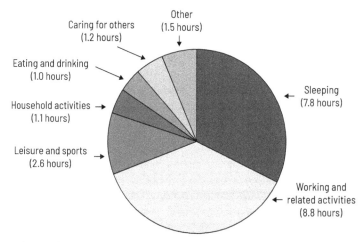

NOTE: Data include employed persons on days they worked, aged 25 to 54, who lived in households with children under 18. Data include non-holiday weekdays and are annual averages for 2015. Data include related travel for each activity.
SOURCE: Bureau of Labor Statistics, American Time Use Survey

Figure 1.2: *Time use on an average work day for employed persons aged 25–54 with children*

Since as adults we spend most of our day at work, it makes sense that this is where we find most of our friends after high school and college. Friends at work make the day more enjoyable, and they help us out when we need it. They are the people that we like to hang out with at lunch and after work, and make plans with on the weekends. Not having a job limits our opportunities to meet people that we can learn to depend on and care about.

Research shows that most jobs are secured through referrals. A report by the Federal Reserve Bank of New York concluded that between 52 percent and 58 percent of male workers under the age of 45 learned about their current job from a friend or relative. For first-time jobs, the percentage increased to between 55 percent and 67 percent. The report also stated that referred candidates were hired at a higher percentage, experienced an initial wage advantage, stayed on the job longer, and were more productive than non-referred workers (Brown, Setren, and Topa 2012).

How are individuals with autism affected in their ability to find and keep a job?

Autism Speaks, a United States advocacy organization dedicated to autism research, awareness, and outreach describes ASD as "a broad range of conditions characterized by challenges with social skills, repetitive behaviors, speech and nonverbal communication" (Autism Speaks 2024). There are no medical tests that can determine if an individual is autistic. Instead, a trained professional (usually a therapist or psychologist) uses autism-specific assessments and evaluations to make the determination of an autism diagnosis. Autism can be accompanied by comorbid medical or psychiatric conditions, which can make it difficult to develop an accurate diagnosis and an effective support plan. How much an individual is affected by their autism is specific to the individual and can vary greatly.

By far the biggest challenge for individuals with autism is the area of social communication. Communication development for children with autism happens, but differently and more slowly than it does for their non-autistic peers. Throughout their lifespan, these individuals may have difficulties reading verbal and nonverbal social cues as well as making eye contact. Individuals who are less impacted may be able to comprehend the thoughts and feelings of others, but their social responses are often perceived by others as not typical or expected.

Another big challenge for autistic individuals is their difficulty in understanding the emotional states and corresponding thoughts, intentions, and feelings of other people. This is called "Theory of Mind," a concept that was developed by researcher Simon Baron-Cohen, Professor of Developmental Psychopathology at the University of Cambridge in the United Kingdom, Director of the University's Autism Research Centre, and a Fellow of Trinity College. Baron-Cohen concluded that children with autism suffer from "mindblindness" or the inability to be able to interpret what others are feeling or thinking because of a selective impairment in mindreading, and, for these children, the world is essentially devoid of mental things (Baron-Cohen 1997).

Many individuals with autism have problems with their capacity to stay organized, complete tasks, and adapt to new ways of doing things. They tend to be good at retaining facts and pieces of information, but they may have challenges applying information to a larger context. This results in difficulties with "seeing the big picture" also known as the "gestalt." These types of skills fall under the term "executive functioning," but "executive functionings" is a more accurate description because the term covers a variety of different functions. As cited by Paula Moraine, executive functionings are a "set of mental processes that help connect experience with present action. People use it to perform activities such as planning, organizing, strategizing, paying attention to and remembering details, solving problems, and managing time and space" (Moraine 2015, p.93).

Many autistic individuals have a dysregulation in their sensory system, which can make them over- or under-responsive to elements in their environment. Their vestibular system may be affected, which affects their ability to balance, or their proprioceptive system, which affects their ability to sense where their body is in space. Because of the way that the brains of these individuals process sensory information, they may find ordinary situations overwhelming, which can cause them to withdraw from daily activities.

All the unique challenges faced by individuals with autism have a direct impact on their ability to secure and sustain meaningful employment. If a person has a hard time forming friendships, job referrals don't materialize. If they are successful in getting a job, they may behave in ways that aren't expected by their coworkers, which can interfere with their ability to form friendships and workplace alliances. If they have difficulty understanding the thoughts and feelings of their coworkers and supervisors, they will have a hard time anticipating what they are expected to do or reacting in socially appropriate ways to information that is shared with them by their coworkers. Problems with time management make it tough to get to work promptly and know when to return from break. Having challenges understanding the big picture makes it difficult to understand the importance of the job. As research has shown, understanding how to do our work, what we contribute to our workplace and how our work fits within our company's big picture is a prerequisite for us to find meaning in our work. Without this, individuals with autism can have difficulty finding their life's purpose.

What workplace supports are available for autistic individuals? How can these be implemented?

Because individuals with autism are affected in ways that are specific to each person, it is said that if you meet one autistic individual, you've met one individual with autism. Support plans must include interventions that are tailored to address each of the individual's core deficits or needs. Step-by-step instruction, or a task analysis (breakdown of a skill set with instructions for each step of the process) when learning a new skill can be beneficial. When we break down larger tasks into smaller components, we can often learn the skill faster.

A universal challenge for individuals with autism is their ability to generalize the use of acquired skills across multiple environments, meaning to replicate a skill learned in one environment in a totally new setting. For instance, mastering how to operate a scanning machine in one office building then being asked to perform the task of scanning papers in a totally different office building for a new company or organization can become problematic, with the individual not knowing which step to perform first. In this case, the skill of scanning documents needs to be re-taught in the new setting.

Teaching a skill in the classroom is the beginning, but it is usually not enough for the individual to be proficient when the skill set is required in a new setting. It needs to be practiced multiple times in a variety of community-based settings so the individual can retain what they've learned and improve on the skill over time. Teaching workplace readiness skills in a classroom setting is a good way to introduce concepts like proper workplace attire, appropriate conversation topics, and the essentials of interview preparation. With appropriate support, a facilitated meeting with a business professional or human resource director is an excellent opportunity for the individual to practice the skills that they've been taught in an actual workplace setting.

The reason why treatments for autism are effective lies in the unique structure of the brain itself. In *Autism Movement Therapy® Method: Waking Up the Brain!*, Joanne Lara tells us that:

> Our brain has the amazing natural capacity to compensate for injury or disease throughout our life. The ability to reorganize and form new connections, synapses (chemical or electrical connection points between brain cells) or create neural pathways in our nervous system is called "neuroplasticity." Though controversial, the science of neuroplasticity is based on the idea that the adult brain can improve cognition and/or restore lost mental abilities and function through regular, continual physical and mental activities. (Lara 2015, p.27)

An example of neuroplasticity in action is Gabby Giffords, the congressional member of congress from Arizona who was shot in the head during a constituent meeting in 2011. Shortly after the attack, she began simple physical and music therapy and progressed to intensive rehabilitation treatments as she improved. Due to the neuroplasticity of the brain, the activities she did in therapy enabled her brain to "rewire" and create new neuropathways around the injured areas. This is why she was able to regain her ability to walk and talk, though not to the full ability that she had prior to her brain injury (Giffords Courage to Fight Gun Violence 2023).

Neuroplasticity is the reason why individuals with autism acquire skills that don't come naturally. By practicing these skills multiple times in a variety of community-based settings, the individual's brain creates new neuropathways, and with repetition, the neuropathways get stronger until the behavior becomes the new normal. This includes many important job skills like effective problem-solving techniques, appropriate ways to socially communicate, and proactive methods of emotional self-regulation.

After the individual is placed in a job, a job coach who is knowledgeable about autism is essential for the person to be successful in keeping their job. The role of a job coach is like that of a behavioral interventionist. A behavioralist provides supports to autistic children at school, at home, and in the community to help them achieve their behavioral goals. A job coach supports the individual in the workplace so they can successfully learn what is expected of them and achieve their goal of maintaining meaningful employment. Once the individual can do their job with minimal support and has developed a positive working relationship with at least one of their coworkers, support is reduced and eventually eliminated altogether when the individual displays mastery of their learned skills. Regular job evaluations or performance reviews are an effective way to help the individual receive constructive criticism about their job performance and reflect on the areas where they can improve.

What are hard and soft job skills? How do these skills affect individuals with autism in the workplace?

Skills that are specific to a job are called hard skills and are typically acquired in college, vocational training programs, and trade schools. But workers must have skills beyond the technical knowledge required by the job. They must be good at interpersonal communication, decision-making, and problem-solving. These are called soft skills and are transferrable to any workplace. To keep a job, an employee must have the hard skills needed to get the job done and the essential soft skills required to keep the workplace running smoothly, efficiently, and without conflict. While an employer may provide training to a new employee on some job-specific hard skills, like the operation of a piece of equipment or a computer program, a new employee is expected to be soft-skills proficient as soon as they are hired.

For individuals with autism, acquiring hard skills for a job may be a relative strength due to the unique wiring of the structure of their brain which makes it easy for them to retain facts and compile information. Conversely, learning soft skills is a universal challenge for almost everyone on the autism spectrum. This means that an effective job training program for this population requires not just teaching the technical skills used in the job but also facilitated instruction of the essential soft skills to help them get along and connect with coworkers, plan and organize job responsibilities, and learn how to self-advocate in the workplace.

What more can be done to help individuals with autism succeed in the workplace?

Autism Works Now (AWN) believes that understanding leads to acceptance and once people in the workplace are aware of what autism is and the contributions that autistic individuals can make to the workplace, they will be more accepting and open to working with individuals with autism. To achieve this goal, autism awareness education should be provided to all employees, including the supervisors and coworkers who will be working directly with the individual. Through these efforts, AWN believes that the result will be workplace environments that are accepting and welcoming of the differences of all employees, not just those with autism.

Why is it important to teach workplace readiness skills to middle and high school students with autism?

As discussed earlier, to adequately support our autistic youth for a successful transition into their adult lives, ITP goals must be established at the start of middle school so that the student can be supported in creating an effective transition plan when they transition out of their high school setting. While some students might be able to obtain a university degree, other students may be better suited to attending a trade school or community college where they can learn a vocational trade. Internships and volunteer jobs with proper support provide excellent opportunities to help these students gain essential job skills, develop professional contacts, and find meaning in the work that they are doing.

How can we address the unmet needs of middle and high school students with autism and improve their ability to secure and sustain meaningful employment?

To help students accomplish their ITP goals, it is essential to start teaching vocational and pre-employment skills starting in middle school. The most effective method of training incorporates classroom instruction with authentic community-based learning opportunities so the student can put into practice the skills they've learned in an authentic work environment. For these students to be fully engaged in the learning process, we must create fun, enjoyable and safe environments where they are given an opportunity to discover the importance of what they are learning. They must be active participants in the learning process so what they are learning is truly meaningful for them.

CHAPTER 2

The Workplace Readiness Workshop

What It Is and How It Works

The Workplace Readiness Workshop was developed by AWN to provide an interactive learning environment to help individuals with autism acquire the pre-employment skills needed to secure and sustain meaningful employment.

How is the workshop structured?

The original workshop met for 28 meetings over eight months and included one field trip per month. The curriculum was designed to build on the skills that were previously acquired, but anyone creating their own workshop can tailor it to include the topics that the instructor feels would be most meaningful for their participants.

How does the workshop for middle and high school students differ from the program for adults?

The original AWN program was created for autistic adults who had already left high school. Classes met once a week, and each class lasted a little over two hours. In contrast, the length of a middle and high school class is typically 50 minutes, so it may be difficult for a class of 14–17-year-olds to stay fully engaged for a two-hour class. If you are developing a program for this population, we suggest offering classes twice a week with each class lasting no longer than one hour. The structure of class meetings is explained in more detail in Chapter 13.

Why are participants in the AWN program called candidates?

AWN believes that words are powerful, and we want our participants to view themselves as viable members of the work community. To help them envision themselves in this light, we address participants as candidates. AWN recommends that a program tailored for middle and high school students should also use the term "candidates" to address the students in their program.

What is the format of class meetings?

There are four parts to each class meeting. These are discussed in more detail in Chapter 13.

Part 1: Agenda and Introductions—length: five minutes

The agenda is reviewed and any guests visiting the class are introduced.

Part 2: Roundtable Discussion (RD)—length: one hour

In group discussions and interactive class activities, candidates learn positive communication skills, proactive stress management techniques, and techniques to create a positive self-image. Guest speakers are scheduled during RD.

RD activities and topics include:

- Sharing information about themselves

- Recalling information about their fellow candidates

- Practicing appropriate workplace conversations

- Initiating conversations

- Assessing their internal state of mind

- Practicing proactive stress management techniques

- Practicing gratitude

- Creating a stronger, more positive self-image

Part 3: Prepare and Practice (P&P)—length: one hour

Workplace topics are presented, discussed and practiced in class activities. Field trip preparation and follow up are scheduled at the start of P&P.

P&P activities include:

- Assessing candidate interests, job preferences, and work knowledge

- Mastering the apps on Google

- Learning about appropriate workplace attire

- Interview essentials

- Networking

- Expected workplace behavior

- State and federal work regulations

- Americans with Disabilities Act (ADA)

- When and how to request workplace accommodations

Part 4: Recall and Review (R&R)—length: ten minutes

The instructor uses the Class Summary Worksheet [23] to review what was covered in class and remind candidates of any assignments that need to be completed by the next class meeting.

Candidates take a quiz consisting of true/false and multiple-choice questions to further review what was covered and assess how much information they have retained.

What is planned for the last two class meetings?

The classes leading up to the end of the program are a time to review what candidates have learned and celebrate the end of the workshop. Parents and caregivers are invited to attend the last two classes.

For the penultimate class, the instructor creates a presentation with pictures from classes and field trips to highlight the positive group experiences that the class shared throughout the program.

Candidates are encouraged to share what they learned, how they'll put it all into practice, and their favorite moments. Candidates take a comprehensive exam composed of questions from past R&R quizzes. Graduation certificates are distributed and a "best of" award is given to each candidate.

Examples of "best of" awards are best attendance, most enthusiastic, best attitude, and most positive. There is no R&R scheduled in this class.

The last class is a time to relax and have fun. For the original AWN program, we met at a restaurant for dinner. For the last meeting of the original program before the Covid pandemic, we had a fun party at a bowling alley.

How does AWN use social media to highlight program activities?

For the original AWN workshop, we maintained a Facebook page and posted pictures from class assignments and field trips. We added our candidates and their parents as Facebook friends and tagged them in any pictures we posted. You may also want to set up an Instagram account or YouTube channel to post any pictures or videos shot in class and on field trips to help publicize your program. We also maintained an AWN account on Pinterest, a visual bookmarking and discovery platform, to reinforce topics that were covered in class so that candidates could access the information at any time. Susan Osborne still maintains the account, which is now titled "Susan Osborne, Autism Advocate."

Prior to the start of the Workshop, you will need to obtain a signed release from anyone who might be included in any of your pictures, granting you permission to use their likeness on social media and in any publicity materials. If anyone refuses to sign a release, you'll have to make sure they are not in any pictures that you use in promotional materials or post online. A sample photo release form is included in the last chapter in the Instructor's Materials section.

What is the format of field trips?

All field trips take place in the workplace of a local company, business, or non-profit organization. Candidates are prepped in advance of the field trip in class to review what they should wear, decide on their method of transportation to the field trip if they are not riding together as a group to the location on a school bus, and conduct internet research on the establishment or organization they will be visiting. Field trips are explained in more detail in Chapter 14.

What activity do you incorporate to encourage motivation?

To motivate candidates to complete workshop activities and assignments, we created the "Shout Out Count." A Shout Out point was awarded for good work and effort. The candidate with the most points for the month became the Shout Out Count Champ and won a $5 Starbucks™ gift card. The Shout Out Count is explained in more detail in the Instructor's Material section in the final chapter.

Are candidates required to finish any assignments outside class?

Most class assignments are completed in class, and, if a candidate can work on their own without support, we ask them to complete them outside class before the next class meeting. To help remind the candidate, we add the assignment to the candidate's Google Task and due date the day before the next class. (A great feature on Google Tasks: any due dates can be automatically added to the user's Google calendar.) We also send candidates an email at least two days prior to class to remind them of what is due and what they need to complete. If a candidate cannot finish the work on their own, they will need someone at home to support them. Chapter 10 on group and candidate requirements covers the topic of candidate support.

We refer to any outside assignments as "recommended assignments." We also have "recommended daily assignments," which are daily life skills that we want candidates to schedule each day as part of a daily routine. These are:

- checking their email once per day

- writing in their gratitude journal (explained in Chapter 8)

- meditating or practicing some form of stress management.

To help these tasks become a habit, we encourage candidates to schedule them at the same time every day. We then add them as an event to the candidate's Google calendar. If the candidate has anyone who regularly supports them, it's a good idea to share the event invitation with them so they can help remind the candidate to complete their daily routine.

Do you allow parents or caregivers to attend class with their child?

For observation of a class, we allow parents and guardians to attend with their child. Parents and guardians are also welcome to attend social events, meals scheduled after field trips, and the last two classes of the workshop. But once their child becomes a candidate in the workshop, it is strongly recommended that parents and caregivers not attend classes with their child for two reasons:

1. The goal of the workshop is for candidates to secure meaningful employment and transfer their dependence from their primary parent or caregiver to a community of friends in the workplace who accept the candidate for who they are. To practice making friends at work, we want friendships to also develop between candidates in the workshop. Depending on their relationship, a parent who attends the workshop with the child can create a barrier to the candidate creating friendships with other candidates, especially if there is friction in the relationship between the parent/caregiver and child.

2. Once the candidate has a job, a parent/caregiver does not and should not accompany their child to their workplace. The workshop is structured to replicate a workplace setting as much as possible. Since the parent/caregiver does not go to work with their child, they should also not attend workshop classes with their child.

How is this book formatted?

This AWN method book is divided into two parts:

Part 1 reviews the topics featured in Roundtable Discussions and Prepare and Practice and explains how candidates can be helped to generalize the use of the soft and hard skill sets that are taught in the workshop.

Part 2 provides information about the nuts and bolts of the AWN Workplace Readiness Workshop and how to adapt a similar program in any community. Information is included on how to create a safe learning environment, behavioral management techniques, room and equipment requirements, the structure and content of class meetings, and field trip preparation, coordination, and follow-up. The final chapter also contains a copy of all instructional documents and instructor's materials that are referenced throughout the book and explains how to organize a candidate AWN workshop binder.

Please note that all pages marked with ✳ can be downloaded at https://library.jkp.com/redeem using the code SPXLNPH for personal use with this program/me, but may not be reproduced for any other purposes without the permission of the publisher.

How does the workshop accommodate the needs of middle and high school students with autism?

The authors, Joanne Lara and Susan Osborne, have years of experience working with individuals with autism of all ages, from toddlers to adults. The workshop was created to meet the needs of adults with autism to help them acquire the skills they need to secure and sustain meaningful employment. The AWN instructional materials that were created for adults are also appropriate for middle and high school students, but there is some subject matter that is sensitive in nature (i.e. sexual harassment). If minors will be attending your workshop, it is recommended that the instructor gets the written permission of the student's parent or guardian allowing their child to participate in the class when these topics are covered. A sample parental permission form is included in the final chapter in the Instructor's Materials section.

CHAPTER 3

Matching the Job to the Individual and Filling in the Blanks

How to Assess an Individual's Interests, Skills, and Abilities
for Job Placement and Workplace Paperwork

Even the most accomplished people in the business world started working in an entry-level job. Warren Buffett, CEO of Berkshire Hathaway who has a current net worth of $140 billion (Bloomberg Billionaires Index 2024) was a paperboy. Oprah Winfrey, one of the richest, self-made women in America, worked at a corner grocery store next to her dad's barber shop. Former President Barack Obama scooped ice cream at a Baskin-Robbins.

Just like these highly successful individuals, most of us didn't view our first job as one where we would stay employed for our entire working lives. Our first job was an opportunity to make money, gain work experience, and meet new people. Our job helped us to learn many important life skills like budgeting, time management, working with others, and understanding the value of hard work. Our first job was also an important part of our transition to adulthood because it provided us with an opportunity to become a member of a community separate and apart from the family we knew growing up.

Why is it important to match an individual with autism to a job that is matched to their skills, abilities and interests?

To find purpose in our lives, we need to have a meaningful connection to the work that we do. To do this, we need to like our work and find it interesting. Our level of job satisfaction is a direct result of these two factors, and once we find satisfaction in our work, we often find our life's purpose.

Autistic individuals have the same need to feel a meaningful connection to their job and like what they do. In fact, it may be even more important to place them in jobs that are connected to their special interests. Many of these individuals are highly knowledgeable about one specific subject. This is referred to as having splintered skill sets, and this type of extreme knowledge in one specific area or reservoir of information can be an asset for companies and organizations that specialize in work related to that topic. This hyper-focus can also present challenges in job placements. Because their level of interest can be very intensified, it may be difficult for the individual to be motivated to do something they don't like or that falls outside their area of interest.

How do you determine an individual's skills, abilities, and interests?

Assessments are the best way to identify what the individual likes to do and the types of jobs that would be a good match for their skills, abilities, and interests. In the Workplace Readiness Workshop, we use several assessments to get an understanding of who the candidate is and the type of work that would be meaningful to them.

Beginning in middle school, students need to be assessed to determine the types of jobs that would be a good match for their natural talents. It's also essential that they be counseled on which classes to enroll in until the end of high school so that they can work towards achieving the career and vocational goals in their IEPs.

An overview of the assessments used by AWN is included below and a copy of each assessment is included in Chapter 15. There are many more assessment tools available so incorporate any that you think will work best in meeting the needs of the individuals that you are supporting or have enrolled in your program.

Plan to complete all assessments during the four class meetings to establish each candidate's baseline work knowledge, skill sets, and types of jobs that each would be best suited to. Due to time constraints, some assignments may need to be completed outside class; some students, depending on their abilities, may need one-on-one support to help complete their assignments by the next class meeting.

AWN Assessments

General Work Knowledge [1]

Purpose: To assess each candidate's baseline general work knowledge and experience, technical abilities, and general knowledge about the interview process.

How to interpret the results: Used to determine a candidate's baseline work knowledge and the amount and type of support a candidate may require to stay focused in class and on field trips.

Google Knowledge [2]

Purpose: Used to determine a candidate's proficiency in the use of Google and its many free apps, including Gmail, Drive, Contacts, Calendar, Maps, and Tasks.

How to interpret the results: Used to determine each candidate's area of proficiency using the free apps on Google that we use in class.

Interests Inventory [3]

Purpose: Used to identify a candidate's top interests, leisure activities, and things they like to do for extended periods of time. It is used to identify common interests among candidates in the group.

How to interpret the results: This assessment will identify the interests of each candidate and help candidates identify which interests they share with other members of the group.

Potential Job Worksheet [4]

Purpose: Used to help candidates identify the types of places they'd like to work and to consider places they already visit to shop or spend time.

How to interpret the results: Information is used for future assignments, for informational interviews or a potential organization to visit for a field trip.

Preferred Workplace Profile [5]

Purpose: Used to identify a candidate's preferred workplace environment and desired workplace characteristics.

How to interpret the results: Used to identify the types of workplace environments that are suited to each candidate and determine the focus of the candidate's job search for appropriate job placements.

Ikigai Worksheet: Finding Your Purpose [5a]

Purpose: Used to identify your ikigai.

How to interpret the results: Used to identify a job that brings your life meaning and purpose.

Work Smarts—Using Multiple Intelligences to Make Better Career Choices [6]

This is ideal for use as an occupational exploration and career development tool. It can also have value in workforce programs looking for a holistic way to assess an individual's occupational interests as well as their potential strengths as an employee.

Based on Howard Gardner's (1991) Theory of Multiple Intelligences, this assessment identifies eight distinct intelligences and learning styles. This theory has emerged from recent cognitive research and documents the extent to which students possess different kinds of minds and therefore learn, remember, perform, and understand in different ways.

The Theory of Multiple Intelligences breaks down into the following eight distinct learning styles:

PEOPLE SMART: INTRAPERSONAL INTELLIGENCE

People who are strong in this area are good at empathizing with others, person-to-person communication, and working in groups. They are skilled at helping others achieve their goals through motivation, teaching, training, counseling, mentoring, and guiding. They typically have many friends, empathy for others, and are street smart. They are best taught through group activities, seminars, and dialogues and learn best through interaction. They benefit from using tools like telephones, audio conferencing, video conferencing, writing, computer conferencing, and email.

SELF-SMART: INTRAPERSONAL INTELLIGENCE

People who are strong in this area can quickly and easily access and understand feelings, motives, and ideas. They are good at looking inside themselves and overcoming their weaknesses and capitalizing on their strengths. They use information about themselves to make effective decisions. They can understand their own interests, are in tune with their feelings, and tend to shy away from others. They have wisdom, intuition, and motivation as well as a strong will, confidence, and opinions. They can be taught through independent study and introspection and benefit from using tools like books, creative materials, and diaries. They are the most independent of the learners.

LOGIC SMART OR LOGICAL MATHEMATICAL INTELLIGENCE

People with strong logic and mathematical skills like reasoning and calculating. They think conceptually and abstractly and can see and explore patterns and relationships. They can perform inductive and deductive thinking and reasoning as well as having the ability to understand patterns and relationships. They like to experiment, solve puzzles, and ask cosmic questions. They need to learn and form concepts before they can deal with details. They are good at solving complex analytical problems and experimenting using scientific principles. They are skilled at recognizing and manipulating abstract patterns and relationships and performing mathematical calculations. They are best taught using logic games, investigations, and mysteries.

PICTURE SMART OR SPATIAL INTELLIGENCE

People strong in this area think in terms of physical space. They are very aware of their environments. They like to draw, do jigsaw puzzles, read maps, and daydream. They like to visualize objects and create mental pictures and images. They are strong at seeing and mentally manipulating forms or objects in their mind. They are skilled at creating visual representations of the world, often visualizing the product then working to create that product. They can be taught through drawings and verbal and physical imagery. They benefit from using tools like models, graphics, charts, photographs, drawings, 3D modeling, video, video conferencing, television, multimedia, and texts with pictures/charts/graphs.

BODY SMART OR BODILY-KINESTHETIC INTELLIGENCE

People who are strong in this area like to use their body and have a keen sense of body awareness. They like movement, making and touching things. They like to control the physical motion of their own body using fine and gross motor skills. They are good at using their hands to solve problems, create products, or convey emotions and ideas. They are skilled at both physical activities such as sports and fine-motor activities such as arts and crafts. They communicate well through body language and are best taught through physical activity, hands-on learning, acting out, and role playing.

WORD SMART: LINGUISTIC INTELLIGENCE

Individuals who are strong in this area like to use words effectively. They have highly developed auditory skills and often think in words. They like reading, playing word games, and creating poetry or stories. They have a strong ability to use language through writing and speaking. They are good at using language to convey information as well as to convince, excite, and persuade people. They are skilled at activities that involve reading, writing, listening, and talking. They can best be taught by encouraging them to say and see words, read books, and using computers, games, books, tape recorders, and lectures.

MUSIC SMART: MUSICAL INTELLIGENCE

People who are strong in this area have a sensitivity to rhythm, sounds, and tones. They love music and have a good sense of musical pitch. They like to sing, play musical instruments, and write and compose music. They think in sounds, rhythms, and tonal patterns. They may study better with music in the background. They can be taught by turning lessons into lyrics, speaking rhythmically, and tapping out time using musical instruments.

NATURE SMART: NATURALIST INTELLIGENCE

People who are strong in this area like the outdoors and have an ability to understand and work effectively in nature and the natural world. They have a strong appreciation for the environment and respect for the beauty of nature. They typically are interested in plants, animals, the environment, and other natural resources. They tend to choose activities such as hiking, camping, hunting, star gazing, swimming, and scuba diving as hobbies (Liptak and Allen 2009).

How to interpret the results: The areas of intelligence where candidates score highest will be a good indicator of the types of jobs and workplace environments where they are best suited. This can be especially helpful for candidates who don't yet have an idea of the type of work they want to do or companies where they'd like to work.

Where to purchase: Work Smarts is a product of JIST Publishing and can be ordered online. JIST has a full selection of other career exploration products including assessments, videos, workbooks, and books that can also be adapted for use in the workshop.

What online resources are available to supplement instruction?

The **California Career Resource Network** from the California Department of Education's California Career Resource Network (CalCRN) provides career development information and resources to support the development of critical career self-management skills necessary for success in today's world of work. Included in its resources are lesson plans and training videos from grade levels five to 12 (California Department of Education 2023).

The **California Career Zone** is available from CalCRN and is designed to help job seekers learn more about the world of work and how to be successful in it. It is extremely user friendly, easy to use, and a great resource for instructors, who can serve as the administrator of the site. Instructors can assign lessons on a variety of topics including career exploration, interest assessments, skills profile, creating a resume, and setting goals. There is no cost to access the site (California Department of Education n.d.b.).

Available from the U.S. Bureau of Labor Statistics, the *Occupational Outlook Handbook* (United States Department of Labor, Bureau of Statistics 2015) is a comprehensive list of occupations in hundreds of industries with job pay ranges, work experience requirements, and prospective employment outlooks.

How do you use a candidate's preferences in exploring possible job options?

Almost all autistic individuals have a clear idea of what they like, and their interests can be used to match them to potential jobs. For instance, many of our candidates enjoyed anime so a job at a retail comic bookstore might be their preference. Some individuals liked movies, so a job at a local movie theatre would match their interests. If the individual likes fashion, an internship with a retail clothing store might be a good fit. But a job that requires frequent contact with the public may be too stressful or over-stimulating. A better fit would be as a stock or inventory clerk, any job that has a slower pace and a more predictable work environment. As the candidate shows mastery in these beginning roles, they can be gradually introduced to jobs with more responsibility and interaction with customers. We also use the ikigai concept to gauge if the job meets the four Ps: *purpose* (what you are good at), *profit* (what you can get paid for), *problems* (what the world needs), and *passion* (what you love).

What workplace paperwork is covered in the workshop?

To help candidates understand the documents and paperwork that are required before starting a new job, we review the following information.

Social Security number

To help candidates understand the importance of a Social Security number, they need to be instructed of its purpose and reason for keeping the number confidential. Prior to the start of the workshop, check with the candidate's parent or caregiver to confirm that the candidate has a Social Security number.

WHAT IT IS

A Social Security number is a nine-digit number that is issued to everyone by the U.S. government. The government uses this number to keep track of an individual's lifetime earnings and number of years worked. When an individual retires or if ever needs to receive Social Security disability income, the government uses the information about the individual's contributions to determine benefit eligibility and to calculate payments.

Social Security numbers are required any time a person files a state or federal tax return or applies for any of the following:

- U.S. passport
- loans
- line of credit
- driver's license
- public assistance.

IMPORTANCE OF CONFIDENTIALITY
A social security number should always be kept confidential and used as infrequently as possible. It should not be carried around unless it is for a specific purpose, like filling out employment paperwork for a new job. The card should always be stored in a safe place at home or in a safe deposit box at a bank. If a card is lost or stolen, the individual will need to apply for a new one from the Social Security Administration.

Employment application [7]
A copy of an AWN employment application is included for candidates to practice filling out.

W-4 [8]
A form W-4 is used by an employer to determine how much federal income tax should be withheld from an employee's paycheck. The IRS recommends that employees submit a new W-4 tax form each year, or any time their personal or financial situation changes.

I-9 [9]
A form I-9 is issued by the Department of Homeland Security to verify that a person is legally authorized to work in the United States. All U.S. employers must have all employees complete a form I-9 on being hired. Verification of their employment status requires an employee to present documents that confirm they are eligible to work in the United States. The most common documents used for verification are a state issued driver's license or ID and a U.S.-issued Social Security card. A U.S.-issued passport is also common.

Resume
For an individual with little or no work experience, the best choice is a simple one-page chronological resume that highlights any paid or volunteer work experience, diplomas or certificates received by the student, and their special skills and talents. In lieu of work experience, middle and high school students should also highlight any scholastic awards and community service projects. A resume template [10] is included in the final chapter.

Portfolios

If a student is creative or artistic, a portfolio of their work is essential in demonstrating to employers what they can do. If the student is technologically savvy, a website can be created to display their artwork and musical compositions. The social media site, Pinterest, is also an excellent resource to display a student's artwork and talents.

CHAPTER 4

Getting Organized with Google

Using Google's Free Apps to Stay Organized,
on Time, and in Communication

The process of finding a job requires many essential life skills, particularly in areas of planning and preparation. To be successful in finding a job, you need to know how to locate a job opening, get to your interview on time, dress appropriately, and make a good impression. As discussed in Chapter 1, these skills fall under the term "executive functioning," and these are weak for many individuals with autism.

Once hired, many employers expect their workers to be familiar with, or be willing to be trained in, the use of business software like *Word*, *Excel*, and *PowerPoint*. While not all jobs require the use of a computer, candidates with experience with any of these programs can improve their chances of getting hired as well as increase their earning potential.

How do you help candidates improve their executive functioning skills?

In the Workplace Readiness Workshop, we use Google for its many free apps to help our candidates improve their skills in time management, task completion, and email communication. They also learn how to store important personal information and workshop materials using Google's cloud service. Google also has its own versions of the business software programs *Word*, *Excel*, and *PowerPoint* which we use to create our workshop materials and help our candidates create their resume and other documents. Using a feature on Google called "share," we're able to give our candidates immediate online access to any information presented in class. Since all information is stored in the cloud, candidates have access to it at any time and any place using a computer, smartphone, or device with a wifi connection.

What are the various Google apps used in the Workplace Readiness Workshop?

Google is one of the biggest brands in the world and its search engine is the one of the most popular and widely used—it covers 91 percent of the worldwide search engine market. But Google is not just a search engine. There are many free products and services available from Google that are excellent for support in time management, locating addresses, finding directions, estimating time travel, and professional email communication.

Below is a list of Google apps that we use most often in the workshop and what executive functions are incorporated with their use.

Google's search engine

Google's search engine is an essential tool for students, opening a world of knowledge about any topic imaginable. By middle school, most students are extremely experienced at conducting internet research and accessing the web, and almost all students are familiar with Google. In the workshop, we utilize the search engine to prepare for field trips by researching the background of the company and the individual that we will be meeting. We also use it to help candidates research job opportunities at companies in their community where they may want to apply.

HOW GMAIL SEARCH ENGINE IS INCORPORATED INTO THE WORKSHOP

- To conduct internet research for upcoming field trips and job searches.

- To research the backgrounds of the field trip hosts that candidates will be meeting and companies where they have interviews.

- To identify available job opportunities.

WORK-RELATED EXECUTIVE FUNCTIONS THAT ARE SUPPORTED

- Researching, retrieving, and organizing information.

Gmail

Gmail is the most popular free email service, used by both individuals and companies around the world. A Gmail account also gives its user access to a free cloud server as well as other apps that are helpful in strengthening executive functioning skills. A user must be a minimum of 13 years old to open a Google/Gmail account.

If a candidate already has a Gmail address and it is appropriate for use in a business setting, we encourage them to keep using it. Some of our candidates already have Gmail with usernames from their youth (e.g. PennielovesPooh), so we help create a username that is more appropriate for use in a business context. All candidates should have an appropriate email address by the second class meeting.

Any candidate that does not have a Gmail account should create one on their own before the start of the workshop or they can be supported in class 1 to create their account. Class activities on using Gmail include reviewing its most useful features, helping with setting up their Gmail and Google accounts, and resetting a password.

HOW DO YOU CHOOSE AN EMAIL ADDRESS FOR A CANDIDATE?

The best choice for an email address contains the candidate's first and last name: jonathansmith@gmail.com or jonathan.smith@gmail.com.

If the candidate's first and last name combined is over 12 letters, we use the candidate's first initial and last name: jsmith@gmail.com.

If neither of these email names is available, we use the candidate's first name (or first initial) and last name followed by one, two, or three numbers, whichever is available using the least amount of numbers, for example: jsmith1@gmail.com or jsmith12@gmail.com (if jsmith1 not available) or jsmith123@gmail.com (if jsmith12 not available).

HOW GMAIL IS INCORPORATED INTO THE WORKSHOP

- To send emails to candidates, parents, and caregivers about upcoming events.

- By candidates to write thank you emails to field trip hosts.

- With Google Drive to send emails to candidates with links to workshop materials.

WORK-RELATED EXECUTIVE FUNCTIONS THAT ARE SUPPORTED

- Composing professional email correspondence.

- Reviewing emails for spelling and grammar errors.

- Reviewing workshop information to reinforce concepts taught in class.

Maps

Maps lets users view any part of the world in an aerial view or at street level. Maps also has a feature that provides directions to and from an address and travel time between the two destinations.

HOW MAPS IS INCORPORATED INTO THE WORKSHOP

- To find the locations where upcoming field trips and interviews will take place.

- To help candidates estimate time travel for upcoming field trips.

WORK-RELATED EXECUTIVE FUNCTIONS THAT ARE SUPPORTED

- Finding an address.

- Planning how to arrive to a location on time.

- Estimating time travel.

Contacts

Contacts allows users to store important contact information of friends and business associates. There is a Google contact worksheet [17.4] included in the final chapter.

HOW CONTACTS IS INCORPORATED INTO THE WORKSHOP

- To store contact information for workshop instructors and fellow candidates.

- To store information from business cards collected from field trip hosts and when meeting a professional in person.

WORK-RELATED EXECUTIVE FUNCTIONS THAT ARE SUPPORTED

- Organizing and storing important information for personal and professional contact.

Calendar

Calendar is an electronic calendar that allows users to input events with detailed information including a location or address which links directly to Google Maps. The event can also be shared with anyone via email, but a word of advice: don't send a Gmail Calendar invitation to a non-Gmail user. We experienced an incompatibility issue with non-Gmail users, and the Calendar email invitation that the person receives will have an incorrect date and time. This is confusing for both you and the invitee and it will require some time on your part to correct. Instead of a Calendar invitation, send an email to the person with the specifics of the meeting.

HOW CALENDAR IS INCORPORATED INTO THE WORKSHOP

- To help candidates to remember workshop events and field trips.

- Synced to candidate's smartphones or tablets so they can access their calendar at any time in the community.

WORK-RELATED EXECUTIVE FUNCTIONS THAT ARE SUPPORTED

- Time and calendar maintenance.

Tasks

Tasks allows users to create to-do lists of ongoing tasks and projects. Tasks also has a feature that allows users to assign a project due date that automatically syncs and displays on the user's Google Calendar. We use Tasks to remind candidates of assignment due dates and upcoming events.

HOW TASKS IS INCORPORATED INTO THE WORKSHOP

- To help candidates keep track of any workshop assignments or project due dates.

WORK-RELATED EXECUTIVE FUNCTIONS THAT ARE SUPPORTED

- Planning and completing projects.

Drive

Drive offers a free cloud storage service and its own versions of Microsoft's software programs *Word*, *Excel*, and *PowerPoint*. Drive allows users to name documents and create folders to store information.

Some of our candidates are already familiar with creating *Word* documents, but not as many have experience with spreadsheets or presentations. If a candidate is interested in individualized instruction in any of these programs, community colleges and adult schools are usually good resources for low-cost options.

We use Drive to create all our workshop materials. We also use another program called *Forms* to create our five-question session review quiz that each candidate completes at the end of each classroom meeting.

HOW DRIVE IS INCORPORATED INTO THE WORKSHOP

- To share workshop materials with candidates.

- To help candidates create and store important documents (e.g. resumes or social security cards).

WORK-RELATED EXECUTIVE FUNCTIONS THAT ARE SUPPORTED

- Organization and creation of important documents.

WORK-RELATED EXECUTIVE FUNCTIONS THAT ARE SUPPORTED

- Sharing information about oneself.

- Finding common interests with others (Biswal 2022).

YouTube

With over one billion people visiting each month, YouTube is one of the most popular websites in the world. So, it is no surprise that without exception, all our candidates know and regularly watch videos on YouTube. With millions of videos posted on the site from people all over the world, YouTube is an incredible resource of information on any subject you can imagine. On October 9, 2006, Google purchased YouTube for $1.65 billion (Google 2006).

HOW YOUTUBE IS INCORPORATED INTO THE WORKSHOP

If you are searching for a video to reinforce a topic, YouTube is a great resource. It is also very popular with our candidates. After several classes, when candidates are better acquainted, we ask candidates to share their favorite YouTube video as an assignment in RD. The video was limited to no longer than three minutes and had to be appropriate viewing for all ages. Candidates were asked to send an email with the link to their video to the instructor at least two days before class to allow the instructor to view the video. The instructor then emailed the candidate to let them know if it was approved. In class, candidates introduced the clip and shared why they liked it. Depending on the size of your class, this assignment may happen over the next several class meetings.

CHAPTER 5

Dress for Success

Knowing What to Wear to Make a Favorable Impression

For better or worse, we will always be judged by the way we look and the clothes that we wear, so our appearance is an important part of the image we present. First impressions are extremely powerful, and our attire speaks volumes about who we are, the type of work we do, and the lifestyle we lead. And, when we dress sharply, we feel better about ourselves. This helps to boost our self-confidence, which radiates an image of self-worth and self-respect (Devine 2015).

Why is it important to discuss dressing well on the job?

When we go to work, it is essential that we match what we wear to the company culture. If we work in the legal or financial industries, we wear a suit to meet the expectations of our boss and clients and to match our attire to what our coworkers are wearing. If we work in a creative field like tech, advertising, or fashion, our clothing choices are more individualized and expected to be an expression of our own personal style. Dressing for the job is the first step to fitting in at work, and, to maintain a positive professional image, it's essential that we stick to the style conventions of the culture of the company for which we work.

How important is dress for a job interview?

In an interview, your goal is to sell yourself as the best match for the job by answering the interviewer's question, "Why should I hire you?" Dressing well for an interview in a style that matches the company's culture shows that you know how to fit in and are a good match for the organization. If you wear clothes that are ill-fitting, in disrepair, or don't match what everyone else in the company is wearing, you'll most likely be disqualified for the position before you even get to speak, no matter if you are the most qualified candidate and come highly recommended with glowing references.

How do you teach the concept of matching attire to the culture of the company?

Community-based field trips provide candidates with an opportunity to meet face to face with potential employers at their place of business. These visits help our candidates put into practice the skills they're learning in the classroom, which are the skills they need to learn in preparation for an actual interview.

In class, we spend a good deal of time discussing what each candidate will wear, and if they don't have something appropriate, we help them develop a plan to go shopping to purchase what they will need. We then follow up our discussion with an email to the candidate's parent or caregiver to make sure the candidate can get the help they need to purchase their interview outfit. To further remind candidates of the time and date of their shopping trip, we create and share a Google Calendar event that appears on the candidate's calendar. If a candidate needs help from their parent or caregiver, we contact them to let them know.

If any candidates need to purchase interview clothing, a field trip to a discount store like TJ Maxx®, Target®, or Ross Dress for Less® are good, low-cost options. The ideal time to schedule the field trip is the month when Dress for Success is that month's topic.

How do you teach the importance of wearing clothes that fit properly?

Knowing your correct body measurements is the key to finding clothes that fit well. It's helpful when trying on clothing in a store's fitting room and a necessary part of ordering clothing from an online retailer. To help our candidates understand what size they are in the different types of work clothing, we have created measurement worksheets for both men and women [18.1 and 18.2] where we record their information. We then compare these to the **Men's and Women's Size Chart** [18.3] to help candidates identify their correct clothing sizes.

How do you teach dress variations within a company's culture?

There are occasions where there are variations in the workplace dress code expectations, and it's important to teach candidates what these variations are. The worksheet **Variations in Workplace Attire** [18.4] summarizes these topics.

Casual Fridays

In companies with a more conservative style of dress, some have a policy called "casual Friday" where the dress code is relaxed but still professional. It doesn't mean to dress very casually, so candidates need to understand that it's never alright to wear flip flops, gym clothes, or graphic tee shirts to work.

Staff and client meetings

Usually, the same attire worn to the office is appropriate for meetings, but candidates may want to learn that they'll make the best impression when they look their best. For these situations, they may want to put more effort into their clothing choices and pick an outfit that they think looks best on them and makes them feel confident.

Social events

Candidates need to learn that their clothing selections for events outside the office need to match what is typically worn at similar events. If the event is a company picnic at a park, jeans, a polo shirt and tennis shoes would be acceptable. If the event is the annual company holiday party at an upscale restaurant, men will be expected to wear a business suit or a nice-fitting sports jacket with slacks, and women a business-appropriate dress or suit. As is true for typical workplace attire, all candidates' clothing worn to company social outings needs to be clean and in good repair.

Halloween

Some companies celebrate Halloween where employees wear costumes or dress up. Any costume worn to work must be appropriate and comfortable to wear. A mask should not be worn to work, even if it is part of the costume.

How do you reinforce the topic of dressing for the workplace?

Our presentation, **Can I Wear This to Work?** shows the differences between formal versus less formal workplace attire and the style of dress suited for various industries. A template of the presentation is included in the final chapter in the Instructor's Materials section. To help reinforce the topic of appropriate workplace attire, we created an activity with a worksheet called **Shopping Online at Old Navy**® [18.5]. This is a class activity where candidates visit the Old Navy® website and choose a shirt, pants, shoes and jacket that would be appropriate to wear to an interview for a barista job at Starbucks®. Candidates copy the link to each item and share with the class what's in their shopping cart.

CHAPTER 6

Interview Essentials

What to Do Before, During, and After an Interview

A job interview is a stressful situation for almost everyone. If you're lucky, you've been referred to the job by someone who has spoken highly of your career attributes and stellar work ethic. If you applied for the job through the company's website or answered an advert posted on Craigslist, you may not know with whom you'll be interviewing or how many other people are also interviewing for the job. From start to finish, the entire job search experience is filled with waiting and anticipation, but planning and preparation can help make the process go more smoothly with a better chance of success in landing your dream job.

The main goal in any job interview is to convince the hiring manager that you are the best choice for the job and a good fit for the organization. To get the job, you must make a positive impression on the interviewer, which means wearing the right clothes, asking insightful questions, and presenting a positive self-image. But none of this happens by chance. It requires planning and preparation on the part of interviewees to increase their chance of getting the job.

What are the biggest fears people have about job interviews?

LaSalle Network, a staffing and recruiting firm headquartered in Chicago, surveyed nearly 1600 people regarding their feelings about job interviews. Not surprisingly, 81 percent of the respondents reported that they got nervous before an interview, and they listed their top fears as saying the wrong thing (50%), making a bad impression (44%), being unable to sell themselves (36%), and being unprepared (28%).

As Tom Gimble, LaSalle Network Founder and CEO, said:

Being nervous for a job interview is a result of being underprepared. Feeling "perfectly" prepared isn't enough. People who study the statistics of their favorite sports team know who the coaches are, the wins vs losses for their favorite teams, and their team's ranking. People need to take the same approach when going for a job. Nearly all their fears listed in our study are preventable depending on how long a candidate prepares. Preparation trumps nerves. (LaSalle 2015)

What are the key steps in preparing for an interview?

On monthly field trips, candidates meet with professionals at their workplace and practice the essential interview skills they've learned in class. In preparation, candidates conduct online research, are assigned questions, instructed on what to wear, determine time travel, and decide on their method of transportation to and from the location if transportation is not being provided. After the field trip, during the next class meeting at the start of Prepare and Practice, the first activity is an email composed by the group thanking the field trip host for their time and expressing appreciation for what they learned. This experience is an excellent opportunity for candidates to generalize the skills they've learned about writing a follow-up email after a job interview. A sample of a group email is included in Chapter 14.

Below is a list of executive functioning skill sets taught in conjunction with our field trips.

Time management

To help candidates understand the concept of time management, AWN created a **Time Management Worksheet** [19.1.1] that includes everything that needs to be completed to be on time for an appointment.

One concept we continually stress is the importance of arriving at least 15 minutes early. To emphasize this point, we use a quote by the great football coach, Vince Lombardi: "If you are five minutes early to an appointment, you are ten minutes late." This 15-minute rule is used for all field trips to put into practice this concept.

Research

To highlight the importance of research in preparation for an interview, the group conducts a Google search in class on the company and the person at the organization who will be hosting the group. This research includes looking at the company's website and reading information about the organization or anything written by the field trip host. At least two days prior to the field trip, the instructor sends an email to candidates with links to the information and the assignment of reviewing the material on their own outside class. The practice of checking their Gmail account each day is something that many of our candidates need to be reminded about, so this exercise serves twofold: to get our candidates into the habit of checking their email each day and practicing online research in preparation for an interview.

Create and assign questions

Instructors conduct their own research on the company, create a list of questions and assign each candidate at least one question to ask during the field trip. Candidates are encouraged to come up with their own questions, but we've found that on-the-spot thinking is a challenge for almost all of them. Preparing the questions in advance and assigning one to each candidate is a good way to help them learn the types of questions that are good to ask during an interview. For each field trip, instructors take notes, transcribe information on a Google Doc, and share the information with each candidate. This document serves as a resource of questions that candidates can use in their own future interviews.

AUTHOR'S REFLECTION
The importance of assigning questions
On the very first AWN field trip to Fox Studios, 12 candidates attended and were given a list of 15 questions to ask of the field trip host. No questions were assigned—each candidate was allowed to choose any question on the list. When candidates were given time to ask a question, there was silence. Not one candidate spoke. For all future field trips, each candidate was assigned at least one question to ask during the field trip.

A good night's sleep and a healthy breakfast or lunch
To be their best for the meeting, we encourage candidates to get a good night's sleep and have a healthy breakfast or lunch prior to going on the field trip. While the topic of nutrition is not something we go into detail about during class instruction, we have a "healthy eating" board on Susan Osborne's Pinterest page that provides information on how to maintain a well-balanced diet and incorporate a regular exercise routine into their daily schedule.

Turn your phone off
Nothing can spoil a great meeting more than having a phone ring in the middle of the conversation. We tell our candidates to turn their phone off as soon as they arrive at the field trip location to avoid this mistake.

Stay calm and relaxed
Meeting new people in an unfamiliar environment can be stressful for many people. For individuals with autism who have challenges with social communication, it can be especially stressful. In class, we practice using various stress management techniques like mindful breathing; this is explained in more detail in Chapter 8. If the meeting is something that causes anxiety for a candidate, we suggest practicing stress management techniques prior to arriving at the field trip location. For an actual interview, we recommend that candidates discretely practice stress management while they are waiting to meet with their interviewer.

Be positive, smile, and use good manners
Smiling and saying please and thank you are essential to making a good impression. We tell candidates that when they smile, it comes through in their voice so they should practice this when asking our field trip host a question.

Use a firm handshake

During class, we practice our handshakes so candidates know what an appropriate handshake should feel like: not too firm or loose with a steady grip. It should be noted that since the onset of Covid, some people are reluctant to shake hands. Candidates are instructed to follow the lead of the interviewer and only shake hands if the interviewer extends their hand first.

Get a business card

AWN instructors ask for the host's business card, and this is shared with candidates during the next class meeting to add to their Google Contacts. But, for workshop-arranged field trips, candidates need to get approval from an instructor before contacting the field trip host. The reason why is explained in more detail in Chapter 14 on field trips.

Send a thank you note

All candidates are advised to follow up every meeting or interview with a thank you email or written note no later than two days afterwards. For the first meeting after a field trip at the start of Prepare and Practice, we compose a group thank you email that we send to our host. By composing the email as a group, we're able to model the appropriate format of a thank you business email. A sample thank you email is included in Chapter 14.

Is there any additional information that is covered in the workshop during Interview Essentials?

Field trips provide the best opportunity for our candidates to put into practice what they've learned in class, but there is more information about interviews that we do not have an opportunity to practice.

Listed below is the information that isn't a part of field trip preparation but is covered in class.

Practice your introduction

To help alleviate the stress associated with an interview, we encourage candidates to practice what they will say when they first meet the company receptionist and when they meet their interviewer. Besides practicing these introductions in class, we encourage our candidates to practice their greetings in front of a mirror so they can see how they appear to others. They are also encouraged to practice their greetings with a trusted adult or friend for their feedback and constructive criticism.

Create a resume

If a candidate doesn't have a resume, we help them create one on Google Docs using the **Resume Worksheet** [10.2]. By the sixth class, all candidates should have created their resume as a group exercise in class.

Create an elevator pitch

An elevator pitch is a 20-second commercial about yourself that quickly and effectively conveys who you are, what you can do, and what value you can bring to an organization. It is useful to use during networking events or in an interview when you are asked the question "Tell me about yourself." To help candidates draft their own elevator pitch, we created the **Elevator Pitch Overview** [19.4.1] and **Elevator Pitch Worksheet** [19.4.2]. After they complete a draft of their pitch, they recite it for the group, who provide constructive feedback on what the candidate did well and anything that needs improvement.

Rehearse answers to commonly asked questions

Candidates are given a list of ten commonly asked interview questions, and we use a class activity to help them practice their answers in class.

Listen to the interviewer's questions

We tell our candidates never to assume anything during an interview. If they don't understand the question, they should ask for an explanation or an example of what the interviewer is thinking. If they don't know the answer to a question, they should not make up an answer or say something that isn't true. Instead, they should admit that they don't know the answer and offer to get back to the interviewer with an answer after the interview.

Know what to say

Being polite and pleasant during an interview is a must, but equally important is knowing what to say and what not to say. This includes:

- never saying anything negative about a former job, coworkers, or supervisors

- using appropriate language and never swearing or using slang

- speaking about their strengths and transferable skills

- discussing experience or skills that are directly related to the job position and not bringing attention to a lack of experience

- speaking about how they will benefit the organization and not how the job will benefit them.

Follow up

If a candidate has not heard from the employer by their decision date, we recommend that candidates call to follow up the day after the decision date. If they reach the person's voice mail, we advise candidates to leave a brief message and to include their phone number.

What activities are used to help candidates generalize information on interview preparation?

To help candidates retain the information they've learned in class, AWN created several worksheets [19.1] to help with understanding interview preparation.

- The **Interview Prep Checklist** outlines the important steps of what to do several days before the interview, what to do during the interview, and how to follow up after the interview. This worksheet is used in conjunction with the **Time Management Worksheet** to help candidates with their time management skills so they arrive to their interview on time.

- The **Day/Night Before Checklist** provides a comprehensive list of tasks to complete before going to bed the night before an interview.

- The **Transportation Checklist** reviews the candidate's method of transportation to an interview and the tasks required for each one.

- The **Interview Reflection Worksheet** helps candidates improve for their next interview. Candidates can reflect on their performance so they can understand what they did well or focus on any areas for improvement in their next interview.

Mock interviews

Using the AWN **Ambassador Job Description** [19.6] as a reference, candidates participate in a mock interview with the instructor. The interview should last about five minutes, and you may substitute the job description for any that you would like to use. The interview should take place in an area away from the class to help the candidate being interviewed feel more comfortable and relaxed. Students not participating in the interview can use the time to complete any unfinished work or conduct internet research on a potential job. After the interview is completed, the group views the video and provides constructive criticism on what the candidate did well and areas where the candidate could improve. It is important that the class view the video the day that the interview happened, so, depending on the class size, mock interviews may take place over the next several classes.

What is a professional and personal reference?

A *professional reference* is a recommendation from a person who can vouch for your job qualifications and work experience. Typically, this is a former supervisor, employer, or coworker who can speak about your work ethic and past job performance. A *personal reference*, also known as a character reference, is an individual who can vouch for your character and abilities. If you are a high school student or recent graduate with limited work experience, character references can provide insight into who you are as a person and your capacities specific to the position (Doyle 2021a, 2021b, 2021c).

The worksheet **Personal and Professional References** [19.5] provides an explanation of both and outlines the process of finding a reference and how to ask someone to be a reference. As a class activity, candidates identify potential personal and professional references.

CHAPTER 7

Landing a Job

Where to Look, Networking, and Creating a Professional Online Presence

The saying "You can never have too many friends" is never more true than when it comes to work. As discussed in Chapter 1, a recommendation from a friend or relative is a key factor in having success in finding a job. Once hired, having friends at our job plays a large part in our level of job satisfaction and a big reason why we stay.

Networking is an important part of any successful job search. Face-to-face meetings with local business owners are a good way to increase your network of professional contacts and your chances for potential job referrals. Job fairs and Chamber of Commerce mixers are excellent places to make new business contacts. Since these events are geared for adult professionals, middle and high school students should be cleared in advance with the event organizer and attend these events as a group. For students, it's essential that the group have enough adult chaperones to adequately supervise them until the event ends and the students have gone home.

Another important element of a job search is maintaining a professional social media presence. As a way of highlighting relevant work skills, abilities, and experience, a well-written profile posted on the right social media sites can serve as an effective marketing tool when seeking employment. Many employers routinely review social media sites of a prospective employee when making hiring decisions, so it's important for job seekers to know what's appropriate to post and what not to post on these sites. Some have age restrictions, with most requiring users to be a minimum age of 13.

The use of social media by middle and high school students with autism can have many benefits, but it's essential that they are taught how to use it safely and responsibly. Adult supervision in the use of social media for all students needs to be ongoing. Independent use of social media should be allowed only after a student has shown that they are mature enough to use it responsibly.

How do you teach networking as part of the job search process?

Looking for a job is one of the hardest jobs there is and takes a lot of planning, perseverance, and persistence. It's important to know which companies in your area are hiring and what jobs are available. To know the right people that can refer you to these potential jobs, it's essential to understand how to network to increase the number of your professional contacts.

The following are the ways we recommend to our candidates to help them develop and expand the contacts within their professional network. Candidates should be accompanied to any meetings by a support person to provide help as needed. If a meeting does not go as planned, candidates will need to reflect on the experience to come up with ideas on how they can be more successful in their next meeting. For candidates of all ages, including middle and high school students, it is recommended that a parent or primary caregiver not be the person providing this support. The activity should be used to help candidates practice their independent work-related life skills. The opportunity to practice these skills independently is lost if the person providing the support is the candidate's primary caregiver.

Talk to the people you know

Because teachers, counselors, and most parents are employed and have their own network of professional contacts, they are an excellent source of referrals for future jobs. To start this process, we help candidates complete a **Google Contact Spreadsheet** [17.4] listing the names of all the adults they know, their occupations, and their contact information. We also include the names of any friends that are employed. We then help them develop a daily and weekly plan of how they will outreach to these contacts. This schedule is then added to the candidate's Google Task list and a due date is assigned which automatically syncs with the candidate's Google Calendar. In preparation for the meeting, we help our candidates develop their "elevator pitch" so they can quickly communicate the type of job they want and ways they can benefit a future employer. Finally, we help our candidates choose who will be helping them to attend the meeting.

Volunteering

Not only is volunteering a good way of giving back to your community, it is also a great way to improve work skills and increase your network of professional contacts. Any work experience, paid or unpaid, looks good on a resume because it shows an employer that the individual has a commitment to work. Even though volunteers do not usually get paid, any volunteer experience can and should be viewed as a way of improving a student's job skills and as a stepping stone to a paying job with additional responsibilities. As Temple Grandin says, the job must be outside the home and have a set schedule.

The best places to start looking for volunteer opportunities are organizations whose missions match the student's likes and passions. Many schools have requirements for service-learning hours, and a school's career center is a good place for recommendations of available volunteer opportunities. If the experience is a success, students should continue in the position since longevity in any job, either paid or unpaid, looks good to a potential employer.

More information on the activity Finding a Volunteer Job is included at the end of this chapter.

Internships and temp jobs

Internships provide excellent opportunities to enter the job market and are well suited for middle or high school students if appropriate on-the-job support is provided. Locating an internship uses the same process as finding a volunteer opportunity. Most internships are unpaid, but some come with a stipend. Temp jobs are an option for adult candidates or students after they leave high school and provide an opportunity to work on a temporary basis before committing to a permanent job. Temp placements are usually handled by an agency who oversees all payroll responsibilities. Unlike permanent employment, temp positions and internships usually last for a specific amount of time.

Attend networking events

Job fairs and Chamber of Commerce mixers are excellent places for candidates to connect with professionals in their field of interest and business owners in their community. Preparing for these events is the same as preparing for an interview, which provides an opportunity for candidates to put into practice the skills they learned in Interview Essentials. To find information about upcoming job fairs, do a "job fair" Google search for your area. For Chamber of Commerce events in your community, check their website for dates and times of their upcoming mixers and social activities. For middle and high school students, it's important to check in advance with the event organizer for any age restrictions. Students should attend the event as a group with enough adult chaperones to adequately supervise all students until the event's conclusion and each one has got a ride home.

Don't forget the business card

Candidates are reminded to always get a business card from any professional they meet and to write down the date and place where the meeting happened. After the meeting, candidates record the information from the business cards into their Google Contacts. One exception about business cards: candidates should not be independently contacting any professionals they may meet through the workshop or while attending workshop activities. This includes field hosts, anyone they meet at a workshop social event, and guest speakers. If a candidate wants to contact the individual they've met through the workshop outside class, establish a rule that they must get prior approval from the instructor before making contact with the professional. This is important because candidates may not fully understand socially appropriate boundaries, so communicating this rule in advance will prevent any misunderstandings in the future.

AUTHOR'S REFLECTION
The importance of setting boundaries

At a gala fundraising event organized by author Joanne Lara, one of our workshop candidates attended as a volunteer. At the event, he met a Hollywood casting agent who was also Joanne's good friend. Because he thought the gala was an opportunity to network, he asked for the agent's business card then contacted her several times to set up a meeting. The agent told Joanne she did not want to speak to him, so I called the young man to let him know why his actions weren't appropriate. I know he wasn't happy, and I'm not sure he fully understood why he shouldn't have made contact. Luckily, because the agent was Joanne's friend, there were no negative consequences for our program, but if the young man had been aware of why he needed to check with his instructors before contacting any professionals he'd meet during workshop activities, the situation could have been prevented.

Candidates should also have their own business card

A simple and nicely designed business card is a must have when attending networking events, job fairs, or any time you want to give out your contact information to someone. A standard business card size is 2" x 3.5".

Below is the essential information for candidates to include on a business card:

- First and last name

- Cell number

- Email address

- LinkedIn profile

- Social media accounts.

Candidates should also include this information if applicable:

- School or university

- Major

- Personal blog or YouTube channel.

An affordable and convenient option to purchase business cards is Vistaprint®. There are hundreds of options from which to choose, and 100 cards can be purchased for under $20 (plus shipping) and delivered in the mail to the candidate's home (Founder n.d.).

What is an informational interview? How can candidates use it in their job search?

An informational interview is an informal conversation with someone working in an area of interest who will give information and advice about their career. It is not a job interview, but it is an opportunity to gain knowledge about a specific career path and occupation. The benefits of informational interviewing include getting first-hand, relevant information about an industry or a specific job, receiving tips on how to prepare and enter a given career, learning what it is like to work for a specific organization, and initiating contact with business professionals (University of California Berkeley, Career Center 2016).

To help candidates understand the steps required to schedule and conduct an informational interview, AWN has created four worksheets [19.1] that review what to do before, during, and after the interview. Our monthly field trips provide our candidates with an excellent opportunity to practice conducting an informational interview in an authentic community-based workplace (Moore Norman Technology Center Employment Guide n.d.). For class instruction, we use two videos from YouTuber Home at 30 (2019a, 2019b) from his series Career Tips for College Students.

How do you help candidates create a professional online presence?

Employers routinely review the social media sites of a prospective employee when making hiring decisions. For this reason, it is important that an individual's online profile contains accurate and updated information about relevant job skills and experience that is consistent across all social media sites.

A candidate's social media presence is not just their personal outlet, it is also their brand that identifies who they are, what they like to do, and the type of activities they like to participate in. For this important reason, candidates must never post anything that could be viewed negatively by a potential employer. To keep track of what others are posting about them, they should adjust their privacy settings so they can control what's posted about them on social media. Rosemary Haefner, Vice President of Human Resources at CareerBuilder, says:

> It's important for job seekers to remember that much of what they post on the Internet—and in some cases what others post about them—can be found by potential employers, and that can affect their chances of getting hired down the road. Job seekers need to stay vigilant and pay attention to privacy updates on all of their social networking accounts so they know what information about them is out there for others to see. Take control of your web presence by limiting who can post to your profile and monitoring posts you've been tagged. (CareerBuilder 2014)

In creating an online profile, we encourage candidates to review the profiles of professionals that they admire to see what they are wearing in their profile picture and how their profile is formatted. For middle and high school students who have limited work experience, it's important that they highlight information about their school projects, club memberships, and any special recognitions and awards they've received. These include blogs to which they regularly contribute, honor roll awards, and competition medals. To be sure that their profile picture looks professional, we remind students to practice proper hygiene before taking their picture, which includes having clean hair with a recent haircut and, for male students, to be clean shaven.

What social media sites do you recommend to candidates?

To help extend their online presence we assist candidates in creating profiles on various social media websites. Although personal social media sites might not seem as important as business sites, some employers also check these before making a hiring decision, so we encourage our candidates to maintain profiles on the most popular ones. These sites are also good places for candidates to connect with coworkers away from the office, which can help in the development of meaningful work friendships.

To help them understand how to use social media responsibly, candidates of all ages must be taught how to use it properly. They must learn the consequence of posting offensive or inappropriate comments, pictures, and materials. This is especially important for individuals with autism who may fail to understand appropriate social cues or have challenges comprehending the consequences of their actions.

Some students may already be regular users of social media. Especially for any middle and high school students, it is highly recommended that a parent or guardian monitor what their child does on social media to ensure that it is being used safely and responsibly until the child demonstrates they are mature enough to use it on their own.

It's important that candidates understand the consequences of abusing social media. Middle and high school students probably already know that it can result in a bad reputation with teachers and fellow students or maybe even get them suspended or expelled if the offense is serious. For work, an inappropriate social media post could cost them a potential job, negatively affect the relationship with coworkers, or, if their post is extremely offensive, get them fired from their current job. It's also essential that they learn how to use social media safely. This includes never giving out their personal information to anyone they meet online or meeting anyone in person that they've only met through social media.

The sites listed below are offered at no cost to the users, although some charge fees for their premium services. Unless noted, the minimum age requirement for these three sites is 13 years. To keep track of their online presence, candidates can use the **Social Media Inventory** [21.5.2] to monitor what sites they are currently on and which site they need to join.

Social media sites

FACEBOOK

This is one of the most popular social sites, with over three billion active monthly users from around the world. When users become friends with other users, they can view what they post and share articles, photos, and videos. Facebook does not offer services for job seekers, but users can include information on their profile about their work history and educational background.

X (FORMALLY KNOWN AS TWITTER)

This is a news and social networking service where users can post 280-character messages called "tweets." It has 250 million active users and is popular with many celebrities, politicians, and social activists. In addition to posting tweets, users can "follow" other users to view their tweets. Like Facebook, X does not offer services for job seekers, but users can create a profile that includes a brief description about themselves. Elon Musk purchased Twitter for $44 billion on October 27, 2022 (Duffy and O'Sullivan 2022).

PINTEREST

This is a photo-sharing website where users can upload, save, sort, and manage images, known as "pins," and other media content, which can be organized into folders or "boards" sorted by a central topic or theme. Users pin pictures or articles that they can share with others. It has more than 500 million monthly active users and offers an endless amount of valuable information on any topic imaginable. Users can also follow other users on Pinterest and browse the content of their feeds. If a candidate is creative or has a special talent or skill, a Pinterest page can be used as an online portfolio to display their artwork and projects.

INSTAGRAM

This is a photo- and video-sharing social networking service that allows users to upload media that can be edited with filters and originated by hashtags. Posts can be shared publicly or with pre-approved followers. Users can browse other users' content, view trending content and follow other users to add their content to a personal feed. With 2.4 billion active users, it ranks fourth among the biggest social media networks.

Business websites

These sites are geared towards working professionals, but it is a good idea to introduce these resources to middle and high school students for their future job search needs. Just as is recommended for personal social media, the use of these sites by students should be monitored by a parent or guardian to ensure that the student is using each one safely and responsibly. Age limits for each of these sites apply.

LINKEDIN

This is a business- and employment-oriented social networking service with more than one billion members in over 200 countries and territories, including more than 30 million students and recent graduates. LinkedIn users can search their job listings, post a professional profile, and view information about potential employers. LinkedIn also allows users to post updates about their activities, share information and articles with other LinkedIn users, and join "groups" that are focused on specific interests and topics. The minimum age requirement is 18.

MONSTER® AND CAREERBUILDER

These are two of the most visited employment websites in the U.S. and around the world. Both sites allow users to search their job listings and company profiles and post online resumes. They also allow users to sign up for their online, career-advice newsletter and offer free services like resume critiques. The minimum age requirement for both sites is 13.

INDEED

This is a worldwide employment-related search engine of job listings that are aggregated from thousands of websites, job boards, staffing firms, associations, and company career pages. The site allows users to search their listings for available job openings and to post their resume online. Indeed also has a Career Guide which is an excellent resource for job-search-related topics. The minimum age requirement is 14 and adult supervision is required for users under 18.

CRAIGSLIST

This is an online resource for almost anything you can imagine, with sites all over the country and around the world. There is a large job-listing section that includes a huge variety of job postings from entry level to senior management. Many employers use the site to advertise jobs. Some of the Craigslist sections on each site are appropriate for adults only, so it is highly recommended that a parent or guardian monitor their child's use of the site.

What is the advantage of having a personal referral for a job interview?

As previously discussed, a personal referral is always the most reliable way to find a job. If you've been referred for a job, there may be only a few people in consideration for the position. Once a job has been posted online, it can be viewed by hundreds and maybe thousands of people, so any time you apply for a job in response to an online job posting, you will be competing against many people for the same job.

For this reason, it is common not to receive a response to an online job inquiry, even if you've written an excellent cover letter and are well qualified for the position.

What other employment services are available to autistic individuals?

Every state in the U.S. has a Department of Vocational Rehabilitation (or DOR) Services which offers a variety of employment services to individuals with disabilities, including direct job placements and job training. Like the IEP, which is created to help students accomplish their academic goals, the DOR develops an Individual Plan for Employment (IPE) for each of their clients to identify employment goals and create a plan of support to accomplish those goals.

DOR services are available to individuals after high school, so students must be within six months of obtaining their diploma or certificate of completion before they can open a case. If a student is interested in pursuing services with DOR, AWN provides information with the address of the office closest to where the candidate lives, a listing of the documents that they need to bring to their meeting, and an overview of the process that is involved in opening their case. If a candidate needs help with transportation and someone to accompany them to the meeting, we help them identify who this will be and coordinate getting the information about the meeting to that person. If it can be coordinated, a field trip for high school students to the local DOR office is a good learning experience to help them understand the process of applying for services.

Do you recommend any companies where candidates can apply for a job?

The worksheet **Companies that Hire People with Special Needs** [21.4] was created from a post on the blog, Noah's Dad. We added information to include the location of each business and the link to each company's website (Smith 2016).

What information do you cover on volunteer jobs?

Because our candidates usually do not have much prior work experience, a volunteer job is an excellent way to get experience and develop a network of professional contacts and references. It is also a great way to give back to your community and meet people with similar interests. Most high school students have service-learning hours as part of their graduation requirements, and their volunteer hours could be used to fill this requirement. To help candidates locate volunteer opportunities, we created the worksheet **How to Find a Volunteer Job** [21.3.1] and the **Volunteer Job Worksheet** [21.3.2].

Some of our candidates considered volunteering as "working for free." To help them change this perspective, we created an activity in R&R called Practicing Kindness. The worksheet **Practicing Kindness** [16] reviews the benefits of practicing kindness and ways to do so.

The benefits of kindness are:

- boosting of feel-good hormones (serotonin and dopamine)
- increased feelings of satisfaction and well being
- fostering of a sense of belonging
- stronger relationships.

Here are some ways to practice kindness:

- Be kind to yourself: practice positive, encouraging self-talk, take time to rest, ask for help, practice gratitude.
- Practice being polite: take turns, say please and thank you often, comfort a friend, practice many small acts of kindness. Let the person behind you in line at the grocery store go ahead if you have a lot of items and they only have a few.
- Show gratitude: show appreciation of others by texting or calling a loved one.
- Listen to understand, not to respond or problem solve; be fully present when someone is talking and let them feel heard and understood (Lancaster 2023).

In the same class where we introduce the concept of kindness, we incorporate the activity Finding a Volunteer Job which is broken down as follows:

- Review the worksheet How to Find a Volunteer Job.

- Next, candidates complete the "Causes I care about" in the volunteering section of the **Networking Worksheet** [21.2] to identify the types of causes and issues that are important to them and help them to find an organization close to their home that focuses on that cause. For instance, if animal welfare is something a candidate is interested in, we help them find a local animal shelter or animal rescue organization that does that work. If a candidate enjoys theatre arts or music, we help them locate a local non-profit organization involved in the arts.

- Candidates complete the worksheet, Volunteer Job Worksheet, to document the information on local organizations where they would like to volunteer.

- The instructor compiles the information for all candidates on the Volunteer Spreadsheet which is then shared in class. A sample of the Volunteer Spreadsheet is included in the final chapter in the Instructor's Materials section.

- Candidates are supported in creating their plan to contact the organization and complete the final steps so they can start volunteering.

What information do you provide on self-employment?

For candidates who want to start their own business, we created the worksheet **So You Want to Start Your Own Business** [21.6]. We only cover this information in class as a discussion if the group expresses interest in the topic.

The following is a summary of what would be covered in a discussion about starting your own business.

Answer questions

- What product will you be selling or what service will you be providing?

- How will you find buyers for your goods and services?

- If you are selling a product, who will be your vendors or suppliers of the items you need to make your product?

- How much do you have to sell your products or services for to make a profit?

- What other businesses are offering a similar product or service and how much do they charge?

Ask questions

If you've identified a similar business or service already in business, call up the owner and ask to schedule an informational interview. The worksheet on **Informational Interviews: Essentials** [21.1.1] will explain how to schedule an interview and what questions to ask.

What you'll need

Once you are ready to launch your business, you'll need the following to get started:

- **Decide on your business structure:** There are four business structures: sole proprietorship, partnerships, limited liability corporations (LLC) and corporations. Most likely, your candidate's business will be a sole proprietor.

- **DBA:** DBA stands for 'doing business as' and allows a business to operate under a name different from the business owner. So, if John Smith's business is named "John Smith's Computer Repairs," he would not need a DBA. But if he named his company "Excellence in Computer Repair," he would. DBA requirements vary by state, county, city, and business structure. Filing fees vary as well. Some states also require a "public notice" to announce your business. Your local county clerk's office can help with paperwork and requirements to file a DBA (Prakash 2022).

- **Business license:** All businesses must have a business license if they are selling goods and services whether they make a profit or not. A business license can usually be purchased from the Finance Office at your local city hall where your company will be operating.

- **Financial transactions:** You'll need to decide how payment will be accepted for your products or services. Accepting payments online is easy using apps like Paypal, Venmo, or Zelle. The minimum age to open an account on these services is 18 years old and each one requires the user's account to be connected to a bank account.

- **Bookkeeping:** For tax purposes, all business transactions, both for incoming and outgoing expenses, need to be documented on paper or electronically. If the company has limited sales and a small amount of expenses, a simple *Excel* spreadsheet that shows credits for income and debits for outgoing expenses is sufficient.

- **Taxes:** According to the IRS, a sole proprietor or independent contractor is required to file an income tax return if their self-employment net earnings are $400 or more. State and local taxes would also be due on any income generated by the business and these rates vary by city and state. Small business owners also owe self-employment taxes based on their income. To cover both income and self-employment taxes, it is recommended that a small business owner set aside 30 percent of their income after business deductions to cover both federal and state income taxes (Nationwide n.d.).

- **Marketing your business:** To generate sales, you'll need to promote your business to find customers to buy your goods and services. Here are some important things to consider.

  - Pitch your business: Create an elevator pitch for your business; keep it to 20 seconds and make it interesting so people want to learn more.

- Website: Establishing a website will require registering a domain name and hosting site. There are three companies that we recommend, and each provides services to register a domain name, web hosting, and website creation. The easiest site to create a website is *Google Sites*, a free website creation app available from Google that allows users to create and edit files online. It is extremely user-friendly and utilizes the apps on Google to create content. The site is free to use, but users have to purchase a domain name for their website from an outside source.

  Other companies that can help with registering a domain name, web hosting and website creation include:

  > IONOS

  > IPage

  > GoDaddy™

- Leverage social media: Create a page on Facebook and accounts on Instagram, Pinterest, TikTok, and X and regularly post new content. Create a channel on YouTube and create a blog to promote your business.

- Get the word out: Hire brand ambassadors who can talk up your business—these can be friends and family who want to support you. Give them T-shirts with your company name—these are free walking billboards! Network at neighborhood events and Chamber of Commerce mixers—your elevator pitch will come in handy. Create a business listing on Yelp.com and Google. Both sites are free, and customers can post reviews of your products and services.

- Advertising: The rule of seven is based on a marketing principle that customers need to see your brand at least seven times before they commit to purchase. Purchasing adverts in local media is expensive, so stick to free resources using social media and attending networking events (Pritchett 2018).

CHAPTER 8

Connecting with Coworkers

Maintaining Positive Workplace Relationships

Positive social connections have a direct impact on our health and well-being. Research has shown that social isolation and lack of social support can have a direct link to an increased risk of various disease outcomes and reduced length of life (House, Landis, and Umberson 1988). Social relationships in the workplace are equally important. A friend on the job can let you in on the inner workings of your office, make the job more enjoyable, and can even enhance your creativity and productivity (Yager 1999).

How are social communication skills affected in individuals with autism?

As we discussed in Chapter 1, autistic individuals benefit greatly from an early intervention program that includes support tailored to their specific needs, but, even with support, a majority of these children have a tough time transitioning into adolescence. In fact, studies have shown that as children with autism age, their challenges can worsen. A study of 185 autistic individuals from ages 5 to 18 years showed the greatest problems in the youngest and oldest cohorts (Rosenthal *et al.* 2013). A study of 120 individuals with autism who were diagnosed in childhood and re-evaluated again at ages 17–40 showed an overall poor outcome in 78 percent of cases (Billstedt, Gillberg, and Gillberg 2005).

How do you teach expected workplace communication skills?

Social communication is dynamic and fluid, influenced by the context in which it occurs. A conversation is an experience that happens spontaneously and can't be scripted or planned. For the conversation to flow, participants must listen to one another, process what is being said, and formulate a response. A conversation is much like a ping pong game where the objective is to keep the ball bouncing between two paddles. In a conversation, responses bounce between participants until the conversation ends.

The first half of the workshop is the Roundtable Discussion, and its purpose is to simulate a workplace setting like a break room. During this part of the workshop, candidates sit around a table and share information about themselves. They also practice recalling information that they learned about other candidates. Sharing information tends not to be too difficult, but remembering information about others is usually not so easy. This can pose a problem in the workplace since our coworkers expect us to remember the information that they've shared and for us to ask about it the next time we see one another.

- **Sharing information about their week:** Each week, candidates share aloud with the group what they did during their week. To help them develop their narrative, AWN created a **Your Week Worksheet/What Happened with You?** [11.1] that asks questions about the who, what, when, where, and favorite part of their activities. We then go around the table and candidates share with the group the highlights of their week. As candidates get to know one another, additional topics are introduced. It is recommended to include this activity each week in the Roundtable Discussion for at least the first three class meetings.

- **Remembering information about others:** After candidates become better acquainted, typically by the fourth or fifth class, candidates are paired, and they interview one another using the **Your Week Worksheet/Interview Your Partner** [11.2.1 and 11.2.2] to learn about their partner and create a narrative of their partner's week. Candidates then take it in turns around the table to share their information about their partner with the group.

- **Icebreakers:** Icebreaker questions are typically about their favorite things like pets, movies, vacations, and restaurants. Their answers are recorded on the **Icebreaker Worksheet** [12] in Google Docs, which is then shared with all candidates. The purpose of this activity is to help candidates share information about themselves and retain information they learn about members of the group. Icebreaker questions are on topics that are appropriate to discuss at work, so the exercise helps candidates learn about what they can ask of their coworkers to get to know them better. A list of icebreaker questions is included in the final chapter.

- **Planned social activities:** Planned outings provide an excellent opportunity for candidates to practice their conversational skills. After field trips, AWN coordinates a place where the instructor and candidates meet to share a meal. These settings are the types of places where coworkers socialize outside the office and, since these are also attended by workshop instructors, these gatherings also provide instructors with an opportunity to gauge how well candidates are generalizing the use of their conversational skills.

  Another opportunity for candidates to practice their communication skills is during AWN-organized parties. During the holiday season, AWN organizes at least one get-together and invites all candidates and their families. If your program meets during the holidays, July 4th and Memorial Day weekend are also good times to organize a group get-together. These events are potluck, which is a common practice for many office parties. For candidates, it's a fun shared experience much like it is for the employees who attend their company's annual holiday party.

  For a group of middle and high school students, planning a group party provides an excellent opportunity to practice many organizational and communication skills that are applicable to the workplace. If possible, it's recommended that the group coordinates with the parents of one of the students to hold a potluck party in one of their homes on a weekend afternoon or evening. This event would provide students with an opportunity to socialize outside school and for parents and guardians to get to know one another. If any student requires support during the party, make sure to have a responsible adult on hand and let students know that this support is available if needed. If a student has an in-class aide, consider inviting the aide as a guest but first check with your school to see if this is allowed. If it is allowed, be sure to agree before the party how many hours the aide will be needed. Also, remember to compensate the aide for the hours worked.

- **Conversation Dos and Don'ts** [20.4] is a summary of appropriate topics for the workplace and how to initiate a conversation. The Roundtable Discussion activity, Interview Your Partner, also provides an opportunity to practice conversational skills. Questions used in the Icebreaker activity are also appropriate questions to use to initiate conversations.

How do you teach the concept of small talk?

Small talk is the opportunity to make a connection with someone you do not know well or have just met to become better acquainted. Because individuals with autism have challenges understanding the thoughts and feelings of others, it can be difficult to initiate a conversation, especially if they don't understand a basic understanding of using small talk. We use a YouTube video called *4 Great Conversation Starters* to introduce and reinforce the concept of small talk. Aaron Marino is a YouTube influencer who goes by the name Alpha M. and has produced a great video on his favorite ways to start a conversation. His style is interesting, but he explains the concept very well. His four great conversation starters are:

- When you're not working, what do you like to do?

- How's your day going?

- Do you have any plans for this weekend?

- Lead with a compliment about something they are wearing (Marino 2015).

AUTHOR'S REFLECTION
The importance of teaching conversational skills
Prior to the first group dinner following a field trip, we had not yet developed any activities on conversational skills. That night at the restaurant, it showed—none of the candidates was having a conversation about anything. To help facilitate their conversation skills, we developed activities in the Roundtable Discussion to

facilitate small talk to sustain a conversation. For anyone developing their own program, this is an area where almost every candidate will need a lot of support. Good conversational skills are an essential skill in doing well in a job, so plan on incorporating a lot of activities that help build these skills.

How do you teach the importance of making a good first impression at work?

As the saying goes, "You never get a second chance to make a first impression," and research has shown this to be true. The results of one study showed that social judgments made from viewing faces are formulated rapidly without much mental effort (Bar, Neta, and Linz 2006; Willis and Todorov 2006). The results from other studies show that social judgments from faces predict important social outcomes ranging from sentencing decisions to electoral success (Blair, Judd, and Chapleau 2004; Eberhardt *et al.* 2006; Little *et al.* 2007; Montepare and Zebrowitz 1998; Zebrowitz and McDonald 1991).

But how long does it take to make a first impression? According to Princeton psychologists Janine Willis and Alexander Todoroc, not much time at all. These researchers found it only took a tenth of a second to form an impression of a stranger after looking at their face. Longer exposures didn't significantly alter those judgments. It only helped the observer to become more confident in their initial judgment (Willis and Todorov 2006). Because making good first impressions is so important, we help candidates practice ways to do this. Our handout **Making a Good First Impression** is used to help our candidates understand the basics of making and maintaining positive connections with coworkers and supervisors.

How do you teach appropriate telephone etiquette?

The cell phone has become an important device in our lives. We use it to text, take pictures, scan the internet, and watch movies and videos. Many young people don't use their phone as a phone anymore, so they don't have an opportunity to learn basic telephone etiquette.

We first review the importance of having an appropriate voice mail greeting on your phone.

Especially if a candidate is applying for work, a potential employer may call, so it's important their greeting clearly identifies them. If the greeting is inappropriate and offends the caller, the candidate could lose out on interviewing for the position. We also review checking voice mail messages and the importance of deleting old emails.

To help candidates learn the concept of telephone etiquette, we created the **Telephone Etiquette Overview Worksheet** [20.2], which reviews the reason for a call, what to say when a person answers, how to end a call, and what information to leave on a voice mail. We also discuss that it's only appropriate to leave one additional voice mail if the first one isn't answered.

Why is it important for candidates to socialize with coworkers outside the workplace?

The workplace provides us with an opportunity to meet people, but we bond as friends during breaks, after work, and on weekends. But before these opportunities to socialize can materialize, we must make positive connections with our coworkers so they will want to get to know us better and spend time with us outside work.

For middle and high school students who have challenges forming friendships with their peers, this may be an area where they will need significant support. An in-class aide or job coach can model appropriate behaviors that can help the student make a good impression and form positive connections to their fellow candidates in class, and, eventually, with coworkers on the job. If a social situation did not go as planned, it's essential that the support person helps the student reflect on what occurred and come up with solutions on what could be done differently in a similar situation in the future.

If a middle or high school student is working and makes plans to socialize with a coworker outside the office, it is highly recommended that a responsible adult accompanies the student on the activity. The most important reason is to ensure the student's safety, but if needed, the chaperone can help facilitate positive communication and help the student problem solve after the event on anything that did not go as planned. It is ideal for the chaperone to be close in age to the student and not be the student's parent or guardian.

What activities do you use to teach stress management?

Studies have shown that autistic children have more severe symptoms of social phobias than their neurotypical peers. Adolescents who are less impacted are even more likely to have a comorbid diagnosis of an anxiety disorder. One theory is that teenagers with high cognitive functioning are more aware of their environment and the way that they are viewed by others, and this becomes more pronounced as they enter adolescence (Alfano, Beidel, and Turner 2006).

In the workplace, it is essential that employees have strategies to self-regulate their emotions so they can proactively manage their stress without negatively affecting the work environment. If they have a meltdown at work, they can disrupt the entire workplace. If they are anxious about meeting new people, it can impede their ability to form meaningful relationships with their coworkers. If they are obsessed about something that happened the night before, they will have a hard time staying focused and completing their work tasks.

Proactive stress management techniques are an effective strategy in helping adolescents and adults take control of their emotions, so their emotions don't take control over them. During the Roundtable Discussion, we address the topic of stress management by helping candidates identify their physical sensations of stress as well as teaching and practicing proactive strategies that will help with managing their stress levels. Below are the strategies that we use with our candidates to help them accomplish this goal.

The Incredible 5-Point Scale

To assess the consequences of our actions, we must be able to determine how to act, react, and interact in each situation, but to do this, we must be self-aware and able to self-regulate. For individuals with autism, these abilities are impacted to varying degrees. The Incredible 5-Point Scale was developed by Kari Dunn Buron and Mitzi Curtis to help these students understand how to match their emotional response to the appropriate social interaction. Using a number rating system, students can identify their feelings in response to a situation (Buron and Curtis 2003). The 5-Point Scale is also an effective technique to use with adolescents and adults with autism to manage their stress.

We begin each workshop by using a 5-Point Scale as adapted by AWN to help candidates self-identify their feelings. After they identify where they are on the scale, the instructor starts by asking, "Who is at a level 1?" and candidates raise their hand if they are at that level. The instructor continues until all candidates have raised their hands. For any candidate that is not at a level 1 or 2, the instructor can ask why, but don't force a candidate to answer if they don't want to. This exercise is also a useful tool for instructors to gauge how motivated each candidate will be to participate in the workshop.

This information is helpful for instructors to understand the candidate's emotional state so they can better know how to support them in class. If a candidate shares any personal information that is upsetting for them, like the death of a pet or feeling frustrated about a poor test score, instructors can use it as an opportunity to model for the class expected appropriate behaviors in response to hearing of another person's misfortune. If the candidate is frustrated or upset and doesn't want to share the reason why with the class, the instructor should approach the candidate privately and provide support as needed.

Below is the rating scale used in the AWN **Incredible 5-Point Group Check-In Scale** [13.1]. As shown, we also match a color to each number/rating:

1. (Blue): I am glad to be here. I will participate and I may even be able to help others.

2. (Green): I am glad to be here and I will participate.

3. (Yellow): I'm here. I might or might not participate.

4. (Orange): I'm here. I will not participate but I will not disrupt.

5. (Red): I will not participate and I may disrupt if I stay.

To help candidates learn how to independently implement the 5-Point Scale, we have them match a level 1 to how they feel when they are doing something they love, which for our candidates can be things like going to Disneyland, seeing a movie, or shopping for Anime. At level 2, they are still feeling good but less excited than they are at level 1. Both levels are appropriate for the workplace. At a level 3, they are starting to feel bothered, frustrated, or annoyed. When they experience these feelings, we advise our candidates to stop, take a break, and use a stress management technique so they can return to level 1 or 2.

The AWN **Incredible 5-Point Stress Meter** [13.2] is used to help candidates match their facial expressions to their feels for each point in the scale. This is an activity where candidates create their own stress meter. For candidates who don't like to draw, you can provide face emoji stickers to represent each emotion. If a candidate is artistically inclined, it is an opportunity to display their talents.

An example of each level could look something like this:

1. Happy face with big smile

2. Happy face with smaller smiler

3. Face with a worried look

4. Angry face

5. Very angry face.

SODA: Stop, Observe, Deliberate, Act

The Social Behavioral Strategy, SODA, was developed by Majorie Bock to address the Theory of Mind impairments for children with autism. Its purpose is to help them stop and reflect before deciding how they will react in a social situation (Bock 2001). It is also an effective strategy for use with adolescents and adults with autism in workplace settings. To help them to stop and think before acting, candidates use SODA to consider the alternate perspectives of their coworkers and supervisors before choosing their own behavior.

The four components of SODA are:

1. Stop: Allows the individual to stop and see what others are doing.

2. Observe: Helps the individual note what social cues are being used by people in that setting.

3. Deliberate: Encourages the individual to consider how they are being perceived by others and think about what they might say or do.

4. Act: Based on this information, the individual makes a choice on how they will interact.

Mindfulness awareness

Mindful awareness can be defined as paying attention to present moment experiences with openness, curiosity, and a willingness to be with what is. It invites us to stop, breathe, observe, and connect with our inner experience. There are many ways to bring mindfulness into our lives, such as meditation, yoga, art, or time in nature. Mindfulness can be implemented in daily life, by people of any age, profession, or background. In the last ten years, significant research has shown that mindfulness can effectively address health issues to lower blood pressure, boost the immune system, increase attention and focus in ADHD, and lower anxiety and depression. It can foster well-being and less emotional reactivity, and thicken the brain in areas in charge of decision-making, emotional flexibility, and empathy (UCLA Mindful Awareness Research Center n.d.).

To help our candidates understand the concept of mindfulness, AWN created a one-page write-up of the steps used in a mindfulness breathing exercise. During the Roundtable Discussion, we practice the mindfulness breathing activity with our candidates, usually during the first class of the month. To help it to become a habit, we encourage our candidates to practice mindful breathing each day for a minimum of three to five minutes.

Free resource: UCLA Mindfulness Awareness Research Center

The Mindful Awareness Research Center (MARC) is located at the University of California, Los Angeles and was founded by internationally acclaimed author, educator, and child psychiatrist, Daniel J. Siegel. MARC's mission is to foster mindful awareness across the lifespan through education and research as well as to promote well-being and a more compassionate society. It offers classes and workshops to the public and provides mindfulness tools and classes for mental health professionals.

MARC's website has a page with eight free guided meditations, which are also available on iTunes.[1]

AWN Stress Management Worksheet

Self-reflection is an effective tool to monitor one's behavior and general state of mind in a situation. For individuals with autism, it can be an especially effective tool in helping them better understand their actions and to come up with more effective ways in which they can handle a stressful situation in the future.

To help our candidates self-reflect on how they react to a stressful situation, AWN created a **Stress Management Worksheet** [13.7] designed to help record the specifics of an incident and the candidate's bodily reactions. The worksheet is most effective if used immediately after an incident once the candidate has calmed down. We recommend giving the candidate's parents, caregivers, and support people a copy of the worksheet so they can help complete it while details of the incident are still fresh. The goal in using the worksheet is to help the candidate self-reflect and come up with effective ways to proactively manage their stress when they are feeling frustrated or confused. For this activity, while it is not ideal, it is okay for a candidate to receive help from a parent or guardian.

Additional worksheets that address stress management

Here are some additional worksheets to help lead discussions on stress management that you can use for a discussion during the Roundtable Discussion:

- **Nine Moments to Appreciate** [13.4] (Kerpen 2020)

- **Seven Ways to Manage Anxiety** [13.5] (AARPRachelA 2020)

---

1   www.uclahealth.org/programs/marc/free-guided-meditations/guided-meditations

In addition to stress management, what other topics can you cover to help candidates maintain an optimistic outlook?

In addition to stress management, we also want to help candidates practice habits that will help them maintain a positive attitude and optimistic outlook on life. The three activities we use to help candidates integrate this into their everyday lives are practicing gratitude, creating a positive self-image, and practicing kindness.

Practicing gratitude

Gratitude is a positive emotion that involves being thankful and appreciative and is associated with several mental and physical health benefits. Feeling grateful for something or someone in your life brings on feelings of kindness, warmth, and other forms of generosity. Gratitude is associated with higher levels of well-being and lower levels of stress (Cherry 2024).

To help teach the concept of gratitude, we use two YouTube videos and the worksheet **Practicing Gratitude** [16], summarizing how to practice gratitude. We then ask candidates to keep a daily gratitude journal to reflect on what is good in their lives. Some take to it enthusiastically, some not so much. For candidates who complete their journals, we reflect on each one to help candidates remember what is positive in their lives and the lives of their fellow candidates.

Adapted from the article "How to practice gratitude" (Cherry 2024) from the website, www.verywellmind.com, this is an explanation of how to practice gratitude:

- Observe the moment: Take a moment to focus on your experience and how you are feeling.

- Write it down: Start a gratitude journal and write down a few things each day for which you are grateful.

- Savor the moment: Take time each day to really enjoy the moment and absorb those good feelings.

- Create gratitude rituals: Pause for a moment each day through meditation, prayer, or mantra.

- Give thanks: Show your appreciation; say thank you and spend time appreciating what you have.

We also use two videos to help reinforce the concept of gratitude. Links to both videos are included in the Instructor's Materials section of the final chapter.

- *Oprah's Gratitude Journal. Oprah's Lifeclass*, Oprah Winfrey Network: From The Golden Eagles (2013).

- *Gratitude Is Good for You*: From the John Templeton Foundation (2015).

Gratitude activity: The instructor leads a discussion on gratitude, shares the two videos that were previously referenced and creates a shared gratitude journal as a Google spreadsheet for each candidate. Their assignment is to write down five things each day for which they are grateful.

Creating a positive self-image

Your self-image is how you see yourself and how you think others see you. Your image can be positive or negative, and the individual is in total control of the narrative they have for themselves.

From the article "10 Rules for Building a Stronger More Positive Self-Image" (Mavi 2018) from the website www.atriumstaff.com we created the worksheet **Creating a Positive Self-Image** [14]. Here are the first four rules:

- Give yourself credit: Attribute your accomplishments to your own hard work and efforts.

- Be present: Stay present in the moment, not on regrets or longing for the future.

- Keep it real: Don't over-exaggerate. Remain level headed when things get complicated or frustrating.

- Don't dwell on things: Don't dwell on negative outcomes. Instead, look for ways to learn from experience and figure out how to improve next time.

To reinforce the concept of a positive self-image, we created an exercise called "What I Like About Me". Each candidate is given an oversized post-it and asked to write down at least five things they do well or like about themselves. We then post on the wall and each candidate shares what they wrote.

Positive self-image activity: Candidates are given a 25" x 30" self-stick post-it easel pad and asked to write down five things they like about themselves. Each candidate then shares with the class what they wrote and why they wrote it.

Practicing kindness

To help our candidates be more empathetic towards others, we created a worksheet called **Practicing Kindness** [16] that we use to lead the discussion. We also use two stories to further elaborate on kindness. Links to both articles are included in the final chapter in the Instructor's Materials section.

- "A Remarkable Gift of Forgiveness" by Luke Broadwater, *Los Angeles Times*, January 7, 2018.

- "On Christmas Eve, A Stolen Bicycle and A Lesson in Giving," by Judy Esty-Kendell and Isabel Dobrin. NPR Story Corp, December 15, 2017.

After the kindness activity in the Roundtable Discussion, we schedule the Finding a Volunteer Job in Prepare and Practice.

CHAPTER 9

Understanding the Workplace

Know Your Rights and Effective Self-Advocacy

The time you've spent planning and preparing has finally paid off. You've aced the interview and you've been hired. You have the technical skills that you need to get the job done. You've improved your soft skills so you can get along with your coworkers and handle the responsibilities of your job.

What more do you need? To understand your legal protections as an employee, it's important to know the state and federal labor laws that protect you from unfair treatment by an employer and a coworker.

To understand your role within an organization, it's important to be familiar with the senior managers of the business. It's also important to know what your role is and how your job fits into the big picture within the structure of the organization. A hierarchy flow chart is a helpful tool to facilitate understanding of your company and how your work contributes to its success.

If you are a worker with a disability, it's also important to be familiar with the Americans with Disabilities Act, so that you understand the regulations that shield you from discrimination as well as the types of accommodations to which you are entitled. Since these accommodations are only available if the individual discloses their disability to their employer, you'll also need to know how and to whom you should disclose. To understand who this is, it's necessary to know the hierarchy of the jobs within your organization and the essential role of your company's human resources department.

To maintain a happy workplace, employees need to know how to respectfully and amicably resolve conflicts. This requires the ability to empathize with another person's viewpoint, but many individuals with autism struggle with understanding the thoughts and feelings of others. To help our candidates learn how to effectively resolve conflicts, we review two methods of conflict resolution: the Interest-Based Relational approach which provides an easy-to-follow, step-by-step conflict resolution technique that is easily adapted for use in the workplace, and the Thomas-Kilmann Conflict Mode Instrument that is a useful tool to use in assessing a conflict and deciding on the proper response to quickly resolve it.

Why is it important to know the organizational structure of the company where you work?

Understanding an organization's structure helps an employee understand how their job fits within the organization and who at their company is responsible for making business decisions. A well-defined organizational structure improves a company's operational efficiency because it helps different departments work more smoothly together to focus their time and energy on completing productive tasks. A company's organizational structure can also provide an easily understood track for employees to advance within the ranks of the organization (Ingram 2016).

As we discussed in Chapter 1, to find meaning in our work, it's important to know how our work fits within the larger context of the company. We need to know the jobs that are performed by our coworkers and how their work relates to what we do. It's also important to know the names of the company's managers and senior managers and their role within the company. Understanding an organization's structure and hierarchy of employees is easy if the company has a small number of workers. It becomes more difficult when the company is large with many departments and multiple layers of management.

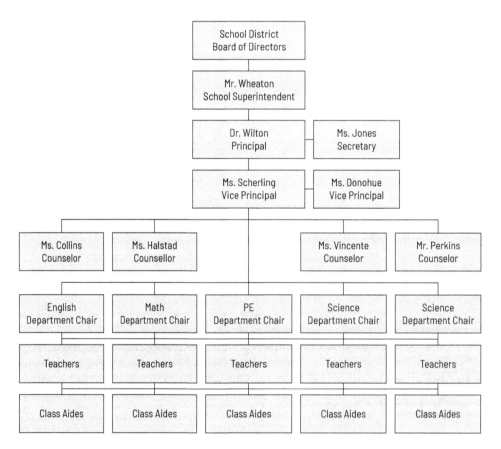

Figure 7.1 ABC High School organizational chart

It's important that candidates learn about the structure of the company for which they work as soon as they are hired so they can understand which employees are at their level as well as the hierarchy of the company's management. Candidates also need to learn how their social interaction with coworkers is different from their interactions with their supervisors and people who are higher up in the company. Since most of our candidates have not yet been employed, we find the best way to teach appropriate social interactions with supervisors and senior management is to role play different scenarios that could happen in the workplace.

For middle and high school students, creating an organizational chart for their school can help them understand the concept of the hierarchy of employees in a company. Ask the principal for a copy of the school's organizational chart or create one yourself. It should list the succession of employees starting with the School District Board of Directors at the top with aides at the bottom. Figure 7.1 gives an example of what a school's organizational chart might look like.

How do you teach about the hierarchy of jobs within an organization?

As we discussed in Chapter 1, to find meaning in the work that we do, it's important that we understand how our daily tasks are connected to the mission of the company for which we work. To help our candidates understand this concept, we break down the structure of a company into four levels. The worksheet **Workplace Hierarchy Chart** [22.1] summarizes this information.

Level 1—Management employees: This group makes plans for the company's growth and manages the work of lower-level employees. They have a vast amount of knowledge and years of experience in their field. This level has employees with job titles like Chief Executive Officer (CEO), Chief Operating Officer (COO), and General Manager.

Level 2—Executive employees: This group has supervisory duties, and these employees are usually the representatives for the company when dealing with the public. They have specialization in their field and work with team members to grow their department within the company. This level has employees with job titles like Executive Director, Chief Technical Officer, Chief Financial Officer, President, Vice President, Community Relations Manager, Treasurer, and Assistant Manager.

Level 3—Entry level and administrative employees: This group does not usually have the authority to make business decisions and workers mainly support the work of the organization's management and executive employees. They mostly work on a fixed schedule and perform work that is assigned to them. This level includes employees with job titles like Clerk, Cashier, Administrative Assistant, Sales Associate, Stock Clerk, Trainee, and Intern.

Level 4—Non-administrative employees: The employees in this group have jobs that require physical strength and the performance of some type of manual labor. They typically have a daily work schedule and may be skilled in a specific trade. This level includes employees with job titles like Security Guard, Custodian, Gardener, Foreman, and Maintenance Worker (Hierarchy Structure n.d.).

What information is covered about the role of a human resources department?

A human resources department (commonly known as HR) is responsible for employee relations and finding candidates to fill job openings. HR conducts interviews, handles the hiring and firing of employees, and completes the necessary paperwork for new hires and exiting employees. HR oversees all matters covering payroll, insurance, benefits, and taxes, and stays up to date on all legal matters affecting employment. HR provides employees with information about assistance programs and is the place where employees can go to ask questions and lodge complaints. When needed, HR provides counseling and mediation to resolve issues within the company.

It's important for candidates to know the function of an organization's HR department and how they can use it to help manage conflicts or problems at work. When hired for a new job, candidates are instructed to get the HR person's business card and enter the information into their Google Contacts (Reference.com 2017).

Which state and federal employment regulations are covered in the workshop?

There are literally hundreds of state and federal laws that cover workers in all 50 states. While it is impossible for someone who is not an HR professional to be familiar with every single one, there are a few that all employees should know and understand. Federal laws apply to employees in all 50 states, but state-mandated regulations apply to workers only in the state where they've been enacted. When creating instructional materials for this portion of the workshop, the curriculum needs to be adapted to the labor laws for the state where the program is being offered.

Employment law, also referred to as labor law, governs the rights and duties between employers and workers. These rules are primarily in place to protect workers' rights to ensure that they are treated fairly, but there are laws that protect an employer's interests as well. Employment laws are based on federal and state constitutions, legislation, administrative rules, and court opinions. An employment relationship may also be governed by a contract (HG.org 2017). The worksheet **Labor Law Overview** [22.2] summarizes this information.

Employment contracts

An employment contract is a legally binding agreement between an employer and an employee regarding a term of employment. The agreement can be oral, written, or implied. We instruct candidates before they start a new job to get a letter from their employer that confirms their rate of pay, employment status, and start date.

At-will employment

Most employees in the United States are presumed to be working at will. This means that the employee can quit or be fired at any time for any reason that isn't illegal under state and federal laws. An at-will employee also has the right to quit their job without penalties. While an employee does not have to provide advance notice of their intentions to leave a job, it is typical and generally expected that an employee gives two weeks' notice when leaving their job. An employee cannot legally be fired for exercising their rights. This includes using family and medical leave, leave to serve in the military, or taking time off to vote. If an at-will employee is fired, it is the responsibility of the employer to prove "just cause" for the termination (Guerin 2017a, 2017b).

Independent contractors

People who are self-employed in an independent trade, business, or profession in which they offer their services to the public are considered independent contractors. Independent contractors who earn more than $400 in a year must pay quarterly self-employment (SE) taxes based on their income. SE taxes are like the Social Security and Medicare taxes paid by employed workers. For any candidate who plans to start their own business, it is essential that they understand their responsibility to set aside money from their earnings so they can pay their quarterly SE taxes on a timely basis or be subject to IRS-imposed fines and penalties (United States Internal Revenue Service 2016).

Exempt vs non-exempt employees

These are the two classifications of employees as determined by the Fair Labor Standards Act (FLSA) which covers rules for employees covering minimum wage requirements, overtime pay, and other protections. Exempt employees are excluded from all FLSA rules. These are typically employees in executive, supervisory, professional, and outside sales jobs that draw a set salary and have a work schedule with varying hours. Non-exempt employees are typically paid an hourly salary, have a set work schedule, and are covered under FLSA regulations. Rules covering safe and healthy workplace environments, equal employment opportunities, and the rights provided under the Family and Medical Leave Act apply to both exempt and non-exempt employees.

All of our candidates that were hired while in our program were hired as non-exempt employees, and so will most of the candidates be in your own program. It's still important that they understand the difference between the status as an exempt and non-exempt employee if they are ever hired in an executive or supervisory role (Monster 2017).

Payroll taxes

Especially for middle and high school students who have limited or no work experience, it's important that they understand that when they receive their paycheck, it won't be for the full amount of their hourly wages. Their employer will be withholding a percentage of their check to cover state and federal taxes. To help our candidates understand the reason for these deductions, it's important to provide an overview of what these are.

FEDERAL INCOME TAX

Employers generally withhold federal income tax from an employee's wages. When a person is hired, a form W-4 is completed by the employee and this information is used to determine the amount of federal income tax that is withheld from each paycheck. Workers that make over $400 in a year must report their earnings to the Internal Revenue Service (commonly known as the IRS) each year by April 15.

STATE INCOME TAX

In all but ten states (Alaska, Florida, Nevada, New Hampshire, South Dakota, Tennessee, Texas, Washington, and Wyoming), workers are required to pay an annual state income tax that is due on April 15 of each year.

SOCIAL SECURITY AND MEDICARE TAXES

Employers also deduct social security and Medicare taxes from each employee's paycheck.

HOW THESE TAXES ARE PAID

It is the responsibility of the employer to deposit all money deducted from the checks of their employees into an account with an authorized bank or financial institution pursuant to Federal Tax Deposit Requirements. The employer must file an annual return reporting the money that was collected and transfer these funds to the IRS on a timely basis (United States Internal Revenue Service 2024).

State laws

As mentioned, regulations vary from state to state, so the information in this portion of the workshop must be matched to the laws of the state where the program is being offered. The regulations that are most important for candidates to be familiar with are:

- state minimum wage rates (if these differ from federal regulations)

- minimum paid rest periods

- minimum meal periods

- payday requirements.

The United States Department of Labor website has the most recent information about the federal labor laws (United States Department of Labor, Wage and Hour Division n.d.a).

The Federal-State Unemployment Insurance Program provides temporary financial benefits to unemployed workers. Each state administers its own program within guidelines established by federal law. The funding for the program in most states is provided by a tax imposed on employers. Benefits paid to recipients must be reported on a federal income tax return (United States Department of Labor, Wage and Hour Division n.d.a).

The United States Department of Labor website has the most recent information about the Unemployment Program for each state (United States Department of Labor, Employment & Training Administration 2015).

WORKER'S COMPENSATION

Workers' compensation (also known as workers' comp) is a state-mandated insurance program that provides financial benefits to employees who suffer job-related injuries and illnesses. The federal government administers the program, which provides replacement benefits, medical treatment, vocational rehabilitation, and other benefits, but each state establishes the rules and regulations for the workman's comp program for their own state. In general, an employee with a work-related illness or injury can get worker's comp benefits regardless of who was at fault. In exchange for these guaranteed benefits, employees usually do not have the right to sue their employer in court for damages for any injuries they've incurred (Hoftfelder 2017).

The United States Department of Labor website has the most recent information about the Workers' Compensation program in your state (United States Department of Labor, Wage and Hour Division n.d.c).

Federal laws

In the United States, the United States Department of Labor administers and enforces federal laws covering workplace activities for about 10 million employers and 125 million workers. Below is a description of the most common federal laws that are covered in the workshop. Candidates are instructed to see their human resources manager if they feel that their employer is in violation of any of these laws or if they would like to take advantage of any of the federal or state employment benefits to which they are entitled.

WAGES AND HOURS

The Fair Labor Standards Act (FLSA) sets the standard for wages and is administered by the Wage and Hour Division (WHD) of the U.S. Department of Labor. For a state or city that has enacted laws setting a higher hourly minimum wage, the higher rate would apply to all workers in that city or state. The Act establishes overtime pay of one-and-a-half times the regular rate of pay when an employee works over 40 hours in one week, but there are no overtime pay requirements for hours worked on weekends or holidays unless the employee has exceeded working 40 hours. The FLSA established 14 years as the minimum age for employment, set the number of hours that children under the age of 16 can work, and banned the employment of children under the age of 18 for jobs deemed too dangerous. The WHD also enforces the labor standard provisions of the Immigration and Nationality Act that applies to aliens working under certain immigrant visa programs.

The federal minimum wage is $7.25 per hour. The most convenient link to determine your state's minimum wage standard is from the United States Department of Labor on State Minimum Wage Laws (United States Department of Labor, Wage and Hour Division n.d.b.).

FAMILY AND MEDICAL LEAVE ACT (FMLA)

Administered by the WHD, the FMLA requires employers of 50 or more employees to give up to 12 weeks of unpaid, job-protected leave to eligible employees for the birth or adoption of a child or for the serious illness of the employee or a spouse, child, or parent. The link on the FMLA is an excellent resource to review the information during class when discussing this topic (United States Department of Labor, Wage and Hour Division n.d.d.).

WORKPLACE SAFETY AND HEALTH

The Occupational Safety and Health (OSH) Act is administered by the Occupational Safety and Health Administration (OSHA). It covers safety and health conditions for most private sector and all public sector employees to guarantee employees a workplace free from recognized, serious hazards (United States Department of Labor, Occupational Safety and Health Administration 2004).

OSHA administers the "whistleblower" protection provisions of 22 states. Under this law, an employee may file a complaint with OSHA if they believe that they have received discrimination or retaliation for exercising any right afforded by OSH. An employee must file a complaint about any health or safety issues within 30 days after the occurrence of the alleged violation (United States Department of Labor, Occupational Safety and Health Administration n.d.).

WORKER ADJUSTMENT AND RETRAINING NOTIFICATION ACT (WARN)

This federal law mandates that workers being laid off be given a written 60-day notice before the date of mass layoffs or plant closings. A worker who does not receive notice per the law may seek damages for back pay and benefits for up to 60 days depending on how many days' notice were received (U.S. Department of Labor, Employment and Training Administration Fact Sheet 1989).

Sensitive workplace topics

The next several topics are sensitive in nature. If your workshop has any candidates that are minors, you should let their parent or guardian know in advance about the material being covered and get their written permission to allow their child to participate. A sample of a parent/guardian permission form is included in the final chapter in the Instructor's Materials section.

HARASSMENT

Harassment in the workplace based on race, color, religion, sex, national origin, age, and disability in any form is prohibited by law. It becomes unlawful when the offensive conduct becomes a condition of continued employment or the conduct is severe or pervasive enough to create a work environment that a reasonable person would consider intimidating, hostile, or abusive. An employer is automatically held liable for harassment by a supervisor that results in a negative employment action such as termination, failure to promote, or be hired. An employer is also held liable if it was known or should have known about the harassment and they failed to take prompt and appropriate corrective action. The Equal Employment Opportunity Commission (or EEOC) handles administration and enforcement of laws covering harassment (U.S. Equal Employment Opportunity Commission n.d.b.).

When offering a workshop to middle and high school students, the topic of harassment might be one that they're familiar with. They may have been bullied at one time or could currently be the target of bullying behavior at school or elsewhere. Especially if the group has bonded and formed any sort of connection, the workshop may become a safe environment for these students, a place where they can share their experiences and their feelings without being judged and can find a place where they are accepted for who they are and their problems are understood.

If a candidate is uncomfortable discussing the topic of harassment or chooses not to participate, their feelings must be respected. If you suspect the candidate is being harmed in any way, initiate a private conversation to get more information. It is possible the student feels embarrassed or ashamed and may not have shared this information with their parents or primary caregiver. Ask the candidate if they would like your help and encourage them to share this information with a trusted adult. If the candidate is a minor and they aren't comfortable speaking to their primary caregiver, encourage them to speak to a counselor or teacher. The student's safety and well-being is your foremost concern, and it's important to let the candidate know that they can trust that you will support them to the best of your abilities.

SEXUAL HARASSMENT

Sexual harassment includes unwelcome sexual advances, requests for sexual favors, remarks about a person's sex, and other verbal or physical harassment of a sexual nature. The victim or abuser can be either a male or female and can be the victim's supervisor, supervisor in another area, a coworker, or non-employee (U.S. Equal Employment Opportunity Commission n.d.b.). Due to the maturity of the subject matter, the instructional materials for this portion of the workshop need to match the social-emotional level of the middle and high school students who make up the class.

If you have reasonable suspicion that a candidate is a victim of sexual abuse or if a candidate shares this information directly with you, it is vital that you act immediately to provide them with the help they need. If you are a mandated reporter, you are required by law to report suspected child abuse to the proper government agency.

What is the Americans with Disabilities Act (ADA)?

The Americans with Disabilities Act (or ADA) of 1990 is a civil rights law that prohibits private employers, state and local governments, employment agencies, and labor unions from discriminating against individuals with disabilities. It contains five titles or sections, and Title 1 covers all aspects of employment including job application procedures, hiring, firing advancement, compensation, and job training. The purpose of the law is to ensure that people with disabilities have the same rights and opportunities as everyone else. It is regulated by the United States EEOC and enforced by the United States Department of Justice. In the workshop, we only cover Title 1.

What disabilities are covered under the ADA?

Under Title 1 of the ADA, an individual with a disability is someone who has a physical or mental impairment that substantially limits one or more major life activities, has a record of an impairment, or is regarded as having an impairment. This includes autism, diabetes, cancer, an intellectual impairment, mobility challenges requiring the use of a wheelchair, cerebral palsy, post-traumatic stress disorder, and multiple sclerosis (U.S. Equal Employment Opportunity Commission n.d.a).

How does the ADA affect individuals in the workplace?

Under the ADA, employers are required to provide to qualified employees "reasonable accommodations" that do not impose an "undue hardship." Reasonable accommodations are defined as adjustments or modifications provided by an employer to ensure that a job applicant or employee with a disability has equal employment opportunities in all aspects of work. This includes applying for a job, performing essential job functions, and enjoying equal access to the workplace. Undue hardship is defined as any actions requiring significant difficulty or expense on the operation of the employer's business considering the size, financial resources, and nature and structure of the operation.

The types of accommodations to which an individual is entitled varies greatly and depends on the needs of the applicant or the employee. An employer is not required to lower quality or production standards to provide an accommodation, nor are they obligated to provide personal items like glasses or hearing aids. After being hired and disclosing a disability, an employer must engage in what the law calls a "flexible inter-active process," a discussion between the employer and the employee on accommodations that would be more effective and practical (U.S. Equal Employment Opportunity Commission 2002). The worksheet **Americans with Disabilities Act** [22.3] summarizes this information.

What is a reasonable accommodation?

A reasonable accommodation is dependent on the agreement reached between an employer and an employee. The types of accommodations vary from individual to individual, and there is no comprehensive list that exists that describes every accommodation that can be provided. The accommodations must be specific to a job and the needs of the individual and cannot impose an undue hardship upon the employer (U.S. Equal Employment Opportunity Commission n.d.a).

What are examples of reasonable accommodations under the ADA?

Below are the types of accommodations that would be easy and inexpensive for an employer to implement regardless of the size of the organization or the nature of the business.

Communication supports

- Allow an employee to provide written responses instead of verbal responses.

- Allow an employee to bring an advocate to a performance review or disciplinary meeting.

Executive functioning/time management supports

- Divide large assignments into smaller tasks.

- Use a wall calendar to help emphasize dates.

- Develop a color-code system to organize files, projects, or activities.

- Use a job coach to teach/reinforce organization skills.

- Provide a list prioritizing job activities and projects.

- Provide written instructions for tasks.

- Help an employee remember the faces of coworkers by providing a directory with pictures and providing coworkers with name tags.

- Provide written instructions for tasks and projects.

- Allow additional training time for learning new tasks.

Supports from a supervisor

- Provide feedback to help an employee to target areas of improvement.

- Prioritize an employee's list of tasks.

- Provide weekly or monthly meetings with the employee to discuss workplace issues.

- Maintain open channels of communication between an employee and a new and old supervisor to help with transitions.

Sensory supports

- Allow an employee to use a hand-held squeeze ball to provide sensory input.

- Provide noise-cancelling headphones to reduce noise that helps the employee focus.

- Relocate an employee's office away from audible or visual distractions.

- Provide a desk lamp in place of overhead fluorescent lighting.

- Allow telecommuting when possible.

Stress management

- Allow an employee to make telephone calls for support.

- Modify an employee's work schedule.

On-the-job social skills support

- Match to a workplace mentor to provide support to the employee when needed.

- Provide a job coach to help learn social cues.

- Use training videos to demonstrate appropriate social cues.

- Make attendance in social functions optional (United States Department of Labor Office of Disability Employment Policy 2013).

What needs to be considered for a reasonable accommodation?

When disclosing a disability, it's important that the employee identifies their specific needs and the accommodation that would best meet these needs. The following questions can help in this process:

1. What limitations does the employee experience?

2. How do these limitations affect the employee's job performance?

3. What specific job tasks are a problem because of these limitations?

4. What accommodations are available to reduce or eliminate these problems?

5. Are all possible resources being used to determine accommodation?

6. Can the employee provide information on possible accommodation solutions?

7. Once an accommodation is in place, would it be useful to meet with the employee to evaluate the effectiveness of the accommodation and determine if additional accommodations are needed?

8. Do supervisory personnel and employees need training regarding the individual's disability?

Can an employer discriminate against an employee because of a disability?

Discrimination in any form is in violation of federal law. Under the ADA, it is illegal to discriminate against an applicant or employee in all aspects of employment including hiring, firing, wages, job assignments, promotions, layoffs, training, benefits, and any other term or condition of employment (United States Department of Labor, Office of Disability Employment Policy 2013).

What questions and actions can and can't an employer ask of an employee with a disability?

Employers are also not allowed to ask an applicant or employee the existence or severity of a disability and cannot ask a job applicant to answer medical questions. Employers may only ask the individual to take a medical exam if it is required for all employees and the exam must be related and consistent with the employer's business needs. After being hired, an employer can only ask medical questions or require a medical exam for documentation supporting an employee's request for accommodations (U.S. Department of Justice, Civil Rights Division 2024).

Is an applicant or employee required to disclose their disability to their employer?

No, it's entirely voluntary for an employee to disclose a disability to their employer, but to benefit from the protections of the ADA, an employee must disclose. Once the employee discloses, the employer and employee enter a discussion to determine what the accommodations will be. If there are multiple accommodation options that would equally meet the needs of the employee, the employer may choose the least expensive option and easiest one to implement (U.S. Equal Employment Opportunity Commission 2002).

When and to whom should an employee disclose?

Employees should disclose their disability on a "need-to-know" basis to a person of authority within the organization who can approve any reasonable accommodations. This is usually the candidate's supervisor, but if they are not comfortable speaking to their boss, they should disclose to an HR manager. Under no circumstances should candidates disclose their disability to a coworker prior to disclosing to their supervisor or someone in HR.

What do you instruct candidates to do when they experience a violation of their rights?

It's important for candidates to know what their rights are as an employee so when they have a problem, they understand it from an informed perspective. If they experience any problems at work, they should always first speak to their immediate supervisor, but if that is not possible or it makes them uncomfortable, they should speak to a human resources representative. They should also speak to HR if they've spoken to their supervisor and the issue is not resolved to their satisfaction. If all these efforts fail, they may choose to report their grievance to the appropriate local, state, or federal government agency that is responsible for overseeing the matter.

Candidates should make all efforts to resolve their issues with their company before reporting the matter to a government agency. If these efforts fail, then this may be necessary. But candidates need to consider the possible consequences that may arise from these actions. This will most likely upset their employer and probably their coworkers, too. Even though they are protected under the law, they may still get fired. They may be ostracized by coworkers that they thought were their friends. By considering all the long-term implications of their actions, they will be better prepared for what might happen next.

What information do you provide on the topic of conflict resolution in the workplace?

Conflict is an inevitable part of any relationship, but workplace conflicts left unresolved can create intense personal animosity and dislike among coworkers. Conversely, workplace conflicts that are effectively resolved can bring hidden problems to the surface and provide an opportunity to clear any unresolved issues so they don't erupt into larger conflicts later. Going through the process of effectively resolving conflicts helps to expand people's awareness and gives them insight into how they can achieve their goals without undermining others.

Effective conflict resolution can help team members develop a stronger sense of mutual respect and a renewed faith in their ability to work together (Mindtools 2011).

What is the Thomas-Kilmann Conflict Mode Instrument?

The Thomas-Kilmann Conflict Mode Instrument (TKI) is the leading measure of conflict-handling behavior. It effectively breaks down the ways to quickly assess a conflict and choose the best way to resolve it (Kilmann and Thomas 1975). For candidates, it provides an easy-to-use tool to quickly assess a workplace conflict and choose the most effective method to resolve it.

These are the five TKI conflict management strategies and the pros and cons associated with each one:

1. Accommodate

This strategy is a form of "giving in" and letting the other person in the conflict have their way.

Pros: It quickly resolves the conflict.

Cons: The person that is doing the accommodating may become resentful.

2. Avoid

This strategy postpones resolving the conflict indefinitely.

Pros: Time may help the conflict resolve itself.

Cons: The conflict and bad feelings may increase the longer the conflict is left unresolved.

3. Collaborate

This strategy requires integrating multiple ideas to help resolve a conflict.

Pros: If effectively used, a solution will be reached that is acceptable to everyone.

Cons: It takes time and may be difficult to get all parties to agree.

4. Compromise

This strategy requires all parties to give up something to find a solution that is acceptable to all parties.

Pros: Once reached, the solution will seem fair to all parties.

Cons: It takes time and may be difficult to get each person to give up something.

5. Compete

This strategy pits coworkers against one another and has a definite winner and loser in the resolution of the conflict.

Pros: It works best in an emergency or crisis when time is of the essence in finding a solution.

Cons: It pits people against one another, and the loser will probably harbor resentment.

What is the Interest-Based Relational Approach?

The Interest-Based Relational (IBR) Approach was developed by Roger Fisher and William Ury, and by Brian Patton as a negotiation strategy, but the basic premise of the IBR Approach makes it well suited for use in workplace conflicts. The IBR Approach requires users to use empathetic listening to effectively resolve conflict. If used effectively, the process can help everyone feel respected, understood, and their point of view acknowledged (Fisher, Ury, and Patton 2011).

The IBR Approach requires all participants to:

- listen with empathy and see the conflict from each other's point of view

- explain issues clearly and concisely

- encourage people to use "I" rather than "you" statements so no one feels attacked

- be clear about their feelings

- remain flexible and adaptable.

The steps in the IBR Approach are set out below.

Step 1. Make sure good relationships are a priority
Treat others with respect and acknowledge their viewpoint, even if you don't agree. Be mindful during your discussion—stay calm, exercise acceptance, and be patient.

Step 2. Separate people from problems
Separate the issue from the person. Put personal feelings aside and address only the matter that is causing the conflict.

Step 3. Listen carefully to different interests
Keep the conversation courteous and don't blame the other person. Ask for the other person's perspective to identify the issue that the person thinks is causing the conflict.

Step 4. Listen first, talk second
Listen to other people's points of view without defending your own. Make sure that each person has finished talking before speaking. Identify what the person thinks is the issue and ask questions if you need clarification.

Step 5. Determine out the facts
Be fair and balanced in the gathering of information. Acknowledge the other person's feelings. Make sure the person feels listened to and has been a part of the discussion.

Step 6. Explore options together
By this point, the conflict may have already been resolved once everyone's views have been heard and understood, but it's important to be open to an alternate position. If needed, brainstorm ideas and be open to all suggestions to come to an agreement that will result in a satisfying outcome (Mindtools 2011).

Putting conflict resolution techniques into action
Role playing is the best way to help candidates practice conflict resolution. The final chapter has a list of scenarios that candidates can use to practice their conflict resolution skills using the TKI and RBI approaches. The worksheets on **Conflict Resolution Role-Playing Techniques** [22.4.1 and 22.4.2] summarize information on TKI and RBI.

What information does the workshop use to help candidates improve their problem-solving abilities in the workplace?
To bring some real-world examples of common situations, AWN created a list of nearly 50 different scenarios that require candidates to answer or come up with a solution to

the situation. The list of questions is included in the Instructor's Materials section in the final chapter.

What information does the workshop cover on dating coworkers?

A decade ago, dating someone at the same company was expressly forbidden, but that is no longer the case. Since adults spend much of their week at their job, the workplace offers the best opportunity to meet people and find friends, and some of these friendships may become romantic.

To be sure that a personal relationship doesn't negatively affect your life at work, we teach candidates the following rules. The worksheet **AWN Rules for Dating Coworkers** [22.5] summarizes this information.

1. Don't date your boss

Most employers have policies that prohibit employees from dating a direct supervisor or a subordinate, and this is for good reason. If the relationship sours, the disgruntled employee could claim a hostile work environment and could sue the company for harassment. A manager-subordinate romance can also create a perception of favoritism for the subordinate, which can upset the other coworkers who also report to the same manager.

2. You can only ask your coworker out one time

If an employee wants to ask out a coworker, they only have one chance. If they continually ask a coworker out after being told no the first time, the coworker could claim a hostile working environment and report the incident to HR. The consequence of these actions at best would be a bad reputation with coworkers and at worst could result in being fired from their job.

3. Avoid public displays of affection

If an employee is dating someone at work, it isn't considered professional to kiss or hug in the office. These actions can make other people uncomfortable and could possibly make some of their coworkers jealous.

4. Tell your company

It's best to disclose to a supervisor when they start dating a coworker. Disclosing a relationship to an employer will keep them from being the focus of office gossip and avoid any awkward situations at work when word finally gets out.

5. Set boundaries

Spending all your time with a boyfriend and girlfriend might not be good for a relationship. If they ever start dating a coworker, we let candidates know it's okay to schedule time for being by themselves and with other friends participating in the hobbies and activities that they enjoy most.

6. Plan for an ending

Relationships do end, which can be a problem if you see someone in a romantic context who you also see every day at work. This could negatively impact you at your job, especially if the relationship ends badly. Before you ask out a coworker, just remember that you're mixing business with pleasure. If the relationship works out, that's great, but if it doesn't, it could create a bad situation at work that might be impossible to fix (Stoeffel 2015).

Part II

WORKSHOP STRUCTURE

CHAPTER 10

Group and Candidate Requirements

Creating a safe environment

One of the most important elements directly correlated to achievement for youth with disabilities that leads to success is the ability for teachers and administrators to create an environment where the student is free to be who they are without fear of being dismissed for their point of view or the way that they think.

Neurotypical children start forming friendships in kindergarten. By third grade, they start to coalesce into social groups based on their common interests. By the end of high school, they have learned how to form solid friendships with their peers, which become the foundation for a successful transition after high school to the next phase of their lives, which is usually college or trade school and ultimately a meaningful job in their field of interest.

This progression of social connectedness often does not happen for autistic individuals. Due to their atypical development and challenges with social communication, many have a difficult time forming friendships or becoming part of a larger social group. Because of these differences, they can be rejected, ostracized, and bullied by their peers. The student can develop deep psychological scars from the experience and this can make it difficult for them to successfully transition after they graduate from high school.

When putting together a group for the workshop, it's important that all candidates feel accepted and welcomed so they are motivated to learn and participate in the workshop. For middle and high school students, this can be especially important, particularly if they are experiencing social isolation or mistreatment by their peers. For these students, the workshop can provide an opportunity to become part of a group of like-minded peers where they are accepted just the way they are.

By creating a safe place for students who are socially stigmatized and labeled as being different or weird, the workshop can become somewhere they are welcomed and appreciated for who they are. By providing these students with this opportunity, we are creating hope and changing lives by giving our candidates the opportunity to feel that they are in a place where they truly belong.

Setting guidelines

To help communicate the expected behaviors in the workshop, AWN created the **Expected Workshop Behavior Chart** [26] which explains the expected behaviors for all candidates. To help establish these guidelines, the chart should be reviewed with candidates at the beginning of the first few class meetings and whenever a new member joins the group. If there are any violations of these expectations, the rules need to be revisited and clear and consistent consequences need to be implemented each time a violation occurs. Learning how to abide by expected behaviors is not just important when interacting in a classroom. These behaviors are also essential life skills that are required in the workplace to keep a job and be accepted by coworkers.

It is helpful to have several laminated copies of the Expected Workshop Behavior Chart placed on the table so candidates can easily view it. Each behavior on the chart is numbered, and if the instructor needs to correct a behavior, the instructor communicates this by mentioning the number of the behavior expectation that is being violated. This serves two purposes: it allows the instructor to quickly communicate to the candidate what the expected behavior is without taking time away from the rest of the class, and it allows the candidate to make a choice to self-regulate and self-correct their own behavior instead of being told what to do.

Candidate requirements

The goal of the workshop is to provide candidates with the pre-employment skill sets they will need to successfully transition into meaningful employment after graduation from high school so they can become active members of their communities. Because individuals with autism can vary widely in their skills and abilities, it's important to make sure that the program is an appropriate placement for every candidate. As mentioned in Chapter 1, it is also important to consider any necessary support or accommodation to ensure that the candidate can successfully access the program curriculum.

The following should be considered when assessing candidates for admission to the workshop.

Candidates must have the ability to attend class meetings and field trips without causing a disruption

The goal of the workshop is to prepare candidates for permanent job placements. To be accepted into the AWN program, candidates must have the ability to attend a one- or two-hour class and participate in a community-based activity without incident. If a candidate does not have this ability, they are not ready for job placement and should not participate in the workshop until they can effectively self-regulate their emotions or can successfully do so with one-on-one support. An individual with aggressive behavioral tendencies will disrupt the learning environment and pose a health and safety issue for anyone participating in class. Candidates with aggressive behaviors also create a public liability while out in the community during activities like field trips and AWN-organized activities.

When considering accepting candidates, it's essential to ask parents and caregivers about the candidate's history regarding outbursts, meltdowns, and aggressive tendencies toward others as well as any incidents of property damage. If there is a history of behavioral or emotional instability, you'll need to gather more information about the candidate, including how recent these incidents were and the severity and frequency of past episodes. If this is an area of concern, ask for permission to speak to a counselor or therapist who is currently treating the candidate and get their opinion about placement in the workshop. For middle or high school students, you should check with the student's counselors and teachers and get their opinion about whether they feel the workshop is an appropriate placement.

Candidates must be able to independently operate a computer or operate a computer with support

The ability to use a computer is an essential life skill, and the workshop incorporates the use of a computer as part of classroom instruction. For candidates to successfully access the AWN program, they must have adequate keyboarding skills to keep up with the pace of the class, a basic understanding of how to use a computer, and knowledge of how to access the internet. For candidates who cannot use a computer independently, but can successfully self-regulate their emotions and are motivated to participate in the workshop, assume that an aide will be required and incorporate this support as part of the workshop for that student.

Candidates should be similar in their functioning abilities

Candidate functioning abilities are an important consideration when creating a class for the AWN program. It is very difficult, if not impossible, to lead a class with a wide variance in candidate functioning levels. The class pace for candidates who are less impacted would be too fast for those who are more impacted. Conversely, class pace for more impacted students would be too slow for less impacted students. The goal is to help all candidates access the workshop curriculum, so it's essential that the pace of the class matches the abilities of all candidates.

Additional considerations
The class length for middle and high school students

As discussed in Chapter 2, a two-hour class with breaks is appropriate for adults because this replicates a typical college class. For middle and high school students, modifying the workshop to a class of an hour may be required because this is closer to the typical length of a middle or high school class. Especially for younger students, consider offering two one-hour classes that meet twice per week instead of one two-hour class that meets once per week.

Class assistants

It cannot be stressed enough how important it is to determine if a candidate will require support to keep pace with the class. Success breeds success, and it also improves a candidate's self-esteem and motivation to stay engaged in the workshop. If a candidate is unable to understand the workshop curriculum and keep pace with the class, they may become frustrated and act out. This damages not just the candidate's self-esteem, who will ultimately feel bad about their behavior, but also the candidate's reputation with fellow classmates. If support is needed, you'll need to determine if the program, school, or parent/caregiver is responsible for providing the aide and if the aide is to be paid or be a volunteer.

For a program for middle and high school students with candidates who are minors, it's recommended that you run a background check on any adult who you are considering hiring. If your program is being offered by a school and the aide is already employed by the school, they should already have a background check in their employment file. If you are unable to run a background check, see if the candidate has a mature older sibling or cousin who could serve as their aide. Students from the high school might also be a good option. In lieu of pay, they may be able to receive serving-learning credits for their time. It is highly recommended that a parent not be the candidate's aide. The workshop should foster a sense of independence for candidates, and it is difficult to foster this when the candidate's main source of class support is their primary caregiver.

AUTHOR'S REFLECTION
The importance of providing classroom support

A candidate who was part of the original program for almost all five years loved coming to class and going on field trips. He was a terrific young man with a warm personality, but he was minimally verbal and had limited computer skills. For almost the entire time, he did not have a support person in class dedicated to help him keep pace. He also failed to make a meaningful social connection to any of his fellow candidates. Occasionally, we were able to provide an aide, but for the most part, he was on his own. I tried to help him when I could, but it was difficult to support him when I was leading the class. I often wondered how much he was gaining from the program or how much information he retained. And because he did not make any meaningful friendship connections, he missed out on the social aspect of the program.

In March 2020, when Covid hit and we had to switch to online classes, he was unable to attend due to his limited computer abilities. Had he had a one-on-one aide, the young man may have been able to attend the online classes and finish the program for what became our final year.

CHAPTER 11

Positive Behavior Supports

The information in this chapter is largely based on an excellent job coach training manual from the North Dakota Statewide Developmental Disability Community Staff Training Program (2020). The manual is divided into several chapters, and concludes with multiple choice, true/false, and essay questions.

There is always a reason why we behave as we do. Our behavior is not random. We choose behaviors that help us to get our needs met. Effective behaviors help us accomplish our goals and get what we want out of life. But when our behaviors are challenging, our actions interfere with our ability to live in harmony with others, which causes conflicts with our families, friends, and coworkers.

But how can we better understand a challenging behavior?

We must start by changing our perspective of behavior. Instead of labeling it as "good" or "bad," "positive" or "negative," "appropriate" or "inappropriate," a more effective way of understanding behaviors is to identify the function of or the reason for the behavior. To do this, we must first examine the cause and effect of the behavior, including where the behavior occurred, the context in which it occurred, what the behavior looked like, and what happened after the behavior stopped. Once we have this information, we can develop a plan to help the individual choose more adaptive behaviors that will be effective in getting their needs met.

The goal of behavior supports is not "to get rid of" the behavior or control what the individual does. Instead, it is to empower the individual with the tools they need to choose more effective behaviors that ultimately help them get what they want. Behavior is a choice, and everyone is capable of learning new ways of choosing behaviors that help them successfully navigate their life, learn from their mistakes, and communicate their needs.

Positive behavior supports (PBS) are ways that help an individual choose more effective behaviors to improve the overall quality of their life. It is an effective technique used to help an individual replace challenging behaviors with more adaptive behaviors. The focus is not just on stopping a single incidence of a behavior but to predict the possibility of future behaviors. The goal is to teach the individual how to choose socially accepted behaviors that can be understood by others.

PBS is based on the following principles:

- **Understanding** that people do not control others.

- **Believing** that there is a reason behind most challenging behaviors.

- **Shifting** from "controlling challenging behavior" to "support for effective behavior."

The goals of PBS are to:

- help people enjoy life

- help people live independent lives

- provide opportunities for choice

- replace challenging behaviors with adaptive, functional behaviors.

PBS approaches are:

- **individualized:** based on the desires, abilities, environments, and preferences of the individual

- **proactive:** steps are taken in advance of an unwanted behavior so it is less likely to occur

- **data-driven:** based on functional assessments to determine the purpose of the challenging behavior

- **capacity building:** teaching replacement skills for any unwanted behavior

- **multi-dimensional:** including a variety of components and methodologies.

Positive behavior support plans

A PBS plan is a roadmap for anyone who supports, interacts, and works with the individual. It explains how to teach the individual ways to make more effective life choices. A PBS plan is tailored specifically to the individual and contains one or more strategies that teach new skills as well as information on how to best support the individual during the occurrence of a challenging behavior. To gauge how well the plan is working, the individual's support staff collect data on the individual's behaviors to determine if the plan is helping them achieve their desired outcomes.

A PBS plan should address these important points for the individual:

- What outcome would they like to see in their life?

- What does a good day look like?

- What can be done to help the individual have greater independence and self-control?

- How can the individual communicate to others what they want?

- What can be done to reduce stress, anger, or frustration?

It is important to remember that a PBS plan is a living document and subject to change. After the individual's support team gets better acquainted with the individual, they can provide valuable insight into what is working as well as make suggestions for improvement. Any changes to the plan must first be agreed to by the individual, the support team, and the staff person responsible for its implementation, which is usually the program manager or executive director of the organization that is providing support.

Functional behavioral assessment

A functional behavioral assessment (FBA) is the foundation of a PBS plan. It is an organized process for looking at behavior to help understand the function of the behavior. To identify a behavior's function, an FBA looks at events as well as the environment where the behavior occurred. It examines any patterns that can predict when a challenging behavior may occur and is a way of looking at behavior from the individual's point of view and to better understand the reason why the individual chose their behavior.

An FBA is based on three core beliefs:

- Every individual is unique.

- Behavior that persists serves some purpose.

- The best way to support behavior change is to understand the reason behind the behavior.

There is important information to be gathered about the individual for an FBA:

- **Strengths:** What skills does the individual have that could become a source of success and esteem (i.e. get the person hired or help them make friends)?

- **Likes/Dislikes:** What does the individual enjoy (i.e. interests, events, foods, or music)?

- **Health:** Is the individual sensitive to a particular sound or texture? Are they on any medication or have dietary restrictions?

- **Preferred learning style:** Does the person learn best by doing, watching, listening, or reading/writing, or a combination of styles?

- **Relationships:** Does the individual have friends, have meaningful connections to others, and belong to a community of like-minded people? What type of person is the individual most attracted to or do they choose to avoid?

- **Intervention history:** What interventions have been previously used? Were these successful? Why or why not? A good FBA learns from the past.

- **Social/Emotional characteristics:** Does the individual seem withdrawn or apathetic? Do they believe their problems are caused by others?

The first step in creating an FBA is to define the challenging behavior. The second step is to observe the behavior. This also includes interviews with friends, family members, support staff, siblings, and peers because they know the person well and can be a valuable information source on the individual's behavior. The third step is to create the PBS plan. It's important to remember that a PBS plan is not a 'fix all' and won't take care of any behavioral issues right away or all at once. The FBA takes time to create, and in some cases, it may not produce a clear answer. Severe or persistent behaviors rarely have a single cause or function. But, an FBA will usually give the individual's support team a direction on where to start when developing a support plan.

Identifying a behavior

The targeted behavior must be something that can be observed, assessed, and measured and can be described in an action word. Specific observable behaviors would be yelling, swearing, throwing, or causing property damage. General descriptors like "mad" or "angry" describe feelings and are assumptions that cannot be observed or documented as objective data. An example: instead of describing someone as angry, specific observable behaviors would be furrowed brow, yelling, pacing and swearing, throwing or breaking objects.

There are four main categories for the function of a behavior.

1. Attention

- Examples for children: misbehaving, overreacting to a minor incident, asking a lot of questions.

- Examples for teens and adults: seeking sympathy, feigning lack of ability to get someone to help you, "fishing" for compliments.

2. Escape

- Examples for children: running away, tantruming, putting head down on their desk.

- Examples for teens and adults: self-isolation, drug or alcohol use, or leaving a gathering early.

3. Sensory stimulation

- Examples for children: hand flapping, finger wiggling.

- Examples for teens and adults: fast sports, using drugs and alcohol.

4. Seeking access to tangibles or activities

- Examples for children: crying or screaming for a desired object.

- Examples for teens and adults: playing video games, viewing YouTube videos.

Systematic observation: Gathering data

After a behavior has been identified, data is gathered about the individual's behavior. An A-B-C analysis is a widely used method in data collection. A-B-C stands for:

- **Antecedent:** What happened right before the target behavior as well as any occurrence or event in the environment that may have caused the behavior.

- **Behavior:** What the person said or did and the length of time that the target behavior occurred.

- **Consequence:** What happened immediately after the target behavior.

The team supporting the individual are the best people to collect A-B-C data. Anyone taking data must be trained on how to properly record the data so everyone will be consistent in their work. It is also extremely important that data collection must occur within minutes of when the behavior occurs. Important information could be lost, misreported, or distorted if not recorded promptly.

Antecedents and consequences can influence behavior in several ways.

- Antecedents prompt or trigger a behavior (e.g. a loud sound).

- Consequences can maintain a behavior (e.g. if a person is having an outburst and a support person continues talking to them instead of letting them calm down).

- Consequences can decrease a behavior (e.g. slowing down your driving after receiving a speeding ticket).

- Consequences and antecedents can be manipulated to teach new skills (e.g. prompting an individual to put on clean clothes then praising them for looking nice).

- Consequences can be positive (e.g. praise and encouragement).

Creating the PBS plan

After determining the antecedents and/or consequences that are influencing the behavior, the PBS plan is written. The plan is developed through the joint efforts of anyone who works or is involved with the individual, including direct support staff, teachers, job coaches, parents, case managers, and anyone else who knows and interacts with the individual. The identified outcomes for the individual must be agreed by the individual and anyone who is providing support.

A PBS plan considers how the following factors affect quality of life.

Environment

The quality of the environment where the individual lives, works, and plays affects behavior. A helpful environment supports skills development and personal growth. There are five ways to assess the quality of an environment:

- Does it support participation in activities the individual enjoys?

- Is it functional, age-appropriate, and meaningful?

- Does it help the individual to use skills and accomplish goals?

- Is it a pleasant and comfortable place with positive and enjoyable events?

- Is it safe?

Communication

Breakdown in communication occurs when the individual is not able to understand or process what other people are saying. Cognitive and physical disabilities affect an individual's ability to process information. This can result in difficulty in processing long sentences, understanding the difference of certain words such as "wh" words (e.g. what, who, where, why, or when), and having difficulty expressing ideas. An individual with auditory processing delays requires more time to understand what is being said. Individuals with short-term memory challenges may have difficulties remembering what another person says. To avoid problems in communication, it is important to adjust our message to match the individual's communication needs. Slowing down our delivery allows the individual more time to process what is being said and respond without feeling pressured and frustrated. Individuals with ADHD are easily distracted by background noises that you may not notice, like the hum of an air conditioner or running water in a sink. A good rule is to wait at least thirty seconds to allow the person time to respond.

Opportunities for choice

Types of choices that enhance quality of life include decisions on:

- who they spend time with

- schedules and routines

- activities and equipment for the activity

- how to use and decorate personal space (e.g. bedroom)

- access to personal property

- privacy

- hiring staff and personal assistants.

Social skills

Social skills refer to behaviors that lead to being accepted by others and experiencing success in the workplace and in other areas of life. Social skills are embedded in our lives and are the foundation of meaningful connections with others. These skills range from simple nonverbal communication like eye contact and head nods to complex problem-solving and communication strategies. A lack of social skills can lead to difficulties at work, emotional problems, aggression, and poor self-image. Cultural differences can also contribute to social and communication differences.

Language and social skill deficits can result in choosing unacceptable behaviors when responding to social situations and interactions. This includes being unable to adapt to new social situations, interpreting and inferring the language of others, self-regulating emotions in stressful situations, and self-isolating to avoid people and social demands. Unfortunately, if the individual has limited opportunity to interact with others in childhood, they will most likely have challenges in social skills as an adult.

There are many important social skills, but these are the four main categories:

- Survival—listening, following directions, ignoring distractions, using assertive talk, rewarding yourself.

- Interpersonal—sharing, asking for permission, joining an activity, waiting your turn.

- Problem-solving—asking for help, apologizing, accepting consequences, deciding on what to do.

- Conflict resolution—dealing with waiting, teasing, losing, accusations, being left out, peer pressure.

Relationships and community
The quality of our relationships has a direct impact on our quality of life, but this extends beyond our individual relationships. It's equally important that we belong to a community of like-minded people. Feeling a sense of community is essential to the human experience and embraces our spirit, character, and pride. Our community gives us a sense of importance and allows us to share our personal relatedness and support the growth of others, ourselves, and our environment. It provides us with a place to bond and an outlet for our interests and causes that we are passionate about (Welling People n.d.).

Helping an individual connect to a community is an important element of a behavioral support plan. Being an active member of a community alleviates feelings of isolation and boosts the individual's self-esteem and self-worth. Online communities are a great resource, but in-person connections will always have more impact. A person's ability to understand social cues is learned, and it's easier to teach social skills and understanding nonverbal communication in one-on-one interactions than it is virtually.

Implementing a positive behavioral support plan
"Catch 'em being good" is a phrase coined by PBS people who use positive reinforcement strategies to modify negative or unwanted behavior. The theory is that a reward is given for a desired behavior or the behavior that is appropriate, and nothing is taken

away when an undesired behavior occurs. Positive reinforcement is something good that happens after a desired behavior. Negative reinforcement is when something bad happens after the behavior. It is more likely for a desired behavior to happen when positive reinforcement is used. An easy-to-use positive reinforcer is to say, "I like the way you're thinking!" after the occurrence of a desired behavior.

A behavior increases or decreases based on the consequences that follow it. In most PBS plans, consequences are added to increase the occurrence of a desired behavior. Every time the desired behavior occurs, the consequence is used as the reinforcer. Reinforcers need to be something the individual likes for it to be motivating for them. Reinforcers also need to be used immediately or shortly after the desired behavior, so the individual connects the reinforcer to the behavior. Reinforcers can also be used to teach delayed gratification by incorporating longer wait times as the individual displays use of a new skill. Eventually, the reinforcer is reduced and eliminated (or faded out) when the individual has mastered the desired skill.

It's important to consider the following when using a reinforcer:

- **Individualize the reinforcer:** An individual's preferences can change and what is reinforcing in one activity may not be for another. A person might cook meals for praise but need to be paid to shovel snow.

- **Over-use of a reinforcer can result in saturation:** Using the same reinforcer can lose its effectiveness. Using a variety of reinforcers will avoid satiating the individual with a specific reinforcer.

- **The amount of the reinforcer should match the behavior required:** The value of the consequence needs to match the amount of the expected behavior. The individual won't want to clean their room for a penny, but they're more likely to for $10.

Negative consequences or punishments are avoided and only be used when the behavior presents a significant risk to the individual or others. Physical punishments are not to be used under any circumstance. Punishment has only short-term effects and is not an effective method of teaching positive behaviors because:

- **It forces people to adapt rather than teach positive behavior.** An example is a speeding ticket. The threat of a ticket doesn't eliminate speeding. Motorists just adapt their driving so they don't get caught.

- **It does not teach positive behavior.** It only suppresses the behavior, and the individual finds another behavior (possibly more disruptive or challenging) to replace it.

- **It provides a poor model of social behavior.** The focus should be on encouraging desired behaviors and not on the punitive actions of challenging behaviors.

- **It may produce anger and aggression in the person being punished.** Punishments only increase negative emotions and do not provide opportunities.

Promoting positive behavior

Respect for the individual is essential. Talking about the individual in front of them, demanding instead of asking or suggesting, insisting on having the last word, or controlling how the individual performs a task are all ways that will make the individual feel that they are not in control of their own life. When a person is allowed to exercise more control, they build confidence. Experience helps them learn to make better choices.

Ways to show respect for the individual include:

- making suggestions rather than telling or demanding
- including the individual being supported in conversations
- using the same tone of voice as used in other adult-to-adult interactions
- allowing individuals to complete tasks in their own way
- being willing to admit when you make a mistake and apologizing
- withholding judgment.

Developing a positive rapport is a critical requirement for proactive behavioral support. Ways to do this include:

- be encouraging
- be responsive to the person's attempts to communicate or socialize
- give and take in verbal and nonverbal exchanges.

Creating positive learning environments is essential to help reduce the occurrence of challenging behaviors. To foster a positive learning environment:

- set realistic expectations
- clarify expectations
- teach and reinforce effective alternative behavior
- pay attention to new or infrequent behaviors if you would like them to occur again
- attend to undesired behaviors as little as possible
- reduce reinforcement for challenging behaviors provided by others
- state your verbal instruction in a positive way
- make statements as clear as possible
- let the individual know the long-term consequences for appropriate behavior
- be a role model
- use a matter-of-fact tone when giving instructions

- be respectful, calm, and concerned in responses

- avoid forcing personal values on others

- don't give sermons and lectures about behaviors

- demonstrate that you mean what you say.

Teaching positive behavior

To ensure the PBS plan is being implemented correctly, support teams have a responsibility to follow researched best practices and ethical procedures that ensure that:

- the target behavior is observable and measurable

- the target behavior does not interfere with the goals and outcomes of the individual or the rights of others

- the support plan is free from bias regarding gender, age, or race

- goals are positive (e.g. state an increase as opposed to a decrease)

- the plan's goal is to help the person reach outcomes that are important to them

- the intervention benefits the individual, not the agency or staff providing the support

- legally protected rights are not targeted (e.g. religion, education)

- the plan supports do not deprive the person of items protected by law (e.g. food, bed, bath, privacy, mail, shelter, community access).

We support teaching positive behavior by:

- changing our responses to match the situation

- reducing demands

- observing rather than judging

- ensuring that supports provided "do no harm"

- using positive, proactive methods

- implementing behavior support plans correctly and consistently

- asking for assistance when needed

- recording the outcomes of the plan

- helping the team evaluate whether or not the support plan is working.

Techniques used to teach positive behavior

State the rule: As an example, the adult/teacher/parent says, "The rule is not calling another student an inappropriate name." Then we ask the student to repeat the rule by asking them, "What's the rule?" The student repeats, "I shouldn't call him an inappropriate name." The student states the rule afterwards, allowing them to cognitively "map" the information in the brain. Here comes the important part: immediately after the student verbally states and repeats the rule, reward the student with, "I like the way you are thinking," and/or a high five. We want to model the behavior that we are seeking or have asked for, and then reward (reinforce) the behavior that the student displays.

"If...then" contingencies: "If...then" statements are best stated in the affirmative, or what we expect the student to do and what good things will happen when they follow through with what we have asked for in the "rule." In keeping with our student who has called another student an inappropriate name, you say, "If you do not call anyone by an inappropriate name from now until lunchtime then you can have 15 minutes free time on the computer in the afternoon."

Two choices: When we redirect, we want to give two choices instead of making a choice for the individual. This allows them to have some measure of power and control over their life. We are not empowered when we are told what to do. For example, "Complete this worksheet," is not empowering, but, "Do you want to work on the worksheet or take a break for a few minutes?" is empowering. Always give the option of "two choices."

Modeling is the most basic approach for teaching social skills and using "self-talk" while modeling is an effective teaching method. Self-talk conveys the thinking and decision-making involved in appropriate social skills and prosocial behavior. On an informal basis, self-talk is just verbalizing what you think to yourself in an actual situation. It is proactive strategy, but it is not effective to use self-talk while a challenging behavior is occurring.

Expectations: Expecting positive results for the individual has a significant impact on their self-esteem. Individuals treated with respect are more likely to develop into responsible adults. If positive expectations are conveyed, the individual's self-concept and desire to demonstrate prosocial traits will be reinforced.

Caring and calm: Focus on the desired behavior by stressing what to do rather than what not to do. Follow up with cues and reminders. Provide reasons for instructions.

Using the teachable moment is about talking with the individual after a challenging behavior has finished and when the individual is calm. The purpose is to help them improve their ability to use social skills, and the goal is to give the individual information about how to be successful in a variety of settings. Teachable moments are captured after successful and not-so-successful interactions. These are also used to help the individual see the consequences of their challenging behavior. The benefit of using a teachable moment is that it provides practice, immediate feedback, and positive reinforcement.

Predictability and social articles: Making social routines more predictable helps the individual understand what others expect of them. Rehearsing common social situations helps them predict what will happen.

Responding to challenging behaviors

Challenging behaviors can occur even with the best PBS plan. In these situations, we need to respond in a way that limits the impact of the behavior. Ignoring the behavior is often the best response, but this isn't an option when the behavior poses a safety issue for the individual or others. The goal is to reduce the power of the behavior, because, if the behavior doesn't have power, the individual won't continue to use it. When staff understand how to de-escalate, interrupt, redirect, and withhold reinforcement, they will be better skilled at remaining calm and will feel confident in their ability to support the individual.

Responding appropriately and effectively to a challenging behavior takes training and practice. The individual is in control of their own behavior, so if a power struggle ensues, the result is a win-lose situation with the individual having the upper hand. At the start of any power struggle, it's essential that the person supporting the individual withdraws from the struggle as soon as they realize that it is happening.

The following strategies can help to interrupt angry emotions to reduce a potential confrontation.

Blocking refers to preventing a behavior from occurring or continuing and is only used when there is the potential of harm and other methods have not worked. Blocking may be physical (i.e. stopping a person's arm from hitting another person). It can also refer to moving a piece of furniture between you and the other person.

Disengaging tactics: The support person must remain outwardly calm. They should take a moment to pause, take deep breaths, then respond in a neutral, calm voice. Responses are brief, don't dwell on what the person did wrong, and don't ask a lot of questions. It is important that support staff stay in control and are not drawn into a power struggle. Ignore any remarks the individual makes that are targeted at another person.

Interrupting tactics: When a person is upset, they aren't in control of their emotions. A respectful and positive interruption can be a supportive technique to stop the person from escalating. Tactics include:

- getting the person to think about something else (e.g. a favorite topic or passion)

- removing yourself or the individual from the settings; if this fails, remove anyone who is in close proximity

- restating the individual's concerns—paraphrasing what the person is saying to show respect for their point of view.

Social disapproval is telling someone that a specific behavior should stop. It is important to state the behavior you want to cease. This technique is typically used for extreme behaviors like swearing, hitting, yelling, or threatening. First state the person's name then say "No," "Do not," or "Stop" and the behavior that needs to stop in a non-emotional tone. Use eye contact and make the statement once. After the situation has passed, the individual can meet with staff who can explain and teach them.

Extinction is defined as making sure a challenging behavior is never reinforced and usually results in a decrease of a challenging behavior until it stops altogether. The individual learns that a behavior that previously worked no longer receives reinforcement. The individual may increase their use of the behavior to get their desired payoff, but once they realize that they will no longer receive a reinforcer, the behavior eventually stops and is "extinguished." Extinction only works when the reinforcers are consistently withheld. Every extinction procedure should include a plan to teach an appropriate replacement behavior that provides a payoff that the individual wants. The person needs to see clearly that the appropriate behaviors will bring the payoff they want.

What to do after a challenging behavior

After the occurrence of a challenging behavior, it is important to reassure the individuals of your concern about their welfare. If necessary, speak to the individual in private to discuss the incident. Restate what happened and what would be a better choice. Stay calm and avoid any power struggles. To help the individual gain insight, use active listening to reflect—pay close attention and ask questions to identify why the individual behaved as they did. Listen carefully and reflect on what you thought the individual meant.

Conclusion

The goal of the Workplace Readiness Workshop is to empower autistic individuals with the skills they need to get and keep a job, and we emphasize that employees must always display acceptable behaviors at work. The consequence of a tantrum or outburst at work would be a negative performance review from a supervisor or they might even be fired if the behavior was extreme. If they injure someone or damage or destroy property, they could get arrested or incarcerated. The general rule for AWN's expected behavior is that if the behavior is not acceptable in the workplace, it will not be tolerated in a workshop class, on a field trip, or during any workshop activity.

Any behavior that can potentially harm the individual or someone else must be corrected immediately. Ideally, any harmful behaviors were managed before the individual reached puberty. It's easier to handle a four-year-old who weighs 40 pounds who is hitting or throwing things than it is to manage a 14-year-old who weighs 140 pounds. If the individual is a teen or an adult exhibiting these types of behaviors, it is essential that they work with an experienced behavior therapist to extinguish the behaviors before they cause harm to themselves or another person.

The previous chapter reviewed the expected behaviors for candidates while they are participating in any workshop activities. In the instructor's section, there is an **Expected Behavior Agreement** that reviews expected behaviors. It is recommended that you have every candidate read and sign the agreement before they begin participating in your program. It's also important to review the expected behavior document at the start of the Roundtable Discussion for the first several classes, to make sure everyone understands what behaviors are expected. Teaching candidates expected workplace behaviors is an important element of teaching work-readiness skills.

CHAPTER 12

Classroom Requirements

Room set-up

To help give candidates the sense that they are at a job, the environment should simulate as closely as possible a workplace conference room or break room. It's important that all candidates are facing one another. If the program is being offered in a school classroom, desks should be arranged in a circle so that candidates can see each other during classroom instruction.

Wifi

Confirm that the location where your class is being held provides wifi and there isn't a firewall that prevents access to the internet. If wifi is not available, many smartphones can be used as a mobile wifi hotspot. Make sure the plan for the phone that you are using has enough data available, so class usage doesn't exceed the minutes on the plan. Overuse fees can be expensive, and switching to a plan with more minutes may be less expensive than the overuse fees.

Equipment

Computers

Each student will need a computer with wifi capabilities. If you are purchasing computers for your program, Chromebook computers are a great choice due to their relatively low cost (most can be purchased for between $125 and $200) and their ease in connecting to Google and the apps that are used in class. For the instructor's computer, it must be compatible with an HDMI cable to connect to the projector.

Projector

During instruction using the computer, materials are projected on a blank wall so all candidates can view together the materials that are being covered. The projector must be HDMI compatible and have sound capabilities.

Screen

If the room does not have a blank wall or a pull-down screen where classroom materials can be projected, you will need to purchase a portable screen.

CHAPTER 13

Classroom Meetings

Program structure

Each class has a specific structure and time allocation. This chapter is an example of the schedule of classes, subject covered, and activities for a 28-class program. All the classroom materials referenced in this chapter are included in the final chapter.

Breaks

It's important to include scheduled break periods for each class, and the time and number of breaks depend on the age of your candidates and the length of the class. For a one-hour class for junior high school and younger high school candidates, it's good to schedule a five-minute break after 30 minutes. For a two-hour class for older candidates, a ten-minute break scheduled between the Roundtable Discussion and Prepare and Practice works well.

Class structure

The following is a suggested listing of topics and activities for the Roundtable Discussion and Prepare and Practice segments for a program of 28 classes. All activities are explained in more detail in Chapter 8.

Part 1: Agenda and introductions

Time allocation: five minutes

Purpose: The agenda is reviewed and any guests who are visiting the class and are not guest speakers are introduced.

Part 2: The Roundtable Discussion (RD)

Time allocation: 60 minutes

Activities

- Candidates practice managing stress and controlling their emotional regulation.

- Candidates practice appropriate workplace conversations.
- The Shout Out Count starts after the first four classes.
- Guest speakers are scheduled after the group check.

Activity 1: Assessing a candidate's internal state of mind

- AWN Incredible 5-Point Group Check-In Scale [13.1]
- Create an AWN Incredible 5-Point Stress Meter [13.2]

Activity 2: Practicing proactive stress management techniques

- Mindfulness Breathing Exercise [13.6]
- Seven Ways to Manage Anxiety [13.5]
- Nine Moments to Appreciate [13.4]

Activity 3: Practicing appropriate conversational skills

- What Happened with You [11.1]
- Interview Your Partner [11.2]
- Conservation Do and Don'ts [20.4]

Activity 4: Practicing gratitude

- Create a Gratitude Journal [15.2]

Activity 5: Creating a Positive Self-Image [14]

- What I Like About Me

Activity 6: Practicing Kindness [16]—this is scheduled for the same class that the activity on finding a volunteer job is scheduled

- Practicing Kindness

Part 3: Prepare and Practice (P&P)

Time allocation: 60 minutes

Activities

- Work-related topics are presented, discussed and practiced in class activities.
- Field trip preparation and follow-up is scheduled at the start of P&P.

TOPICS: ASSESSMENTS, GETTING ORGANIZED WITH GOOGLE AND WORKPLACE PAPERWORK

All assessments should be completed in class during the first four classes of P&P. Instructors should collect all assessments and review them prior to the next class meeting to get an understanding of each candidate's level of knowledge and get a better sense of each candidate's skills, abilities, and interests.

For the meetings at the beginning, these are the candidate goals:

- First meeting: have a working Gmail account.

- First four meetings: complete all assessments.

- Sixth meeting to have a final draft of their resume.

Note: If you are using any substitute assessments or the online resources referenced in Chapter 3, you will need to replace the activities listed for classes 1–5 with the online resources you'll be using.

Class 1

- Complete assessments

- General Work Knowledge [1]

- Google Knowledge [2] or create a Gmail account

- Interests Inventory [3]: start in class and complete outside of class if needed

- Create Gmail account: for candidates who don't have one

Class 2

- Google Formatting Options worksheet (17.2)

- Google account settings

- Account: Personal data, changing a password

- Sync cell phones to Google account

- Complete assessment: Preferred Workplace Profile [5]—start in class and complete outside class if needed

Class 3

- Review results of the Interests Inventory

- Based on the results, candidates are paired with someone of similar interests to share information

- Assignment: Complete Work Smarts [6]—candidates may start in class and take home to complete and return in the next class meeting

- Activity: Ikagi Worksheet [5a]

Class 4

- Assignment: Fill out each of the following documents:

    - Employment Application [7]

    - W-4 [8]

    - I-9 [9]

    - Activity: Ikagi Worksheet [5a] (if not completed in class 3)

Class 5

- Complete: Resume Worksheet [10.2]—candidates may start in class and take home to complete and return in the next class meeting

Class 6 (Volunteer job activity same day as Kindness activity in RD)

- Complete: Final drafts of resumes

- Discussion: Benefits of volunteering

- Review: Steps in How to Find a Volunteer Job [21.3.1]

- Activity: Complete "Causes I Care About" on the Networking Worksheet [21.2]

TOPIC: DRESS FOR SUCCESS

The next two classes will cover appropriate workplace attire. Candidates identify their correct sizes for various articles of clothing and do an activity shopping online on the Old Navy® website for an interview outfit. Dress for Success worksheets are located in section 18 in the candidate binder.

Class 7

- Presentation: "Can I Wear This to Work"

- Discussion: Variations in Workplace Attire [18.4]

- Complete: Measurement worksheets [18.1 and 18.2]

- Assignment: Worksheets on Landing a Job/Volunteering [21.3]

Class 8

- Discussion: Size for shirts, pants, jackets, and shoes

- Assignment: Shopping Online at Old Navy® [18.5]

- Identify: Organization to volunteer with

TOPIC: INTERVIEW ESSENTIALS

Candidates learn what to do before, during, and after to improve their performance in their next interview. Candidates participate in mock interviews that are videotaped and played back in class for constructive feedback on the candidate's interview performance. Candidates also create a 30 second elevator pitch about themselves. Interview Essential worksheets are located in section 19 in the candidate binder.

Class 9

- Review: The Art of Interviewing

- Complete: Personal and Professional References [19.5]

- Activity: Identify Personal and Professional References

- Review: Ten Questions Frequently Asked Questions [19.2]

- Review: Questions to Ask Your Interviewer [19.3]

Class 10

- Review Interview Essentials worksheets [19.1]

  - Interview Prep

  - Day/Night Before/Transportation Checklist

  - Reflection

- Assignment: Elevator Pitch Worksheet [19.4.1]—may start in class, take home to complete

Class 11

- Assignment: Complete Elevator Pitch Worksheet [19.4.1]

- Recite: Elevator pitches

- Provide: Feedback from class

- Preparation for mock interview

Classes 12–14

- Conduct: mock interviews

- Done in separate location from group and videotaped

- Candidates who are not interviewing finish any unfinished assignments

- Playback of interviews with group feedback

- Assignment: candidate self-assessment of their mock interview with Interview Reflection Checklist

TOPIC: CONNECTING WITH COWORKERS (CTC)

The focus of instruction in CTC is making a good first impression and learning to self-regulate one's emotional state to maintain positive relationships with coworkers and supervisors. Conflict resolution techniques are introduced and covered more in depth during Understanding the Workplace. Connecting with Coworkers worksheets are located in section 20 in the candidate binder. Rules for Dating Coworkers is located in Understanding the Workplace in section 22.

Class 15

- Review worksheet: Making a Good First Impression [20.1]

- Review worksheet: AWN Rules for Dating Coworkers [22.5]

- Discussion: How to put what you learned into practice

Class 16

- Review worksheet: Telephone Etiquette [20.2]

- Activity: Review each candidate's voice mail greeting

- Conversation Dos and Don'ts [20.4]

TOPIC: LANDING A JOB

The essentials of scheduling and conducting an informational interview are covered in this section. Candidates have been practicing their informational interview skills during the monthly field trips, so they have already been introduced to the process. Candidates also learn the elements of networking and how to use social media as part of their job search. Landing a Job worksheets are located in section 21 in the candidate binder.

Class 17

- Review worksheet: Informational Interviews: Essentials [21.1.1]

- View video *How to Make an Elevator Pitch*

- Complete Informational Interviews: Contact List [21.1.2]

Class 18

- View video *Elevator Pitch Examples for Students*

- Review: Informational Interviews: Scripts and Correspondence [21.1.3]

- Assignment: Draft elevator pitch

Class 19

- Complete elevator pitch

- Recite elevator pitch

- Research potential locations and professions for informational interview

Class 20

- Review: Social Media: Overview [21.5.1]

- Discussion: Your social media footprint

- Complete: Social Media: Inventory [21.5.2]

- Take headshot to post on profile

Class 21

- Create a LinkedIn profile

- View profiles

Class 22

- Discussion: Professional websites and social media sites

- Assignment: Finish LinkedIn profile

TOPIC: UNDERSTANDING THE WORKPLACE

Candidates learn about the structure of an organization and about the roles that a variety of jobs play within that structure. Candidates also learn about important labor laws and review the Americans with Disabilities Act and how it is relevant in the workplace. Conflict resolution techniques are reviewed, and role-playing activities are used to help candidates put these techniques into practice. Understanding the Workplace worksheets are located in section 22 of the candidate binder.

Class 23

- Review: Labor Law Overview [22.2]

- Review: Workplace Hierarchy Chart [22.1]

- Discussion: Which laws do you think will most apply to you?

Class 24

- Review: Americans with Disabilities Act (ADA) Overview [22.3]

- Discussion: Accommodations—what could benefit you and how would you request these of your employers?

- Course review

- Networking

- Social media

Class 25

- Review worksheet: Thomas-Kilmann Strategy [22.4.1]

- Discussion: Sample scenarios and apply best strategy to situation

Class 26

- Review worksheet: Interest-Based Relational Approach [22.4.2]

- Discussion: Sample scenarios and apply best strategy to situation

WORKSHOP REVIEW

The penultimate class is used to review all the information that was covered in the workshop. For candidates who did not start the program from the beginning, this is an opportunity to review any information that was missed.

Classes 27–28

- Review: Content and highlights of program

- Final quiz: Compiled from questions from all class quizzes

- Awards ceremony

- Final meeting: Dinner/Party

Part 4: Recall and Review (R&R)

Time allocation: ten minutes

Purpose and activities

- Review information that was covered in class

- Take quiz to assess knowledge retention

- File paperwork in binders

Note to instructors—reminders to candidates

To remind candidates about activities or assignments they need to complete by the next class, it is recommended that the instructor send an email within two days of the class to all candidates and anyone who supports the candidate. The email should outline what they are expected to complete or do. It's recommended that you also BCC parents or caregivers as well to keep them informed. Ask candidates to confirm that they received the email and award a Shout Out point to any candidates who respond.

Here is a sample email to send to candidates:

Subject: AWN Reminders and Required Assignments

Hi everyone,

Here are your reminders for this Thursday's workshop:

AWN Assignments

- Textbook, Chapter 3: Read "Getting Organized with Google."

- Assessments: If you still need to complete an assessment, please complete it and bring it with you on Thursday. Contact your instructor if you have questions or need more information.

AWN daily recommended habits

- Check your email.

- Meditate at least one time per day.

- Write in your gratitude journal.

Candidates, so we know that you received and read this email, please respond with a "Thank you" or "Got it."

Thanks so much everyone. We look forward to seeing you on Thursday!

CHAPTER 14

Field Trips

Frequency and purpose

Field trips should be scheduled once per month. These visits provide candidates with an opportunity to put into practice the skills they have learned in class so they can generalize the use of their skills in an actual office setting. These skills include estimating time travel, choosing attire that matches the company culture, conducting research on an organization, and preparing questions for an interview. Field trips are scheduled starting in the second month of the program and then once a month afterwards.

If time allows, arrange for the group to meet for lunch or dinner before or after the meeting. This provides a fun, shared experience for the group and an opportunity for candidates to practice their conversational skills over a meal. It also allows instructors an opportunity to observe how well candidates are generalizing the use of their conversational skills outside the classroom. Parents and caregivers are not allowed to accompany their son or daughter on the field trip, but they may be invited to social events like the meal before or after the field trip. This provides a time for parents and caregivers to socialize with each other, candidates, and the program instructors.

Choosing a business

Almost any business is suitable for a field trip visit. The most motivating places for candidates will be with a company that hires in their preferred field of interest. The easiest to schedule are places where you have a direct contact. It is possible to successfully schedule a field trip with an organization where you don't have a contact, but you'll need to practice the elevator pitch about your program so you can quickly communicate what you want and the mission of your organization. Review the website of the company you want to visit prior to making your call so you are familiar with what the company does, the goods and services it provides, and the names of the senior managers of the company.

Scheduling a field trip

Once you have identified a business you would like to visit, do a Google search for the organization's address and phone number. A phone call is the best way to make your initial contact, so make sure you sound professional and have no interruptions during your call. If the organization is large and you do not have the name of anyone who is employed within the organization, ask to be connected to the human resources department. If it is a small company, ask for the owner or the manager of the store.

Below is a sample telephone introduction that you can use when making your initial call.

SAMPLE TELEPHONE INTRODUCTION SCRIPT

Hello Ms. Jones.

My name is Susan Osborne, and I am calling from Autism Works Now. Our organization teaches middle and high school students with autism the skills they need to get and keep a job. The current statistics for this population after they leave high school are not good, with over 80 percent never holding a job or attending college within eight years of leaving high school. Our program is attempting to help these students, so they have the skills to transition to meaningful employment after high school.

An important part of our program is a monthly field trip to a business, and I was hoping we could schedule a visit with your company. These visits are an important part of our program because they provide our candidates an opportunity to practice the skills they've learned in class in an authentic workplace setting and give them a hiring perspective of business owners and human resources managers. I was hoping you might be willing to host a field trip for our group on a day and time that is most convenient for you.

If your contact says yes to arranging a visit, schedule the date and time during the call. If possible, try to schedule the visit on the same day and time as the workshop; however, as you want the visit to have as low an impact as possible on the person's schedule, be flexible on the date and time. If you are not speaking to the owner of the business, president of the company, or the head of a division within the company, your contact will probably have to check with their supervisor for approval to schedule the visit. Confirm the date that your contact will have an answer and be sure to call back on this date. Sometimes your contact will request additional information so be sure to send the email either right away or no more than 24 hours after your conversation.

Follow-up emails
After your call, send a follow-up email to confirm the date and time you scheduled your field trip for, or an email recapping your conversation and the date you will be calling back.

SAMPLE EMAIL SCRIPT: FIELD TRIP CONFIRMATION

Dear Ms. Jones,

Thank you for your time on the phone today and thank you for hosting our next field trip with the candidates of Autism Works Now on May 5 at 2:00pm.

Our visits typically last around two hours and include a tour of the facility. Our candidates also prepare questions to ask during the visit, and if you'd like, we would be happy to send a list of these in advance. Our group will include two adults and between five and eight candidates aged 14–18 years old.

Thank you again for hosting our visit to the Pacific Coast Theatre in Springfield. Please let me know if you need any additional information, and I look forward to meeting you in May.

Sincerely,
Susan Osborne
Autism Works Now

SAMPLE EMAIL SCRIPT: FOLLOW-UP CALL BACK

Dear Ms. Jones,

Thank you for your time on the phone the other day. I've attached a copy of a brochure for Autism Works Now, and if you'd like to learn more about our organization, please visit our website at www.autismworksnow.org.

Thanks so much for considering a visit from the candidates from Autism Works Now to the Pacific Coast Theatre in Springfield, CA. Our Workplace Readiness Workshop teaches adults with autism the skills they need to get and keep jobs. Field trip visits are an important part of our program as these provide useful opportunities for our candidates to put into practice the skills that they've learned in the classroom as well as learn about the hiring perspectives of business managers and employers.

Visits typically last around two hours and include a tour of the facility. Our candidates also prepare questions to ask during the visit, and if you'd like, we would be happy to send a list of these questions in advance. Our group will include two adults and between five and eight candidates aged 14–18 years old. Our past visits have included meetings with the owner of Donner Ranch, the general manager of KTTT Channel 2, and the Executive Director of Home Bodies, a non-profit organization that helps the elderly.

Thank you again for any help in arranging a visit for Autism Works Now to the Pacific Coast Theatre in Springfield. I will be calling next Wednesday to follow up. Please let me know if you need any additional information, and I look forward to confirming our visit.

Sincerely,
Susan Osborne
Autism Works Now

Field trip preparation

Create and share a calendar event

At the next class meeting, create a Google Calendar event and share it with candidates. Also, share the event with the person who is transporting each candidate if you are not using school-arranged transportation. The event will include the date, time, and address where the field trip is taking place. If candidates live close to one another, arrange for those candidates to carpool. Do not share the event with anyone who does not have a Gmail account. There is an incompatibility issue with Google and non-Gmail accounts. These recipients will receive a notification of the event but it will contain an incorrect date and time.

Estimate travel time

Help each candidate determine travel time to the business address using Google Maps. If needed, use the Time Management Worksheet [19.1.1] to help candidates decide what time they need to leave so they aren't late for the field trip. All candidates should be at the location at least 15 minutes prior to the start time of the field trip.

Review the company website

Pull up the website with the class as it is projected and review the website together. Be sure to go over the company's mission, the products and services they provide, and the senior managers of the company. Set a homework assignment for candidates to review the website several times before the next class or before the field trip if the meeting is happening before the next class.

Match attire to the company's culture

Discuss the type of business that is being visited and decide what type of attire would be appropriate. If you would like to share a visual reference of the type of attire that candidates can wear on the field trip, do a Google search for a company in a similar industry and share that information with the class during your field trip preparation.

Assign questions

Prior to class, create enough questions to assign one per candidate. To help create your questions, review the company's website and research the company's senior managers and the person who helped arrange your field trip. A list of sample questions is included in the final chapter under Instructor's Materials.

Confirm the field trip information by email

In addition to the shared Calendar event, send an email confirmation with the date, time, address, and parking instructions at least a week prior to when the field trip is happening. Drivers do not accompany their child on the field trip, so ask if any of the drivers need a place to wait while the field trip is taking place.

Confirm lunch or dinner reservations

If the group is going to dinner after the field trip, provide the address of the restaurant and the time of the reservation in your confirmation email. Also, include the list of questions and the name of the candidate who is assigned to each question. Decide if the group wants to meet for dinner. Get an estimate of the number of people who will be attending and locate a restaurant in the neighborhood close to the organization you are visiting.

SAMPLE EMAIL SCRIPT: CANDIDATE AND DRIVER EMAIL

Hi everyone,
Here is the information for our field trip and dinner on Thursday, April 21.

Field trip to Pacific Coast Theatre
Location: 123 River Street, Springfield, CA 91001
Time: 2:00pm

Early dinner at John's Grill
Location: 345 River Street (across the street from Pacific Coast)
Time: 4:30pm

Parking
Free parking is available in the garage next to the theatre.

Candidates, these are your questions. We will also have a print out of your question at the theatre.

Cathy: What is your favorite movie?

Clark: What are the various jobs at Pacific Coast Theatre?

Lucy: What is your favorite thing about working at Pacific Coast Theatre?

Parker: What career advice do you have for someone wanting to work at Pacific Coast Theatre?

Steven: How did you get started at the Pacific Coast Theatre?

Wyatt: What is a typical day like at Pacific Coast Theatre?

Thank you and we look forward to seeing everyone on Wednesday!
Sincerely,

Susan and Joanne

During the field trip

Instructors should meet all candidates prior to meeting with your field trip host so you can enter as a group. Let the receptionist or a company associate know that you have arrived and the name of the person you are scheduled to meet. Greet the field trip host and introduce the host to each of the candidates. Each candidate should shake the hand of the host, smile, and say hello. At the end of the field trip, thank the host for their time and let them know how much you appreciated meeting with the group. Ask for the card of the field trip host before you leave.

Take notes

Instructors should take notes during the question-and-answer portion of the field trip. The notes are transcribed afterwards onto a Google Doc and include each candidate's question and the host's answers. These become a good resource of the types of questions that candidates can ask when they have an actual job interview.

Pictures

Take as many pictures as you can during the field trip. Be sure to take a picture at the end of the meeting with all candidates and the field trip host.

Follow-up

Instructors should email the host after the field trip, preferably the same day, thanking the host for their time and expressing how much the candidates learned during the visit. Attach a picture taken during the field trip, preferably one taken with the host and all candidates. In the next class at the start of Prepare and Practice, project the instructor's Gmail account and compose a group email thanking the host. Get input from the group for suggestions for the email and include each candidate's Gmail name in the CC of the email. Include a picture with the group and the field trip host with your thank you email.

SAMPLE THANK YOU EMAIL SCRIPT: FROM INSTRUCTORS

Dear Mary,

We can't thank you enough for making everyone from Autism Works Now feel so welcome during our visit to Pacific Coast Theatre. The tour was so much fun, especially the projection room, and you were so generous in answering our candidates' questions. You made a very positive impact and the information you provided will serve them well in their job search.

Thanks again. You made our visit so memorable! We hope to see you next time we visit the Pacific Coast Theatre!

Sincerely,
Joanne Lara and Susan Osborne
Autism Works Now

SAMPLE THANK YOU EMAIL SCRIPT: FROM THE GROUP

Dear Mary,

Thank you so much for hosting our field trip at the Pacific Coast Theatre on Wednesday. We are all avid movie goers, and it was very informative to get a behind-the-scenes look at the projection room and the employees' break room.

We really liked the talk session at the end of our visit.

We look forward to possibly one day being hired as an associate with the Pacific Coast Theatre!

Sincerely,
Cathy Anderson
Clark Davis
Lucy Johnson
Parker Smith
Steven Thompson
Wyatt Wilson
Joanne Lara, Executive Director
Susan Osborne, Workplace Readiness Director

CHAPTER 15

Instructional Materials

Candidate binders

At the start of the program, all candidates receive their own binder. Each binder is divided into eight sections where classroom materials are filed. At the beginning of each class, materials are distributed, and during Recall and Review, candidates file all materials in the correct section of their binder. Be sure to provide support for any candidates with organizational challenges.

Binder materials

- One half-inch three-ring binder: white (or your preferred color) with a pocket on the front

- Binder dividers: eight tabs

- Table of content dividers 1–31 tabs

- Lined paper

All materials can be purchased at any office supply store, but for reference, we have included links and item numbers from Office Depot®.

Binder: item 208243 www.officedepot.com/a/products/208243/ Office-Depot-Brand-Durable-View-3

Binder dividers (eight tabs): item 592057(Avery 11901) www.officedepot.com/a/products/592057/Avery-Dividers-for-3-Ring-Binders

Table of content dividers (1–31 tabs): item 740245 (Avery 11129) www.officedepot.com/a/products/470245/Avery-Ready-Index-1-31-Tab

Lined three-hole punch paper: item 589483 (Pack of 150) www.officedepot.com/a/products/589483/Office-Depot-Brand-Notebook-Filler-Paper

Create a binder cover page

Create a personalized cover page for the binder that includes the candidate's name and program name. If your program has a logo or trademark, also include that on the binder cover. A sample cover page is included in the section with Instructor's Materials.

Create binder tabs

These are the titles for each of the eight tabs:

- Agendas

- Assessments

- Workplace Paperwork

- Roundtable Discussion

- Prepare and Practice

- Recall and Review

- Expectations

- Fieldtrips and Guest Speakers

Avery has a website with free templates that allow you to print the tabs on your computer. You'll also be able to save your work so you can print out more tabs in the future. Here's what you need to do to print out your tabs.

- Create an account on the Avery site: www.avery.com/templates.

- Input the number of the Avery product (for the eight-tab dividers, it's 11901).

- Create the eight tabs listed above and print.

Print the table of contents for binder and sections

Print out one each of the following:

- Table of contents for full binder

- Table of contents for the eight tabbed sections

Below is the table of contents for full binder and each tabbed section.

- AGENDAS

- ASSESSMENTS

Assessment Checklist

1. General Work Knowledge

2. Google Knowledge

3. Interest Inventory

4. Potential Job Worksheet

5. Preferred Workplace Profile

5a. Ikigai Worksheet

6. Work Smarts Assessment

WORKPLACE PAPERWORK

7. Employment Application

8. Form W-4

9. Form I-9

10. Resume

ROUNDTABLE DISCUSSION

11. Your Week Worksheet

- What Happened with You

- Interview Your Partner

12. AWN Icebreaker Worksheet

13. Stress Management

14. Creating a Positive Self-Image

15. Practicing Gratitude

16. Practicing Kindness

PREPARE AND PRACTICE

17. Getting Organized with Google

18. Dress for Success

19. Interview Essentials

20. Connecting with Coworkers

21. Landing a Job

22. Understanding the Workplace

REVIEW AND RECALL

23. Class Summary

24. Workshop Quiz

EXPECTATIONS

25. Workshop Syllabus

26. Expected Workshop Behavior Chart

27. Workplace Habits and Expectation

FIELD TRIPS AND GUEST SPEAKERS

28. Field Trip Recaps

29. Guest Speakers

30. Notes/Blank Paper

31. Miscellaneous

Assemble the binder

- Insert tabs in dividers and place in binder

- Place the table of contents (TOC) dividers in this order

  - In Assessments, add tabs 1–6

  - In Workplace Paperwork, add tabs 7–10

  - In Roundtable Discussion, add numbered tabs 11–16

  - In Prepare and Practice, add numbered tabs 17– 22

  - In Review and Recall, add numbered tabs 23– 24

  - In Expectations, add numbered tabs 25–27

  - In Field Trips and Guest Speakers, add numbered tabs 28–31

Inserting the table of contents

- Place the full binder table of contents on top of the agenda tab. This is the first page of the binder.

- Place the section tables of contents on top of the first numbered tab in that section; it is the first page in each section.

- Place ten pages of blank lined paper in number 30.

Worksheets and study guides

The following section contains the instructional materials that are used during Workshop classroom instruction and referenced throughout the book. They can be downloaded at https://library.jkp.com/redeem using the code SPXLNPH.

Worksheets and study guide table of contents

Assessments

Assessment Checklist

1. General Work Knowledge

2. Google Knowledge

3. Interests Inventory

4. Potential Job Worksheet

5. Preferred Workplace Profile

5a. Ikigai Worksheet

6. Work Smarts Assessment and Other Assessments

Workplace Paperwork

7. Employment Application

8. Form W-4

9. Form I-9

10. Resume

    a. Resume Example

    b. Resume Worksheet

Roundtable Discussion

11. Your Week Worksheet

    a. What Happened with You?

    b. Interview Your Partner

12. AWN Icebreaker Worksheet

13. Stress Management

    a. AWN Incredible 5-Point Group Check in Scale

    b. AWN Incredible 5-Point Stress Meter

    c. AWN SODA Chart (Stop, Observe, Deliberate, Act)

    d. Nine Moments to Appreciate

    e. Seven Ways to Manage Anxiety

    f. Mindfulness Breathing Exercise

    g. Stress Management Worksheet

14. Creating a Positive Self-Image

15. Practicing Gratitude

    a. Gratitude Journal

16. Practicing Kindness

Prepare and Practice

17. Getting Organized with Google

    a. Gmail Account Settings

    b. Gmail Formatting Options

    c. Google Account Settings

    d. Google Contact Worksheet

18. Dress for Success

    a. Men's Measurement Worksheet

    b. Women's Measurement Worksheet

    c. Men's and Women's Size Charts

    d. Variations in Workplace Attire

    e. Activity: Shopping Online at Old Navy®

19. Interview Essentials

    Intro: The Art of Interviewing

    a. Interview Checklists

        – Time Management

        – Interview Prep

        – Day/Night Before/Transportation Checklist

        – Reflection Worksheet

    b. Ten Frequently Asked Questions

    c. Questions to Ask Your Interviewer

    d. Elevator Pitch

        – Elevator Pitch Overview

        – Elevator Pitch Worksheet

    e. Personal and Professional References

    f. AWN Ambassador Job Description

20. Connecting with Coworkers

    a. Making a Good First Impression

    b. Telephone Etiquette

    c. Voice Mail Manners

    d. Conversation Dos and Don'ts

21. Landing a Job

    a. Informational Interviews

       – Essentials

       – Contact List

       – Scripts and Correspondence

       – Worksheet

    b. Networking Worksheet

    c. Volunteering

       – How to Find a Volunteer Job

       – Volunteer Job Worksheet

    d. Companies that Hire People with Special Needs

    e. Social Media

       – Overview

       – Inventory

    f. So You Want to Start Your Own Business

22. Understanding the Workplace

    a. Workplace Hierarchy Chart

    b. Labor Law Overview

    c. Americans with Disabilities Act (ADA) Overview

    d. Conflict Resolution Role-Playing Techniques

       – Thomas-Kilmann Strategy

       – Interest-Based Relational Approach

    e. AWN Rules for Dating Coworkers

Recall and Review

23. Workshop Summary

24. Workshop Quiz

Expectations

25. Workshop Syllabus

26. Expected Workshop Behavior Chart

27. Workshop Habits and Expectations

ASSESSMENT CHECKLIST

Name: . . . .

Date completed: . . . .

1. General Work Knowledge

2. Google Knowledge

3. Interest Inventory

4. Potential Job Worksheet

5. Preferred Workplace Profile

5a. Ikigai Worksheet

6. Work Smarts

Other assessments

- . . . .

- . . . .

- . . . .

- . . . .

- . . . .

1. GENERAL WORK KNOWLEDGE

Name: ....

Date completed: ....

Check all items that you have done or know how to do on your own without support.

- ☐ I know how to use a computer or laptop.
- ☐ I have a smartphone.
- ☐ I know how to use a smartphone.
- ☐ I have an email address.
- ☐ I check my email at least once a day.
- ☐ I use a calendar to keep track of my appointments.
- ☐ I know how to do internet research.
- ☐ I know how to find an address using the internet.
- ☐ I know how to use the program *Word* to type documents.
- ☐ I know how to use the program *Excel* to draft spreadsheets.
- ☐ I know how to arrive to an appointment on time.
- ☐ I have a resume.
- ☐ I have applied for a job.
- ☐ I have worked as a volunteer.
- ☐ I have worked in a paying job.
- ☐ I know the type of job that I want and/or have a career goal.
- ☐ I have at least two adult personal references.
- ☐ I have at least two work references.

An interview should take how many minutes:

- ☐ 15 minutes
- ☐ 1 hour
- ☐ 2 hours

Should I bring my resume to an interview?

- ☐ Yes
- ☐ No

Generally I get .... hours of sleep each night.

For breakfast I eat: ....

2. GOOGLE KNOWLEDGE

Name: ....

Date completed: ....

Check all items that you can do on your own without support

- Google
    - ☐ Create a new account
    - ☐ Change my personal information
    - ☐ Change my password

- Gmail
    - ☐ Compose and send an email
    - ☐ Format an email (i.e. change text, indent, add bullets)
    - ☐ Search for an email
    - ☐ Create and edit a label
    - ☐ Set filters
    - ☐ I do not have a Gmail account
    - ☐ Manage settings
        - ☐ Change default text settings
        - ☐ Add my picture
        - ☐ Create a signature
        - ☐ Create a vacation responder
        - ☐ Create a folder
        - ☐ Create a filter
        - ☐ Forward emails
        - ☐ Set a theme
        - ☐ Set the "undo" send feature

- Maps
    - ☐ Find an address and directions
    - ☐ Estimate travel time
    - ☐ Check traffic

- Calendar
    - ☐ Create an event with a time, date, and location
    - ☐ Share an event
    - ☐ Add repeat to an event
    - ☐ Add location
    - ☐ Add description
    - ☐ Add notifications
    - ☐ Change event time zone

- ☐ Change event color
- ☐ Create a calendar
- ☐ Share a calendar

- Drive
  - ☐ Create a document on Docs (like *Word*)
  - ☐ Create a spreadsheet on Sheets (like *Excel*)
  - ☐ Create a presentation on Slides (like *PowerPoint*)
  - ☐ Create a survey on Forms
  - ☐ Search for a document, spreadsheet, or presentation
  - ☐ Share a document/sheet/slide/survey
  - ☐ Create a folder
  - ☐ Move a document/sheet/slide/survey to a folder

- Tasks
  - ☐ Access Gmail
  - ☐ Access Calendar
  - ☐ Add/delete a task
  - ☐ Add a task due date

- Contacts
  - ☐ Create a new contact
  - ☐ Edit a contact
  - ☐ Create a contact group

3. INTERESTS INVENTORY

Name: ....

Date completed: ....

When you have free time and no one is telling you what to do, what do you like to do?

1. ....

2. ....

3. ....

What do you like to talk about, read about, or do for a long period of time?

1. ....

2. ....

3. ....

What was/is your favorite subject in school?

1. ....

2. ....

3. ....

If you are at a bookstore or magazine stand, what type of book or magazine would you pick up?

1. ....

2. ....

3. ....

What are your favorite sports, hobbies, or recreational activities?

1. ....

2. ....

3. ....

What are your favorite internet sites and subject matter on those sites?

1. ....

2. ....

3. ....

4. POTENTIAL JOB WORKSHEET

Name: ....

List the professional people in any industry that you admire or you'd like to meet.

1. ....
2. ....
3. ....

List the companies where you would like to work.

1. ....
2. ....
3. ....

List the stores where you shop for fun.

1. ....
2. ....
3. ....

List the stores where you buy groceries, clothes, or essential items.

1. ....
2. ....
3. ....

List the places where you like to spend time.

1. ....
2. ....
3. ....

List the events that you'd like to attend.

1. ....
2. ....
3. ....

List the companies that you'd like to visit.

1. ....
2. ....
3. ....

5. PREFERRED WORKPLACE PROFILE

Name: ....

Date completed: ....

1. What jobs and careers are you most interested? List up to ten.

....

....

....

....

....

....

....

....

....

....

2. List your job-specific skills, degrees or certificate that you've received, computer programs that you are proficient in, and foreign languages that you are conversant in.
Skills

....

....

Degrees or certificates

....

....

Computer software programs

....

....

Foreign languages

....

....

Your job-related talents and skills
Circle the words that are most applicable to you

Acting

Advising

Analyzing (ideas, situations)

Assembling

Budgeting

Building

Calculating

Caring for animals

Caring for people

Caring for things (plants, artwork)

Categorizing

Classifying

Compiling

Composing music

Coordinating (events, work)

Counseling

Creating

Decorating

Deciding

Demonstrating

Designing

Drawing

Editing

Estimating

Evaluating (a performance)

Examining (information, patient)

Explaining

Handling complaints

Influencing

Initiating

Innovating

Inspecting

Interpreting (data, languages)

Inventing

Investigating

Leading

Listening

Meeting deadlines

Meeting the public

Monitoring

Motivating

Negotiating

Observing

Operating (equipment)

Organizing

Persuading

Photographing

Presenting

Proofreading

Public speaking

Reasoning

Recording information

Repairing

Researching

Scheduling

Selling

Summarizing

Supervising

Teaching

Testing

Troubleshootng

Updating

Visualizing

Writing

Additional skills:

. . . .

. . . .

. . . .

Important criteria and ideal work environment
How many hours do you want to work per week?

- ☐ Fewer than 10 hours
- ☐ Between 10 and 20 hours
- ☐ Between 20 and 40 hours
- ☐ 40 hours or more

What is your maximum commute (time and distance)?

Time: .... minutes/hours

Distance: .... miles

How will you get to and from work?

- ☐ Drive my own car
- ☐ Use public transport
- ☐ Walk

How much money do you need to make? (*choose at least one*)

$............. per hour
$............. per week
$............. per month
$............. per year

How much money do you want to make? (*choose at least one*)

$............. per hour
$............. per week
$............. per month
$............. per year

Are you willing/able to obtain further training or education in order to qualify for a particular job?

- ☐ Yes
- ☐ No

Do you prefer to perform the same duties every day, different duties every day, or a combination of both?

- ☐ Same duties every day
- ☐ Different duties every day
- ☐ Combination of both

Do you need a job that is very structured, where you know exactly what you need to do, or one that allows you to decide what tasks to do and when?

- ☐ Structured environment where you know what to do
- ☐ Allows you to decide what tasks to do and when

Do you prefer a job with a slow and steady pace or one that is fast paced?
- ☐ Slow and steady pace
- ☐ Fast paced

Can you manage a job with tight deadlines and surprise projects?

- ☐ Yes
- ☐ No

How do you prefer to work?

- ☐ Alone for most of the day
- ☐ Minimal interaction with coworkers
- ☐ Lots of interaction with coworkers
- ☐ Interaction with people inside and outside the organization

What kind of supervision do you need?

- ☐ Close, including contact with my supervisor several times per year
- ☐ Daily check-ins
- ☐ Weekly supervision
- ☐ Prefer to be self-employed

Do you want to work indoors or outdoors?

- ☐ Indoors
- ☐ Outdoors

Do you prefer an environment that is formal or informal?

- ☐ Formal
- ☐ Informal

Do you prefer detailed, well-defined work or creative/strategic work?

- ☐ Detailed and well-defined
- ☐ Creative/strategic

Which of the following do you prefer working with?

- ☐ Animals
- ☐ Facts and information
- ☐ Ideas
- ☐ Numbers
- ☐ People
- ☐ Your hands

What other criteria are important to you?

....

....

....

....

....

Adapted by AWN from *The Complete Guide to Getting a Job for People with Asperger's Syndrome* by Barbara Bissonnette (2013).

5A. IKIGAI WORKSHEET: FINDING YOUR PURPOSE

Ikigai is a Japanese concept meaning "a reason for being" and roughly translates in English to "a reason to get out of bed in the morning." It evolved from the basic health and wellness principles of traditional Japanese medicine. Neuroscientist Ken Mogi says that ikigai can simply be translated as "a reason to get up in the morning" or "waking up to joy." It is the key to living a life of meaning and purpose and brings us happiness and joy.

The concept of ikigai is divided into elements or "Ps":

- PASSION: Do what you love

- PURPOSE: Do what you're good at

- PROFIT: Do what you can be paid for

- PROBLEMS: Do what the world needs

Once you identify something that overlaps in all four circles, you have found your ikigai.

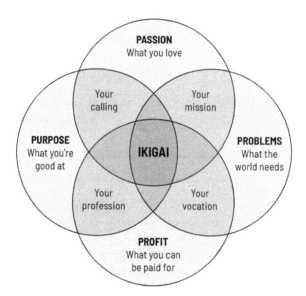

Figure 15.1: Ikigai

Questions to help you find your Ikigai

PASSION: WHAT YOU LOVE TO DO	PROFIT: WHAT CAN YOU BE PAID FOR
What do you like doing?	What are you skilled at doing?
What do you wish you could do more of?	What have you been trained to do?
What is something you do in your spare time? What brings a smile to your face? What are your hobbies?	What do people compliment you on?

PURPOSE: WHAT YOU ARE GOOD AT	PROBLEMS: WHAT THE WORLD NEEDS
What are people always asking you for advice about?	What do you dislike to see happening?
Why do people want to spend time with you?	What is something you notice or despise?
What have you overcome that others struggle with? What are your strengths?	What would you like to see more of in the world?

Ikigai activity

- Answer the questions in the table.

- Write the answer to each question in the corresponding circle below.

- Write anything that is listed in all four circles in the center oval.

- This is your ikigai.

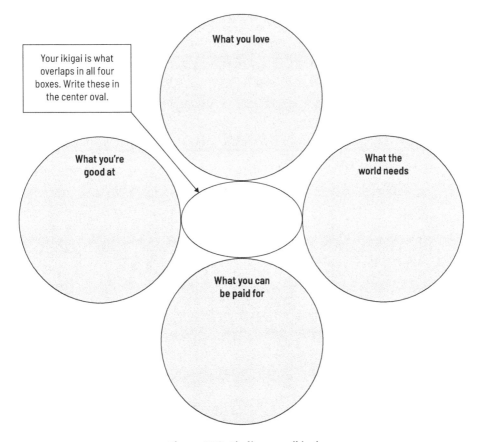

Figure 15.2: Finding your ikigai

6. WORK SMARTS

After the Work Smarts Assessment is completed, it is three-holed punched and filed in this section of the binder.

7. EMPLOYMENT APPLICATION

Employment Application

Applicant Information

Full Name: _____ Date:_____
Last   First   M.I.

Address: _____
Street Address   Apartment/Unit #

_____
City   State   ZIP Code

Phone: _____ Email_____

Date Available: _____ Social Security No.:_____ Desired Salary:$_____

Position Applied for: _____

                           YES NO   YES NO
Are you a citizen of the United States?   ☐   ☐   If no, are you authorized to work in the U.S.? ☐   ☐

                           YES NO
Have you ever worked for this company?   ☐   ☐   If yes, when?_____

                           YES NO
Have you ever been convicted of a felony? ☐   ☐

If yes, explain: _____

Education

High School: _____ Address:_____

                                   YES NO
From: _____ To:_____ Did you graduate? ☐   ☐   Diploma::_____

College: _____ Address:_____

                                   YES NO
From: _____ To:_____ Did you graduate? ☐   ☐   Degree:_____

Other: _____ Address:_____

                                   YES NO
From: _____ To:_____ Did you graduate? ☐   ☐   Degree:_____

References

Please list three professional references.

Full Name: _____   Relationship:_____
Company: _____   Phone:_____
Address: _____
_____

Full Name: _____   Relationship:_____
Company: _____   Phone:_____
Address: _____
_____

Full Name: _____   Relationship:_____
Company: _____   Phone:_____
Address: _____

Previous Employment

Company: _____   Phone:_____
Address: _____   Supervisor:_____

Job Title: _____   Starting Salary:$_____   Ending Salary:$_____

Responsibilities: _____

From: _____ To:_____   Reason for Leaving:_____

May we contact your previous supervisor for a reference?   YES ☐   NO ☐

_____

Company: _____   Phone:_____
Address: _____   Supervisor:_____

Job Title: _____   Starting Salary:$_____   Ending Salary:$_____

Responsibilities: _____

From: _____ To:_____   Reason for Leaving:_____

May we contact your previous supervisor for a reference?   YES ☐   NO ☐

_____

Company: _____   Phone:_____
Address: _____   Supervisor:_____

Job Title: _____   Starting Salary:$_____   Ending Salary:$_____

Responsibilities: _____

From: _____ To:_____   Reason for Leaving:_____

2

May we contact your previous supervisor for a reference?   YES ☐   NO ☐

Military Service

Branch: _____   From: _____   To: _____

Rank at Discharge: _____   Type of Discharge: _____

If other than honorable, explain: _____

Disclaimer and Signature

I certify that my answers are true and complete to the best of my knowledge.

If this application leads to employment, I understand that false or misleading information in my application or interview may result in my release.

Signature: _____   Date: _____

8. FORM W-4

Form W-4 (2017)

Purpose. Complete Form W-4 so that your employer can withhold the correct federal income tax from your pay. Consider completing a new Form W-4 each year and when your personal or financial situation changes.

Exemption from withholding. If you are exempt, complete **only** lines 1, 2, 3, 4, and 7 and sign the form to validate it. Your exemption for 2017 expires February 15, 2018. See Pub. 505, Tax Withholding and Estimated Tax.

Note: If another person can claim you as a dependent on his or her tax return, you can't claim exemption from withholding if your total income exceeds $1,050 and includes more than $350 of unearned income (for example, interest and dividends).

Exceptions. An employee may be able to claim exemption from withholding even if the employee is a dependent, if the employee:

• Is age 65 or older,

• Is blind, or

• Will claim adjustments to income; tax credits; or itemized deductions, on his or her tax return.

The exceptions don't apply to supplemental wages greater than $1,000,000.

Basic instructions. If you aren't exempt, complete the **Personal Allowances Worksheet** below. The worksheets on page 2 further adjust your withholding allowances based on itemized deductions, certain credits, adjustments to income, or two-earners/multiple jobs situations.

Complete all worksheets that apply. However, you may claim fewer (or zero) allowances. For regular wages, withholding must be based on allowances you claimed and may not be a flat amount or percentage of wages.

Head of household. Generally, you can claim head of household filing status on your tax return only if you are unmarried and pay more than 50% of the costs of keeping up a home for yourself and your dependent(s) or other qualifying individuals. See Pub. 501, Exemptions, Standard Deduction, and Filing Information, for information.

Tax credits. You can take projected tax credits into account in figuring your allowable number of withholding allowances. Credits for child or dependent care expenses and the child tax credit may be claimed using the **Personal Allowances Worksheet** below. See Pub. 505 for information on converting your other credits into withholding allowances.

Nonwage income. If you have a large amount of nonwage income, such as interest or dividends, consider making estimated tax payments using Form 1040-ES, Estimated Tax for Individuals. Otherwise, you may owe additional tax. If you have pension or annuity income, see Pub. 505 to find out if you should adjust your withholding on Form W-4 or W-4P.

Two earners or multiple jobs. If you have a working spouse or more than one job, figure the total number of allowances you are entitled to claim on all jobs using worksheets from only one Form W-4. Your withholding usually will be most accurate when all allowances are claimed on the Form W-4 for the highest paying job and zero allowances are claimed on the others. See Pub. 505 for details.

Nonresident alien. If you are a nonresident alien, see Notice 1392, Supplemental Form W-4 Instructions for Nonresident Aliens, before completing this form.

Check your withholding. After your Form W-4 takes effect, use Pub. 505 to see how the amount you are having withheld compares to your projected total tax for 2017. See Pub. 505, especially if your earnings exceed $130,000 (Single) or $180,000 (Married).

Future developments. Information about any future developments affecting Form W-4 (such as legislation enacted after we release it) will be posted at *www.irs.gov/w4*.

Personal Allowances Worksheet (Keep for your records.)

A   Enter "1" for **yourself** if no one else can claim you as a dependent . . . . **A** _____

B   Enter "1" if:
- You're single and have only one job; or
- You're married, have only one job, and your spouse doesn't work; or
- Your wages from a second job or your spouse's wages (or the total of both) are $1,500 or less.

} . . . **B** _____

C   Enter "1" for your **spouse.** But, you may choose to enter "-0-" if you are married and have either a working spouse or more than one job. (Entering "-0-" may help you avoid having too little tax withheld.) . . . . **C** _____

D   Enter number of **dependents** (other than your spouse or yourself) you will claim on your tax return . . . . **D** _____

E   Enter "1" if you will file as **head of household** on your tax return (see conditions under **Head of household** above) . . **E** _____

F   Enter "1" if you have at least $2,000 of **child or dependent care expenses** for which you plan to claim a credit . . . **F** _____
    (**Note:** Do **not** include child support payments. See Pub. 503, Child and Dependent Care Expenses, for details.)

G   **Child Tax Credit** (including additional child tax credit). See Pub. 972, Child Tax Credit, for more information.
- If your total income will be less than $70,000 ($100,000 if married), enter "2" for each eligible child; then **less** "1" if you have two to four eligible children or **less** "2" if you have five or more eligible children.
- If your total income will be between $70,000 and $84,000 ($100,000 and $119,000 if married), enter "1" for each eligible child. **G** _____

H   Add lines A through G and enter total here. (**Note:** This may be different from the number of exemptions you claim on your tax return.) ▶ **H** _____

For accuracy, complete all worksheets that apply.
- If you plan to **itemize** or **claim adjustments to income** and want to reduce your withholding, see the **Deductions and Adjustments Worksheet** on page 2.
- If you are **single and have more than one job** or are **married and you and your spouse both work** and the combined earnings from all jobs exceed $50,000 ($20,000 if married), see the **Two-Earners/Multiple Jobs Worksheet** on page 2 to avoid having too little tax withheld.
- If **neither** of the above situations applies, **stop here** and enter the number from line H on line 5 of Form W-4 below.

---------------------------- Separate here and give Form W-4 to your employer. Keep the top part for your records. ----------------------------

Form W-4
Department of the Treasury
Internal Revenue Service

Employee's Withholding Allowance Certificate

▶ Whether you are entitled to claim a certain number of allowances or exemption from withholding is subject to review by the IRS. Your employer may be required to send a copy of this form to the IRS.

OMB No. 1545-0074

2017

1 Your first name and middle initial	Last name		2 Your social security number

Home address (number and street or rural route)	3 ☐ Single ☐ Married ☐ Married, but withhold at higher Single rate.
	Note: If married, but legally separated, or spouse is a nonresident alien, check the "Single" box.
City or town, state, and ZIP code	4 If your last name differs from that shown on your social security card, check here. You must call 1-800-772-1213 for a replacement card. ▶ ☐

5   Total number of allowances you are claiming (from line **H** above **or** from the applicable worksheet on page 2)   **5** _____

6   Additional amount, if any, you want withheld from each paycheck . . . . **6** $ _____

7   I claim exemption from withholding for 2017, and I certify that I meet **both** of the following conditions for exemption.
- Last year I had a right to a refund of **all** federal income tax withheld because I had **no** tax liability, **and**
- This year I expect a refund of **all** federal income tax withheld because I expect to have **no** tax liability.

If you meet both conditions, write "Exempt" here . . . . ▶ **7** _____

Under penalties of perjury, I declare that I have examined this certificate and, to the best of my knowledge and belief, it is true, correct, and complete.

Employee's signature
(This form is not valid unless you sign it.) ▶   Date ▶

8 Employer's name and address (Employer: Complete lines 8 and 10 only if sending to the IRS.)	9 Office code (optional)	10 Employer identification number (EIN)

For Privacy Act and Paperwork Reduction Act Notice, see page 2.   Cat. No. 10220Q   Form **W-4** (2017)

Deductions and Adjustments Worksheet

Note: Use this worksheet *only* if you plan to itemize deductions or claim certain credits or adjustments to income.

1	Enter an estimate of your 2017 itemized deductions. These include qualifying home mortgage interest, charitable contributions, state and local taxes, medical expenses in excess of 10% of your income, and miscellaneous deductions. For 2017, you may have to reduce your itemized deductions if your income is over $313,800 and you're married filing jointly or you're a qualifying widow(er); $287,650 if you're head of household; $261,500 if you're single, not head of household and not a qualifying widow(er); or $156,900 if you're married filing separately. See Pub. 505 for details	1	$
2	Enter: { $12,700 if married filing jointly or qualifying widow(er) / $9,350 if head of household / $6,350 if single or married filing separately }	2	$
3	**Subtract** line 2 from line 1. If zero or less, enter "-0-"	3	$
4	Enter an estimate of your 2017 adjustments to income and any additional standard deduction (see Pub. 505)	4	$
5	**Add** lines 3 and 4 and enter the total. (Include any amount for credits from the *Converting Credits to Withholding Allowances for 2017 Form W-4* worksheet in Pub. 505.)	5	$
6	Enter an estimate of your 2017 nonwage income (such as dividends or interest)	6	$
7	**Subtract** line 6 from line 5. If zero or less, enter "-0-"	7	$
8	**Divide** the amount on line 7 by $4,050 and enter the result here. Drop any fraction	8	
9	Enter the number from the **Personal Allowances Worksheet,** line H, page 1	9	
10	**Add** lines 8 and 9 and enter the total here. If you plan to use the **Two-Earners/Multiple Jobs Worksheet,** also enter this total on line 1 below. Otherwise, **stop here** and enter this total on Form W-4, line 5, page 1	10	

Two-Earners/Multiple Jobs Worksheet (See *Two earners or multiple jobs* on page 1.)

Note: Use this worksheet *only* if the instructions under line H on page 1 direct you here.

1	Enter the number from line H, page 1 (or from line 10 above if you used the **Deductions and Adjustments Worksheet**)	1	
2	Find the number in **Table 1** below that applies to the **LOWEST** paying job and enter it here. **However,** if you are married filing jointly and wages from the highest paying job are $65,000 or less, do not enter more than "3"	2	
3	If line 1 is **more than or equal to** line 2, subtract line 2 from line 1. Enter the result here (if zero, enter "-0-") and on Form W-4, line 5, page 1. **Do not** use the rest of this worksheet	3	

Note: If line 1 is **less than** line 2, enter "-0-" on Form W-4, line 5, page 1. Complete lines 4 through 9 below to figure the additional withholding amount necessary to avoid a year-end tax bill.

4	Enter the number from line 2 of this worksheet	4	
5	Enter the number from line 1 of this worksheet	5	
6	**Subtract** line 5 from line 4	6	
7	Find the amount in **Table 2** below that applies to the **HIGHEST** paying job and enter it here	7	$
8	**Multiply** line 7 by line 6 and enter the result here. This is the additional annual withholding needed	8	$
9	Divide line 8 by the number of pay periods remaining in 2017. For example, divide by 25 if you are paid every two weeks and you complete this form on a date in January when there are 25 pay periods remaining in 2017. Enter the result here and on Form W-4, line 6, page 1. This is the additional amount to be withheld from each paycheck	9	$

Table 1

Married Filing Jointly		All Others	
If wages from **LOWEST** paying job are—	Enter on line 2 above	If wages from **LOWEST** paying job are—	Enter on line 2 above
$0 - $7,000	0	$0 - $8,000	0
7,001 - 14,000	1	8,001 - 16,000	1
14,001 - 22,000	2	16,001 - 26,000	2
22,001 - 27,000	3	26,001 - 34,000	3
27,001 - 35,000	4	34,001 - 44,000	4
35,001 - 44,000	5	44,001 - 70,000	5
44,001 - 55,000	6	70,001 - 85,000	6
55,001 - 65,000	7	85,001 - 110,000	7
65,001 - 75,000	8	110,001 - 125,000	8
75,001 - 80,000	9	125,001 - 140,000	9
80,001 - 95,000	10	140,001 and over	10
95,001 - 115,000	11		
115,001 - 130,000	12		
130,001 - 140,000	13		
140,001 - 150,000	14		
150,001 and over	15		

Table 2

Married Filing Jointly		All Others	
If wages from **HIGHEST** paying job are—	Enter on line 7 above	If wages from **HIGHEST** paying job are—	Enter on line 7 above
$0 - $75,000	$610	$0 - $38,000	$610
75,001 - 135,000	1,010	38,001 - 85,000	1,010
135,001 - 205,000	1,130	85,001 - 185,000	1,130
205,001 - 360,000	1,340	185,001 - 400,000	1,340
360,001 - 405,000	1,420	400,001 and over	1,600
405,001 and over	1,600		

Privacy Act and Paperwork Reduction Act Notice. We ask for the information on this form to carry out the Internal Revenue laws of the United States. Internal Revenue Code sections 3402(f)(2) and 6109 and their regulations require you to provide this information; your employer uses it to determine your federal income tax withholding. Failure to provide a properly completed form will result in your being treated as a single person who claims no withholding allowances; providing fraudulent information may subject you to penalties. Routine uses of this information include giving it to the Department of Justice for civil and criminal litigation; to cities, states, the District of Columbia, and U.S. commonwealths and possessions for use in administering their tax laws; and to the Department of Health and Human Services for use in the National Directory of New Hires. We may also disclose this information to other countries under a tax treaty, to federal and state agencies to enforce federal nontax criminal laws, or to federal law enforcement and intelligence agencies to combat terrorism.

You are not required to provide the information requested on a form that is subject to the Paperwork Reduction Act unless the form displays a valid OMB control number. Books or records relating to a form or its instructions must be retained as long as their contents may become material in the administration of any Internal Revenue law. Generally, tax returns and return information are confidential, as required by Code section 6103.

The average time and expenses required to complete and file this form will vary depending on individual circumstances. For estimated averages, see the instructions for your income tax return.

If you have suggestions for making this form simpler, we would be happy to hear from you. See the instructions for your income tax return.

9. FORM I-9

Employment Eligibility Verification
Department of Homeland Security
U.S. Citizenship and Immigration Services

USCIS
Form I-9
OMB No. 1615-0047
Expires 08/31/2019

► **START HERE:** Read instructions carefully before completing this form. The instructions must be available, either in paper or electronically, during completion of this form. Employers are liable for errors in the completion of this form.

ANTI-DISCRIMINATION NOTICE: It is illegal to discriminate against work-authorized individuals. Employers **CANNOT** specify which document(s) an employee may present to establish employment authorization and identity. The refusal to hire or continue to employ an individual because the documentation presented has a future expiration date may also constitute illegal discrimination.

Section 1. Employee Information and Attestation *(Employees must complete and sign Section 1 of Form I-9 no later than the first day of employment, but not before accepting a job offer.)*

Last Name *(Family Name)*	First Name *(Given Name)*	Middle Initial	Other Last Names Used *(if any)*

Address *(Street Number and Name)*	Apt. Number	City or Town	State	ZIP Code

Date of Birth *(mm/dd/yyyy)*	U.S. Social Security Number	Employee's E-mail Address	Employee's Telephone Number
	☐☐☐-☐☐-☐☐☐☐		

I am aware that federal law provides for imprisonment and/or fines for false statements or use of false documents in connection with the completion of this form.

I attest, under penalty of perjury, that I am (check one of the following boxes):

☐ 1. A citizen of the United States

☐ 2. A noncitizen national of the United States *(See instructions)*

☐ 3. A lawful permanent resident (Alien Registration Number/USCIS Number): _____

☐ 4. An alien authorized to work until (expiration date, if applicable, mm/dd/yyyy): _____
Some aliens may write "N/A" in the expiration date field. *(See instructions)*

Aliens authorized to work must provide only one of the following document numbers to complete Form I-9:
An Alien Registration Number/USCIS Number OR Form I-94 Admission Number OR Foreign Passport Number.

QR Code - Section 1
Do Not Write In This Space

1. Alien Registration Number/USCIS Number: _____
OR
2. Form I-94 Admission Number: _____
OR
3. Foreign Passport Number: _____

Country of Issuance: _____

Signature of Employee	Today's Date *(mm/dd/yyyy)*

Preparer and/or Translator Certification (check one):
☐ I did not use a preparer or translator.   ☐ A preparer(s) and/or translator(s) assisted the employee in completing Section 1.
(Fields below must be completed and signed when preparers and/or translators assist an employee in completing Section 1.)

I attest, under penalty of perjury, that I have assisted in the completion of Section 1 of this form and that to the best of my knowledge the information is true and correct.

Signature of Preparer or Translator	Today's Date *(mm/dd/yyyy)*

Last Name *(Family Name)*	First Name *(Given Name)*

Address *(Street Number and Name)*	City or Town	State	ZIP Code

STOP *Employer Completes Next Page* STOP

Employment Eligibility Verification
Department of Homeland Security
U.S. Citizenship and Immigration Services

USCIS
Form I-9
OMB No. 1615-0047
Expires 08/31/2019

Section 2. Employer or Authorized Representative Review and Verification

(Employers or their authorized representative must complete and sign Section 2 within 3 business days of the employee's first day of employment. You must physically examine one document from List A OR a combination of one document from List B and one document from List C as listed on the "Lists of Acceptable Documents.")

Employee Info from Section 1	Last Name *(Family Name)*	First Name *(Given Name)*	M.I.	Citizenship/Immigration Status

List A Identity and Employment Authorization	OR	List B Identity	AND	List C Employment Authorization
Document Title		Document Title		Document Title
Issuing Authority		Issuing Authority		Issuing Authority
Document Number		Document Number		Document Number
Expiration Date *(if any)(mm/dd/yyyy)*		Expiration Date *(if any)(mm/dd/yyyy)*		Expiration Date *(if any)(mm/dd/yyyy)*
Document Title				
Issuing Authority		Additional Information		QR Code - Sections 2 & 3 Do Not Write In This Space
Document Number				
Expiration Date *(if any)(mm/dd/yyyy)*				
Document Title				
Issuing Authority				
Document Number				
Expiration Date *(if any)(mm/dd/yyyy)*				

Certification: I attest, under penalty of perjury, that (1) I have examined the document(s) presented by the above-named employee, (2) the above-listed document(s) appear to be genuine and to relate to the employee named, and (3) to the best of my knowledge the employee is authorized to work in the United States.

The employee's first day of employment *(mm/dd/yyyy)*: _____   *(See instructions for exemptions)*

Signature of Employer or Authorized Representative	Today's Date*(mm/dd/yyyy)*	Title of Employer or Authorized Representative
Last Name of Employer or Authorized Representative	First Name of Employer or Authorized Representative	Employer's Business or Organization Name
Employer's Business or Organization Address (Street Number and Name)	City or Town	State	ZIP Code

Section 3. Reverification and Rehires *(To be completed and signed by employer or authorized representative.)*

A. New Name *(if applicable)*			B. Date of Rehire *(if applicable)*
Last Name *(Family Name)*	First Name *(Given Name)*	Middle Initial	Date *(mm/dd/yyyy)*

C. If the employee's previous grant of employment authorization has expired, provide the information for the document or receipt that establishes continuing employment authorization in the space provided below.

Document Title	Document Number	Expiration Date *(if any) (mm/dd/yyyy)*

I attest, under penalty of perjury, that to the best of my knowledge, this employee is authorized to work in the United States, and if the employee presented document(s), the document(s) I have examined appear to be genuine and to relate to the individual.

Signature of Employer or Authorized Representative	Today's Date *(mm/dd/yyyy)*	Name of Employer or Authorized Representative

LISTS OF ACCEPTABLE DOCUMENTS
All documents must be UNEXPIRED

Employees may present one selection from List A
or a combination of one selection from List B and one selection from List C.

LIST A		LIST B		LIST C
Documents that Establish Both Identity and Employment Authorization	**OR**	**Documents that Establish Identity**	**AND**	**Documents that Establish Employment Authorization**
1. U.S. Passport or U.S. Passport Card		1. Driver's license or ID card issued by a State or outlying possession of the United States provided it contains a photograph or information such as name, date of birth, gender, height, eye color, and address		1. A Social Security Account Number card, unless the card includes one of the following restrictions: (1) NOT VALID FOR EMPLOYMENT (2) VALID FOR WORK ONLY WITH INS AUTHORIZATION (3) VALID FOR WORK ONLY WITH DHS AUTHORIZATION
2. Permanent Resident Card or Alien Registration Receipt Card (Form I-551)				
3. Foreign passport that contains a temporary I-551 stamp or temporary I-551 printed notation on a machine-readable immigrant visa		2. ID card issued by federal, state or local government agencies or entities, provided it contains a photograph or information such as name, date of birth, gender, height, eye color, and address		
4. Employment Authorization Document that contains a photograph (Form I-766)		3. School ID card with a photograph		2. Certification of Birth Abroad issued by the Department of State (Form FS-545)
5. For a nonimmigrant alien authorized to work for a specific employer because of his or her status: a. Foreign passport; and b. Form I-94 or Form I-94A that has the following: (1) The same name as the passport; and (2) An endorsement of the alien's nonimmigrant status as long as that period of endorsement has not yet expired and the proposed employment is not in conflict with any restrictions or limitations identified on the form.		4. Voter's registration card		3. Certification of Report of Birth issued by the Department of State (Form DS-1350)
		5. U.S. Military card or draft record		4. Original or certified copy of birth certificate issued by a State, county, municipal authority, or territory of the United States bearing an official seal
		6. Military dependent's ID card		
		7. U.S. Coast Guard Merchant Mariner Card		
		8. Native American tribal document		5. Native American tribal document
		9. Driver's license issued by a Canadian government authority		6. U.S. Citizen ID Card (Form I-197)
		For persons under age 18 who are unable to present a document listed above:		7. Identification Card for Use of Resident Citizen in the United States (Form I-179)
6. Passport from the Federated States of Micronesia (FSM) or the Republic of the Marshall Islands (RMI) with Form I-94 or Form I-94A indicating nonimmigrant admission under the Compact of Free Association Between the United States and the FSM or RMI		10. School record or report card 11. Clinic, doctor, or hospital record 12. Day-care or nursery school record		8. Employment authorization document issued by the Department of Homeland Security

Examples of many of these documents appear in Part 8 of the Handbook for Employers (M-274).

Refer to the instructions for more information about acceptable receipts.

10.1. RESUME EXAMPLE

Your name ....

Telephone number...........................

Email address ....

SUMMARY
Example: Energetic, reliable, and hard-working high school graduate who is looking for a full-time or part-time job.

PROFESSIONAL EXPERIENCE

Name of company, city, state	**Year started to present**
Job title • Responsibilities and accomplishments • Responsibilities and accomplishments	
Name of company, city, state	**Year started to year ended**

JOB TITLE

- Responsibilities and accomplishments
- Responsibilities and accomplishments

EDUCATION
College degree
Diploma

ACCOMPLISHMENTS/HONORS/AWARDS

- Awards etc.
- Awards etc.

SKILLS

- Software proficiency
- Typing speed
- Special training

INTERESTS AND HOBBIES

- Interest/hobby
- Interest/hobby

10.2. RESUME WORKSHEET

Name: ....

Telephone number: ....

Email address: ....

SUMMARY

....

....

PROFESSIONAL EXPERIENCE

Name of company, city, state	Year started to present
Job title: • [Responsibilities and accomplishments] • [Responsibilities and accomplishments]	
Name of company, city, state	Year started to year ended
Job title: • [Responsibilities and accomplishments] • [Responsibilities and accomplishments]	

EDUCATION
Diploma/College degree
Certificates

ACCOMPLISHMENTS/HONORS/AWARDS

SKILLS

- Software proficiency:

- Typing speed:

- Special training:

INTERESTS AND HOBBIES

- Interest/hobby:

- Interest/hobby:

11.1. YOUR WEEK WORKSHEET/
WHAT HAPPENED WITH YOU?

Name: . . . .

Date: . . . .

Where did you go?

. . . .

When did you go?

. . . .

Who went with you?

. . . .

What did you do?

. . . .

What was your favorite part of the activity?

. . . .

11.2.1. YOUR WEEK WORKSHEET/INTERVIEW YOUR PARTNER: WHAT DO YOU LIKE TO DO?

Name: . . . .

Name of your partner: . . . .

Date: . . . .

ASK YOUR PARTNER THESE QUESTIONS:
Where did you go?

. . . .

. . . .

. . . .

When did you go?

. . . .

. . . .

. . . .

Who went with you?

. . . .

. . . .

. . . .

What did you do?

. . . .

. . . .

. . . .

What was your favorite part of the activity?

. . . .

. . . .

. . . .

11.2.2. YOUR WEEK WORKSHEET/INTERVIEW YOUR PARTNER: WHAT WOULD YOU LIKE TO DO FOR WORK?

Name: ....

Name of your partner: ....

Date: ....

What company or companies would you like to work for?

....

....

....

What job do you want to do there?

....

....

....

What type of work would you like to do there?

....

....

....

Why would you like to work at this company?

....

....

....

What people do you know that do the same job or work at the same company?

....

....

....

11.2.3. YOUR WEEK WORKSHEET/INTERVIEW YOUR PARTNER: THE WORKSHOP AND YOU

Name: ....

Name of your partner: ....

Date: ....

What was the most useful thing you learned in the workshop?

....

....

....

What did you learn that will help you the most in getting a job?

....

....

....

What was your favorite thing to do in the workshop?

....

....

....

What would you like to have done more of in the workshop?

....

....

....

If you could change anything about the workshop, it would be....

....

....

....

12. AWN ICEBREAKER WORKSHEET

Name: ....

Date: ....

Today's icebreaker: ....

Candidate name	Answer

13.1. STRESS MANAGEMENT/AWN INCREDIBLE 5-POINT GROUP CHECK-IN SCALE

1 I am really glad to be here.

I will participate and I may even be able to help others.

---

2 I am glad to be here and I will participate.

---

3 I'm here. I might or might not participate.

---

4 I'm here. I will not participate but I will not disrupt.

---

5 I will not participate and I may disrupt if I have to stay.

13.2. STRESS MANAGEMENT/AWN
INCREDIBLE 5-POINT STRESS METER

. . . . 's Stress Meter

	What My Face Looks Like	How My Body Feels	What I Can Do to Calm Down
5			
4			
3			
2			No Action Needed
1			No Action Needed

STOP OBSERVE DELIBERATE ACT

THINK BEFORE YOU ACT WITH

Before making a decision ...

  STOP

  OBSERVE

  DELIBERATE

  ACT

13.4. STRESS MANAGEMENT/NINE MOMENTS TO APPRECIATE

Here are nine moments worth experiencing every day if you want to live a happy and more successful life.

A moment of laughter
There is scientific evidence that shows smiling and laughing put you in a better mood. Take time to laugh every day. Surround yourself with funny people, find opportunities to laugh, and think positive thoughts that make you want to smile.

A moment of celebration
Take time to feel good about your successes, big and small. Schedule a time each day to celebrate a "Moment of Rock." Examples of things to celebrate include taking your daily walk, reading a chapter in a book you've been wanting to read, or cooking a delicious meal for your family.

A moment of reflection
Put your phone away, get somewhere by yourself and simply reflect on what happened today, what will happen tomorrow, and what you've learned from the past.

A moment of stillness
Shut everything off and get into a meditative state. Schedule a time each day to spend 15 minutes practicing yoga or meditating, or simply sit still and let your mind go blank.

A moment of pride
Take a moment each day to sit back, appreciate all you've done, and the good person that you are. Take pride in the little things you've accomplished along the way.

A moment of humility
Appreciate the tiny role you play in the profoundly large universe around you. When you take a second to appreciate the amazing world around you, it's easy to be happy for all that you have.

A moment of connection
We are social beings, so take a moment to connect with the people around you: your significant other, friends, and family. Give someone a hug (if this isn't uncomfortable for you), hold someone's hand, and tell someone you love them. It will brighten your day and theirs.

A moment of joy
Take a moment to experience the joy of your family, your pets, and in play, music, and dance.

A moment of gratitude
Take time each day to express gratitude—for the people in your life, the experiences you've had and the world around you.

13.5. STRESS MANAGEMENT/SEVEN WAYS TO MANAGE ANXIETY

Our world as we knew it was upended when Covid-19 struck. But while the virus is not ruling our lives as it once did, the anxiety it caused has not gone away for many of us. Here are some guidelines that experts recommended to adopt at the height of the pandemic, and these are all still good things to do today to keep your anxiety in check.

Limit news consumption
It's important to know what's happening in the world, but obsessively watching the news will heighten your stress levels. Don't ignore current events but accept that it's the current situation and don't let it interfere with your life. Of course, if it's a cause or situation that you can contribute to in some small way, investigate ways to take action.

Practice calming techniques
Try deep breathing, visualizing something positive, taking a warm bath, meditation, or sitting with your pet.

Move your body
Exercise, take a walk, or stretch. Participating in a team sport is a way to exercise and make positive social connections.

Listen to music and find activities that bring you joy
Post-pandemic, many symphonies, opera house, ballets, and theatres started offering their productions online. Classical musical has been proven to release a chemical in the brain called dopamine, which increases feelings of pleasure. If you prefer more modern music, choose something upbeat that makes you want to dance.

Get stuff done
If you have a hobby, start doing it. If not, find a hobby that you enjoy. Tackle a project—organize your closet, sort through your clothes and donate any items that don't fit or you don't wear, or clean out your garage. Keeping yourself busy will take your mind off anything bothering you.

Find ways to laugh
Watch a funny video on TV or YouTube, or hang out with friends who make you laugh.

Connect to loved ones
Call a family member or close friend. To make sure they're available, text them ahead of time to see if they are free and available to talk.

13.6. STRESS MANAGEMENT/MINDFULNESS BREATHING EXERCISE

Definition of mindfulness

Mindfulness is being completely in touch with and aware of the present moment and taking a non-judgmental approach to your inner experience. A mindful approach to one's inner experience is simply viewing "thoughts as thoughts" as opposed to evaluating certain thoughts as positive or negative. The term comes from Eastern spiritual and religious traditions like Zen Buddhism.

How to practice being mindful

Mindfulness is about being completely in touch with the present moment. So often in our lives, we get stuck in our heads, caught up in the anxiety and worries of daily life. This exercise will introduce you to mindfulness and should be helpful in getting you "out of your head" and in touch with the present moment.

It is important to practice this exercise when you are not overly stressed-out or anxious. It's similar to the experience of learning to drive a car. You don't begin driving on a busy freeway during rush hour. You start in an empty parking lot or on the streets in your neighborhood when there is not a lot of activity or many cars on the road. The same goes for the practice of mindfulness.

Remember, it is normal for your mind to wander during this exercise, so don't get discouraged. For times like this, it may be useful to think of mindfulness in this way: if your mind wanders away from your breath one hundred times, mindfulness is about bringing your attention back to the present moment a hundred and one times.

Proper breathing

Before you try your mindful breathing exercise, it is useful to practice proper breathing. This may sound silly, but many people don't breathe properly, which can cause them to become stressed and anxious.

Over time, people forget how to breathe properly and instead take short and shallow breaths, which can increase stress and anxiety. It is never too late to "re-learn" how to breathe to avoid becoming stressed.

Natural breathing involves your diaphragm, a large muscle in your abdomen. When you breathe in, your belly should expand. When you breathe out, your belly should fall.

Mindfulness breathing exercise

Find a comfortable position in a quiet place. Sit in a position that is comfortable enough so you can fully relax your body and completely immerse yourself in your breathing. It should also be quiet enough so you can hear your own breathing.

Begin from a physically relaxed place. Release the thoughts and the stresses from your mind and just let your mind relax. These may be things that have occurred today or have been happening in your life for a while. Don't breathe from a "stressed" place. You may become distracted and try to change it.

Set an alarm. It will be easier for you to let go and relax into your breathing if you have a set end time. Also, if you fall asleep, the alarm will wake you so don't oversleep and miss an appointment.

Relax your shoulders. Before you begin, relax your shoulders and let them fall. They shouldn't rise and fall as you breathe.

Breathe from your diaphragm. Breathe deeply. Your belly should rise with every in-breath and fall with every out-breath. This is the natural way of breathing.

Notice your breathing. Once you've relaxed your breathing, don't try to change it. Eventually, you will find yourself feeling a "oneness" with your breathing.

Focus your attention on your breathing. Let the awareness of your breath keep you anchored in the present moment. As your thoughts come and go, as physical sensations arise, or as noises happen in your environment, return your focus to back to your breathing.

Don't judge yourself when your mind wanders. This is completely normal. Instead, congratulate yourself for noticing that your mind's focus has shifted and gently redirect your attention back to your breathing.

Continue for as long as you like! Three to ten minutes is a good amount of time to practice mindfulness breathing.

Make this a habit. Practice this exercise at least once a day or when you feel the need to destress.

- For more information, click on the UCLA Mindfulness Awareness Research Center at www.uclahealth.org/programs/marc. For additional meditations from the MARC, click on "Free Guided Meditations."

13.7. STRESS MANAGEMENT/STRESS MANAGEMENT WORKSHEET

Name: . . . .

When did you experience stress?

. . . .

Date and time of day: . . . .

What happened before: . . . .

What happened after: . . . .

What level was your stress using the Incredible 5-Point Scale? (*Check one*)

Low stress (1–2)	Medium stress (3)	High stress (4–5)
Not much	*Felt stressed but didn't lose my temper*	*Had a meltdown or lost my temper*
☐	☐	☐

How did your body react?

Face . . . .

Jaws . . . .

Forehead. . . . .

Cheeks . . . .

Ears . . . .

Eyes. . . . .

Throat . . . .

Chest . . . .

Heart . . . .

Arms/Hands . . . .

Feet/Legs . . . .

What did I do to manage my stress?

☐ I took deep breaths
☐ I visualized something to calm myself down
☐ I took a walk outside to clear my head

Something else:. . . . .

What was the outcome?

☐ It went well and I wouldn't change anything
☐ It went okay, but I want to change how I react next time
☐ It didn't go well and I need to change how I react next time

If I want a different outcome next time, what could I do differently?

. . . .

. . . .

14. CREATING A POSITIVE SELF-IMAGE

Having a positive self-image is the foundation for being truly happy in life. But it goes beyond what you see in the mirror each day. It's about having a positive view of our entire self, from our thoughts and feelings to actions and capabilities.

Here are ten rules for creating a stronger, more positive self-image.

Give yourself credit: Attribute your accomplishments to your own hard work and efforts.

Be present: Stay present in the moment, not on regrets or longing for the future.

Keep it real: Don't over-exaggerate. Remain level-headed when things get complicated or frustrating.

Don't dwell on things: Don't dwell on negative outcomes. Instead, look for ways to learn from experience and figure out how to improve next time.

Stay in control of your emotions: Don't let your emotions rule you. Stay calm even when frustrated.

Let go: Grudges and negative feelings only hold you back. Let go of negativity to make room for more positivity in your life.

Don't compare yourself to others: Be happy with your own path, whatever that may be.

Be kind to yourself: Make time for self-care. Don't obsess about things outside your control.

Know that perfection isn't attainable: Strive to better yourself, but make your goals attainable, not out of reach.

Take time to be grateful for what you have: Practicing gratitude will lighten your mood and improve your outlook on life. Practicing gratitude daily will have lasting effects.

15.1. PRACTICING GRATITUDE

Gratitude is a positive emotion that involves being thankful and appreciative. It is associated with several mental and physical health benefits. When you feel grateful for something or someone in your life, you respond with feelings of kindness, warmth, and other forms of generosity.

In general terms, gratitude stems from the recognition that something good happened to you.

Measuring gratitude

Evaluate your tendency to experience gratitude by asking yourself the following questions:

- Do you feel as if you have a lot to be thankful for in your life?

- If you made a list of all the things you are grateful for, how long would it be?

- Do you frequently experience moments where you appreciate something or someone?

- Do you appreciate the people in your life?

Here are some ways you can practice gratitude in your daily life:

- **Observe the moment:** Take a moment to focus on your experience and how you are feeling.

- **Write it down:** Start a gratitude journal and write down a few things each day for which you are grateful.

- **Savor the moment:** Take time each day to really enjoy the moment and absorb those good feelings.

- **Create gratitude rituals:** Pause for a moment each day through mediation, prayer or mantra.

- **Give thanks:** Show your appreciation; say thank you and spend time appreciating what you have.

Benefits of practicing gratitude

Researchers have documented the following benefits of practicing gratitude:

- Better sleep
- Better immunity
- Higher self-esteem
- Decreased stress levels
- Lower blood pressure
- Less anxiety and depression
- Stronger relationships
- Higher levels of optimism.

15.2. PRACTICING GRATITUDE/GRATITUDE JOURNAL

Write down five things each day for which you are grateful

Name: ....

Week of: ....

SUNDAY	1.
	2.
	3.
	4.
	5.
MONDAY	1.
	2.
	3.
	4.
	5.
TUESDAY	1.
	2.
	3.
	4.
	5.
WEDNESDAY	1.
	2.
	3.
	4.
	5.

THURSDAY	1.
	2.
	3.
	4.
	5.
FRIDAY	1.
	2.
	3.
	4.
	5.
SATURDAY	1.
	2.
	3.
	4.
	5.

16. PRACTICING KINDNESS

Kindness is about showing up in the world with compassion and acting in a way that benefits the greater good of all. While being nice is about being polite, pleasant, and agreeable and doing what we think we should, kindness goes a step beyond. It is a universal language that can bring people together and it transcends age, race, ethnicity, socioeconomic status, and identity.

Common sayings include, "Doing good is good for you" and, "It's better to give than receive," and research supports this. Being kind boosts the production of feel-good hormones dopamine and serotonin in the brain, which produces a feeling of satisfaction and well-being. Kindness is also good for our heart because the positive feelings we get generate oxytocin, which can reduce blood pressure and the stress hormone cortisol. Kindness fosters a sense of belonging and helps us build and strengthen our relationships. Kindness can also be contagious. Acting kindly can inspire the people around you to be kind.

Here are some ways to practice kindness.

Be kind to yourself
Practice supportive and encouraging self-talk. Practice self-care and take care of your body: get eight hours of sleep each night, eat healthy and move your body. Ask for help when you need it.

Practice basic good manners
Say please and thank you. Smile and say hello to strangers. Take turns. Comfort a friend. Let someone go ahead of you in line at the store if they have just a few items and you don't. Stop at crosswalks when someone is about to cross the street.

Express gratitude
Show appreciation. Tell someone they are doing a great job. Let someone know when they helped you. Text or call a loved one to tell them they made a difference in your life.

Listen to understand, not to respond or problem-solve
When someone is talking, don't try to solve their problems. Instead, be present and really listen to what they are saying. Acknowledge their feelings. Let them know you care and are there to help. Next time you ask someone how they are, hold space and pay attention to their verbal and nonverbal communication.

Here are two stories about how kindness can make a positive impact on the lives of both parties:

- "A Remarkable Gift of Forgiveness" by Luke Broadwater, *Los Angeles Times*, January 7, 2018. https://enewspaper.latimes.com/infinity/article_popover_share.aspx?guid=6961d391-747d4817-bed1-2e52b0162aa5.

- "On Christmas Eve, A Stolen Bicycle and A Lesson in Giving" by Judy Esty-Kendell and Isabel Dobrin. NPR Story Corp, December 15, 2017. www.npr.org/2017/12/15/570806606/on-christmas-eve-a-stolen-bicycle-and-a-lessonin-giving.

17.1. GETTING ORGANIZED WITH GOOGLE/ GMAIL ACCOUNT SETTINGS

Gmail account settings

- Open Gmail
- Click on gear icon (upper right-hand corner)

Gmail appearance settings: Density and theme (pictures)

- Click "See all settings"

Gmail account settings

- General
- Labels
- Inbox type
- Accounts and imports
- Filters and blocked addresses
- Forwarding and POP/IMAP

17.2. GETTING ORGANIZED WITH GOOGLE/ GMAIL FORMATTING OPTIONS

Composing your email
To/Recipients: Top section
To: Person you are sending the email
CC: Copy of email will be sent and original recipient will know it's been copied
BCC: Copy email will be sent but original recipient won't know it's been copied

Subject: Middle section
Subject: Title of your email

Bottom section
Text of your email

Formatting your email
To open formatting options, click on the A (on bottom right)

Insert File	Picture Hyperlink	Attach Google	Insert Mode	Attach Doc	Confidential

Formatting options

	Undo			Underline										
Fonts	Text Size			Bold	Italics	Strikethru		Colors		Bullet	#	List	Indent	

Fonts

- Fixed Width
- Garamond
- Georgia
- Narrow
- San Serif
- Serif
- Comic Sans
- Tahoma

- Trebuchet MS
- Veranda
- Wide

Text size

Justify

Left   Center   Right

17.3. GETTING ORGANIZED WITH GOOGLE/ GOOGLE ACCOUNT SETTINGS

Open Gmail

- Click on nine dots on upper right-hand corner of screen
- Click on account
- Click on Sign In and Security

Click on personal information

- Add your photo
- Name
- Birthday
- Gender
- Email (second one)
- Phone number
- Address

Data and privacy

- History settings
- Web and app
- Location
- YouTube
- Information shared with others
- Profile
- Location sharing

Security

- Recommendations—protect your account
- Recent security activity
- How you sign in:
  - Two-step verification
  - Passkey
  - Password—this is where you can change your password
  - Recovery phone
  - Recovery email
  - Security question
- Your devices
- Third-party apps with account access

17.4. GETTING ORGANIZED WITH GOOGLE/ CONTACT WORKSHEET

Name: ....

Company: ....

Email: ....

Office phone number: ....

Mobile phone number: ....

Address: ....

Birthday: ....

Website: ....

Notes—to help you remember, include where you met the person:

....

....

....

....

18.1. DRESS FOR SUCCESS/MEN'S MEASUREMENT WORKSHEET

How to measure: Remember to keep tape loose

NECK	Measure around the middle of neck at Adam's apple
CHEST	Measure under arms around the fullest part of chest and relax arms at the side
WAIST	Measure around natural waistline
HIPS	Measure around fullest part of hips and buttocks
INSEAM	Measure from top of inner thigh down to bottom of ankle
ARM LENGTH	Bend elbow 90 degrees and place hand on hip. Hold tape at center of back of the neck. Measure across shoulder down to elbow and down to waist
HEIGHT	Measure from top of head to floor while standing straight

18.2. DRESS FOR SUCCESS/WOMEN'S MEASUREMENT WORKSHEET

How to measure: Remember to keep tape loose

NECK	Measure around middle of neck
CHEST	Measure under arms around fullest part of chest and relax arms at the side
WAIST	Measure around natural waistline
HIPS	Measure around fullest part of hips and buttocks
INSEAM	Measure from top of inner thigh down to bottom of ankle
ARM LENGTH	Bend elbow 90 degrees and place hand on hip. Hold tape at center of back of the neck. Measure across the shoulder down to elbow and down to waist
HEIGHT	Measure from top of head to floor while standing straight
DRESS LENGTH	Measure from nape of neck to desired length
SKIRT LENGTH	Measure from middle of waist to desired length

18.3. DRESS FOR SUCCESS/MEN'S AND WOMEN'S SIZE CHART

All measurements are in inches. For in between measurements, go to the next size up.

MEN	Small	Medium	Large	XL	2XL	3XL	4XL	5XL
Chest	36–38	39–41	42--44	46–48	50–52	54–56	58–60	62–64
Waist	29–31	32–34	35–37	38–41	42–45	46–50	51–54	55–58
Hip	35–37	38–40	41–43	44–46	47–49	51–53	54–57	59–61
Sleeve length	33	34	35	36	36	$36^1/_2$	$37^1/_2$	38
Inseam	32	32	$32^1/_2$	33	$33^1/_2$	$33^1/_2$	$33^1/_2$	$33^1/_2$
Neck	15	$15^3/_4$	$16^1/_2$	$17^1/_2$	$18^1/_2$	$19^1/_2$	$20^1/_2$	$21^1/_2$

WOMEN	X Small	Small	Medium	Large	XL	2XL	3XL
Chest	32–33	34–35	36–38	39–41	42–44	46–48	50–52
Waist	24–25	26–27	28–30	32–34	36–38	40–42	44–46
Hip	34–36	36–38	38–40	41–43	44–46	48–50	52–54
Sleeve length	30	$30^3/_4$	$31^1/_2$	$32^1/_4$	33	$33^1/_2$	34
Inseam	$31^1/_2$	32	32	32	$32^1/_2$	$32^1/_2$	$32^1/_2$
Numeric size	2	4/6	8/10	12/14	16/18	20/22	24/26

18.4. DRESS FOR SUCCESS/VARIATIONS IN WORKPLACE ATTIRE

There are occasions where there are variations in the workplace dress code expectations, and it's important to know what these are.

Casual Fridays
In companies with a more conservative style of dress like finance or law, some have a policy called "casual Friday" where the dress code is relaxed but still professional. A polo or button-down shirt without a tie and khakis with dress shoes are acceptable. Jeans, tennis shoes, flip flops, gym clothes, or graphic tee shirts are never appropriate in an office setting.

Staff and client meetings
For office meetings, you'll want to make the best impression and look your best. Pick something that makes you look good and feel confident.

Social events
If the event is a company picnic at a park, jeans, a polo shirt and tennis shoes are a good choice. If the event is the annual company holiday party at an upscale restaurant, business-appropriate attire is expected.

Halloween
Some companies celebrate Halloween where employees wear costumes or dress up. Any costume worn to work must be appropriate and comfortable to wear. Even if you feel it is an important part of your costume, you shouldn't wear a mask or face paint at work.

18.5. DRESS FOR SUCCESS/SHOPPING AT OLD NAVY®

Scenario: You have an interview for a job at Starbucks.

Your task: Go shopping at Old Navy® for interview clothes.

Instructions

Go to the Old Navy® website: www.oldnavy.com

- On the top line, click on Women or Men.

- Choose a shirt, pants, shoes and jacket that you would choose to purchase for your interview.

- Search the site and add the link for each item in the space provided below.

Shirt: . . . .

Pants: . . . .

Jacket: . . . .

Shoes: . . . .

19. INTERVIEW ESSENTIALS INTRODUCTION: THE ART OF INTERVIEWING

What should I do in an interview to increase my chances of getting hired?
   This is based on the following:

How you look

- Wear the right clothes—match the company culture
- Practice good hygiene—shower, wash hair, brush teeth, clean nails (guys should also shave)

What you say and how you say it

- Prepare answers to common interview questions
- Ask insightful questions—know the company
- Be polite—say please and thank you when appropriate
- Speak with vocal inflections at a comfortable level—not in a monotone, or too loud or too soft

What you do

- Arrive 15 minutes early
- Have a positive attitude—think good thoughts, don't say anything negative
- Project good body language—sit up, with shoulders back
- Have a pleasant demeanor—smile!

Remember your follow-up

- Send a thank you note by mail or email within two days.

19.1.1. INTERVIEW ESSENTIALS/INTERVIEW CHECKLISTS: TIME MANAGEMENT WORKSHEET

Appointment time . . . .

Subtract 15 minutes from your appointment time: −15 . . . .

THIS IS YOUR ARRIVAL TIME . . . .

Subtract travel time (confirm on Google Maps) . . . .

Subtract 20 minutes for parking and finding the location: −20 . . . .

Subtract preparation time . . . .
(total minutes from the Preparation Checklist)

THIS IS WHEN YOU START GETTING READY!

PREPARATION CHECKLIST

Make a list of things you have to do before you leave. Estimate the amount of time needed to complete each item; examples are listed below

	Number of minutes to complete
Shower	. . . .
Shave	. . . .
Put on makeup	. . . .
Get dressed	. . . .
Eat breakfast/lunch/dinner	. . . .
Other	. . . .
Other	. . . .
Other	. . . .
Total preparation time (enter above)	. . . .

19.1.2. INTERVIEW ESSENTIALS/INTERVIEW CHECKLISTS: INTERVIEW PREP

BEFORE INTERVIEW (1–2 days)

- Research the company
    - What does the company do, produce, or create?
    - How long has the company been in business?
    - Who are the senior managers (CEO, COO, President)?
- Prepare five questions to ask the interviewer based on your research
- Prepare answers to list of **Ten Frequently Asked Questions**
- Practice your introduction to the receptionist and greeting to the interviewer
- Prepare and practice your elevator speech
- Complete the **Day/Night Before Checklist** and the **Transportation Checklist**
- Complete the **Time Management Worksheet**

DURING INTERVIEW: Before meeting with interviewer

- Use the **AWN Incredible 5-Point Group Check-In Scale** to assess your internal state
- Stay relaxed using visualization and mindful breathing
- Smile and say hello when meeting anyone who walks by
- Turn your phone off or to silent

DURING INTERVIEW: While meeting with interviewer

- Use a firm handshake
- Listen to interviewer's questions and don't speak until they have finished talking
- Focus your answers on your strengths and transferable skills
- Stay positive—don't say anything negative about former employers or coworkers
- Use appropriate language—don't use slang
- Keep discussion on the benefits you'll bring to employer and your skills related to the job
- Do not make up answers or say anything that isn't true

END OF INTERVIEW

- Ask the interviewer the date by which a decision will be made

- Ask for the interviewer's business card

FOLLOW-UP

- Send a thank you email or mail a written note within *one day* of the interview

- If there is no word, email or call on the date that the interviewer said a decision would be made

- Complete the **Interview Reflection Worksheet** to identify ways to improve in the next interview

19.1.3. INTERVIEW ESSENTIALS/INTERVIEW CHECKLISTS: DAY/NIGHT BEFORE AND TRANSPORTATION

Day/Night Before Checklist
Check the circle next to the item when it is completed

- ☐ On my calendar, I entered an event with a name, location and person I'm meeting into my Google Calendar
- ☐ I picked out my clothes and shoes
- ☐ I checked that my clothes and shoes are clean and don't need repairs
- ☐ I washed my clothes and cleaned my shoes if they needed cleaning
- ☐ I charged my phone
- ☐ I gathered the following items for my appointment:
  - ☐ Resume
  - ☐ References
  - ☐ Paperwork: . . . .
  - ☐ Book(s): . . . .
  - ☐ Notebook
- ☐ I put all the items in a folder or bag
- ☐ I placed the folder or bag where I can easily see it when I leave
- ☐ I need to eat breakfast or lunch, or dinner before I leave   Yes . . . . . . No . . . . . .
  If no, stop here. If yes, go to next question
- ☐ I have the food items I need to make my meal   Yes . . . . . . No . . . . . .
  If yes, stop here. If no, go to next questions
- ☐ I made a list of the food items I need to buy
- ☐ I went grocery shopping the afternoon before my appointment
- ☐ I have completed the Transportation Checklist (below)

Transportation Checklist

- ☐ I am traveling by car
  - ☐ I have enough gas in my car to get home and back
  - ☐ I know where I will park
  - ☐ I have money for garage parking or change for the meter
- ☐ I am traveling by public transportation
  - ☐ I know which bus route to take
  - ☐ I know which bus stop to stop at and get on
  - ☐ I know the bus schedule
  - ☐ I have money for the bus fare
- ☐ I'm getting a ride or taking Access
- ☐ I have confirmed the day and time with my driver or pickup time with Access at least one day before pickup

19.1.4. INTERVIEW ESSENTIALS/INTERVIEW CHECKLIST: REFLECTION WORKSHEET

	Excellent	Room for improvement	I need a do-over
Several days before			
I researched the company	☐	☐	☐
I prepared five questions from my research	☐	☐	☐
I prepped answers for **Ten Frequently Asked Questions**	☐	☐	☐
I practiced my elevator speech	☐	☐	☐
I checked that my clothes were clean/in good repair	☐	☐	☐
I took my clothes to the dry cleaner (if needed)	☐	☐	☐
The day before			
I cleaned my nails/got a manicure (females)	☐	☐	☐
I got a haircut	☐	☐	☐
I practiced my greeting for the receptionist	☐	☐	☐
I practiced my greeting for the interviewer	☐	☐	☐
I added the interview date/time on my Calendar	☐	☐	☐
I estimated the traveling time on Google Maps	☐	☐	☐
I washed my clothes if they were dirty	☐	☐	☐
I picked up my clothes from the dry cleaner if needed	☐	☐	☐
The night before			
I put my resume/references/papers in a bag/folder	☐	☐	☐
I checked that my shoes were clean	☐	☐	☐
I shined/cleaned my shoes (if needed)	☐	☐	☐
I charged my phone	☐	☐	☐
I got eight hours of sleep	☐	☐	☐
The morning of the interview			
I showered/washed my hair/brushed my teeth	☐	☐	☐
I shaved (males)/put on makeup (females)	☐	☐	☐
I ate a healthy breakfast or lunch	☐	☐	☐
I did relaxation/stress management exercises	☐	☐	☐
I remembered my bag/folder with my documents	☐	☐	☐
I put money for transportation in my wallet	☐	☐	☐

Before the interview

I arrived 15 minutes early to the interview	☐	☐	☐
I turned off my cell phone	☐	☐	☐
I said hello to anyone I met	☐	☐	☐
I greeted the receptionist	☐	☐	☐

During the interview

I greeted the interviewer	☐	☐	☐
I shook the interviewer's hand with a firm handshake	☐	☐	☐
I didn't interrupt the interviewer	☐	☐	☐
I stayed on topic	☐	☐	☐
I was relaxed and confident	☐	☐	☐
I smiled	☐	☐	☐
I asked for a business card at the end of the interview	☐	☐	☐

Follow-up

I sent a thank you email or sent a card in the mail	☐	☐	☐
If I didn't hear back, I called one week after the interview	☐	☐	☐

19.2. INTERVIEW ESSENTIALS/TEN FREQUENTLY ASKED QUESTIONS

1. Tell me about yourself.

2. What are your key strengths/skills?

3. What are your weaknesses?

4. What kind of environment would you like to work in?

5. If I were to call your references, what would they say about you?

6. When reading the job description, what interested you in this position?

7. Give me an example of a difficult situation and how you dealt with it?

8. What are your career goals?

9. What do you know about the organization?

10. Why should we hire you?

19.3. INTERVIEW ESSENTIALS/QUESTIONS TO ASK YOUR INTERVIEWER

About the job

1. How do you measure the success of a person in this role?
2. Can you tell me something about the team with which I'd be working?
3. What traits do the most successful employees have in common?
4. What skills would you expect an employee to master in the first 90 days?
5. What is a typical day like?

About the company

6. What is the culture at your workplace?
7. What are the various departments and jobs at your company?
8. What accomplishment are you most proud of?
9. What companies are your biggest competitors?
10. Where do you see your organization in the next five to ten years?

About the interviewer

11. What do you like most about working at your company?
12. How did you get started in this industry?
13. What jobs did you have before working at your company?

19.4.1. INTERVIEW ESSENTIALS/ ELEVATOR PITCH OVERVIEW

Imagine, you're scheduled for an interview for a job that you really want. On arrival, you're instructed to take the elevator to the HR Department on the top floor. At the next stop, to your great surprise, the doors open and in enters the President of the company! Right now, you need a quick and easy way to introduce yourself and summarize how your skill set is a good match for the organization.

An **elevator speech** is a 20-second commercial about yourself that summarizes who you are, what you do, and how you can benefit an employer. Your speech can be used at networking events and social gatherings. It can also be used as the foundation of an introductory email, a cover letter, or a social media profile. If you are attending a networking event, you'll want to close with a call to action or what you would like to happen next. You'll want to practice your pitch so you feel comfortable saying it and adopting it as needed.

An effective elevator speech answers these questions:

- What have you done and what can you do—*what makes you unique?*

    - Include any awards, recognitions, and certifications that you've received as well as transferable work skills and areas of strength.

    - If you are in school, include information on your major, club memberships, people you admire, and favorite subjects.

    - Words that are good for explaining what you can do are:

        > Adept at...

        > Proficient in...

        > Accomplished at...

        > Expertise in...

        > Savvy...

- What are your best skills and abilities—*how can you benefit an employer?*

    - Be specific about what you do best.

    - Consider areas where are you most confident.

    - Focus on positive feedback that you've received about your work.

    - Words that are good for explaining your skills are:

        > Have a knack for...

        > Talented at...

        > Effective at...

- What is your goal? *Make it specific and one sentence long.*

  - You need to communicate what you want so the person will know how to help you. Phrases to use include:

    - > Gain exposure to the industry...

    - > Hoping to find a role in...

    - > Suggestions as to how I can...

    - > Looking for opportunities to develop my skills...

    - > Insight on how I can apply...

- Also consider what motivates you and what motivates you outside the paycheck.

  - Who do you want to help or inspire?

  - Who benefits from your work?

  - Why do you want a job in this industry?

  - Words to describe why you want this type of job:

    - > Because...

    - > On behalf of...

    - > I'm inspired by...

    - > I believe...

The delivery of your elevator pitch might feel awkward at first, but with practice, you will feel more confident and it will feel more natural and authentic. So, practice. A lot. And remember when speaking, a smile on your face will put a smile in your voice.

The following are ways you can practice and improve your elevator speech:

- In front of a mirror to watch your facial expressions.

- Record your speech with your phone and replay later to hear how you sound.

- Videotape yourself with your phone so you can replay it later to see how you look.

- Practice saying your speech to someone you respect and ask for their feedback.

Elevator speech sample

I am seeking an internship in the restaurant industry so I can start my career as a chef. My eventual career goal is to become a fully qualified and experienced professional restaurateur with the longer-term aspiration of running my own business. I have excellent interpersonal skills and I have the ability to quickly learn new skills and acquire more skills. I am looking to meet professionals in the industry to learn more about the business and the skills and education I will need to be successful.

19.4.2. INTERVIEW ESSENTIALS/ ELEVATOR SPEECH WORKSHEET

1. List details about the job you want

Field . . . .

Position . . . .

Location . . . .

Company/Companies . . . .

2. What is your goal—make it one sentence and specific

. . . .

. . . .

List your skills, accomplishments and work experience that are relevant to the job

. . . .

. . . .

3. How can you benefit an employer?

. . . .

. . . .

4. What makes you unique?
Who are you?

. . . .

. . . .

What would you like to do?

. . . .

. . . .

List three adjectives that describe you

. . . .

. . . .

STUDENTS
Who you are and what you have you been doing

You are a Senior/Junior/Sophomore/Freshman (*circle one*) at [name of your school]

Classes/course: which ones did you like the most (completed or currently enrolled)

....
....

Club membership: list any clubs of which you are a member

....
....

Club leadership roles:

....
....

Events or actions you have organized, or your club participated in

....
....

Extracurricular actives or athletic teams

....
....

List any leadership roles

....

List any awards or honors

....

5. If networking, what do you want to happen next?

....
....

19.5. INTERVIEW ESSENTIALS/PERSONAL AND PROFESSIONAL REFERENCES

Professional references

A professional reference is a recommendation from a person who can vouch for your qualifications for a job. A professional reference for an experienced worker is typically from a supervisor, a colleague, former employer, client or someone else who speaks about your work ethic and past job performance.

Recent college graduates might also use professors, coaches, and college personnel who were advisers for their activities. The key is picking references who have observed you acting in a productive capacity where you displayed your skills and qualifications for employment.

The professional reference speaks mainly to the applicant's employability and work-related qualities, as opposed to their personal or character traits. The ideal reference will be able to speak about your attributes and have examples of your work. The best professional reference is one that has a high position within the company.

Personal references

A personal reference, also known as a character reference, is from an individual who knows you and can vouch for your character and abilities. If you're a recent graduate or changing careers, character references may provide insight into your work ethic and capacities specific to the position you're seeking that a former employer or colleague wouldn't be familiar with.

While it's a good idea to have references from people who have worked with you—supervisors, colleagues, and staff—it can be helpful to have some personal references as well. This is particularly true for high school students or recent graduates, who may not have a lot of paid work experience, but who have professors or others who can speak about their qualifications as an employee. More experienced workers who are changing careers may also want to include a personal reference who can recommend them based on familiarity with their skill sets.

Business acquaintances, teachers, professors or academic advisors, volunteer leaders, religious workers, friends, coaches, and neighbors can all provide a personal reference. You should not, however, ask a family member or spouse to provide a personal reference.

Request permission before you use someone as a reference

Be sure to contact your potential references before you give out their information to make sure that they are comfortable and willing to serve as your reference. It's also a good idea to forward them an updated resume and a copy of the job posting. If you haven't talked in a long while, make sure that they are familiar with the specific skills that the job requires so they'll know how to speak specifically about those skills.

Keep your references appraised of your progress and give them a heads up if you think they might be contacted.

When to share your references with employers

Unless specifically mentioned in the job posting, wait until you are asked to provide references to a potential employer.

How to provide references to employers

Prepare your list of references and have a copy printed out to give to the interviewer at the interview.

For professional references, include the person's name, job title, company, address, phone number, and email address.

For personal references, include the person's name, phone number, email address, your relationship to the person, and the number of years you've known them.

Thank your references

Remember that giving you a referral takes some time, consideration, and thought on the part of your referee. Mail a note or send an email to thank the person to show your gratitude.

Letter of reference

It's a good idea to ask an employee for a letter of reference highlighting your positive work qualities. If you are leaving a job and you have a positive relationship with a supervisor, ask for the letter before you depart. Sometimes, the person will ask you to write the letter yourself that they can print on company letter headed paper and sign. Below is a standard format for a letter of reference.

Sample reference letter

To whom it may concern,

As a nanny to my eight-year-old twins for the past three years, Heather Pleat has proven herself to be a remarkably responsible, confident young woman.

I am amazed at the ease with which Heather can fulfill a variety of tasks. She has worked for me not only as a nanny, but also as a tutor to my children and as a housekeeper. She even finds time to volunteer at a local daycare for single mothers. Not once have I seen Heather become overwhelmed by a given task or assignment.

I am confident that Heather's intelligence and maturity will be great assets in any organization. Please do not hesitate to contact me with any questions.

Sincerely,

Janet Monroe
(555) 555-5555
Janet.monroe@email.com

19.6. INTERVIEW ESSENTIALS/AWN AMBASSADOR JOB DESCRIPTION

Overview

The AWN Ambassador's function is to be a representative as a candidate in the Workplace Readiness Workshop at events and conferences where AWN is an exhibitor or is a featured organization. Ambassadors speak to the general public and to potential candidates and their families to share their experience as a candidate in the Workplace Readiness Workshop.

Key responsibilities

- Attend events and conferences as a representative of AWN.

- Answer questions about and share their experience as a candidate in the workshop.

- Create and deliver an "elevator pitch" that summarizes the essential elements of the workshop.

- Maintain proper business casual work attire as the AWN Ambassador.

Desired skills

- Basic keyboarding abilities preferred but not required.

- Knowledge of and experience creating/using word processing documents and spreadsheets preferred but not required.

Mandatory job requirements

- Currently enrolled in AWN's Workplace Readiness Workshop.

- Arrival no later than 30 minutes prior to the start of an event.

- Ability to attend events and conferences with minimal support.

- Ability to lift and/or move up to 25 pounds.

- Ability to stand, walk, sit, use hands and fingers and reach with hands and arms.

- Ability to adhere to AWN policies and procedures.

- Ability to follow instructions in various forms (written, oral, or pictorial).

- Knowledge of basic safety and security procedures.

Qualifications

- To perform this job successfully, an individual must be able to perform each essential duty satisfactorily.

- The requirements listed above are representative of the knowledge, skills, and/or ability required.

- Reasonable accommodations may be made to enable individuals with disabilities to perform the essential functions.

Rate of pay

- $18 per hour.

20.1. CONNECTING WITH COWORKERS/ MAKING A GOOD FIRST IMPRESSION

As the saying goes, you never get a second chance to make a first impression, and research has proven this to be true. Within the first few seconds of meeting someone, people form assumptions about us based on what we wear, how we speak, and our general attitude. In the workplace, these first impressions can have a long-term impact on our reputation and ultimately determine how successful we are in our career.

Below are ways you can make a positive first impression when starting a new job. Practicing these tips every day will help you develop good workplace habits that will help solidify your reputation with your coworkers and supervisors.

Keep your attitude positive

The best defense against the daily stressors that we experience in our job is to maintain a positive attitude. Proactively managing our stress helps us stay calm and focused. Practicing gratitude for our job and our loved ones helps us appreciate what we have. Smiling often improves our mood and is appreciated by everyone at work.

I know what things are good: friendship and work conversation. (Rupert Brooke)

Be mindful of formal and informal workplace policies

Become familiar with general office procedures. Learn about the daily office routine and the way that your coworkers like to maintain their environment. Do they like music on or off? Do they like speaking loudly in the hallways, or are they quiet and reserved? As a newcomer, it is your responsibility to observe and adapt to your new work environment as much as possible. When you don't know something, ask for help. Don't assume. That's when drama starts.

Get to know your coworkers

Work is not a social gathering place, but you should be friendly with all of your coworkers and remember something about them. After meeting a coworker for the first time, make sure you remember their name. If this is difficult, keep a notepad and write down each name as you learn it along with some distinctive information about the person. Here's an example: *Dave, works in the stockroom. Tall and has dark hair. Likes Anime. Worked here five years and is a good person to ask questions.*

Try to go to lunch or take a break with a coworker. Try to find a workplace "buddy," someone who knows what's going on and will keep you informed of what is happening at work. But be mindful with whom you associate. The office gossip or troublemaker is not usually well liked or respected, so if you hang out with one, your coworkers might see you as a gossip or a troublemaker too.

Watch your manners

Say thank you to the people who help you and say please when making a request. Do not tell off-color jokes. Do not get into petty arguments.

> Do all the good you can, by all the means you can, in all the ways you can, in all the places you can, at all the times you can, to all the people you can, as long as ever you can. (John Wesley)

Listen carefully

Really listen to what others are saying. Be mindful and attentive to their words. Let your coworkers know that you appreciate and value their opinion. Make eye contact when this is possible.

> We have two ears and one mouth so that we can listen twice as much as we speak. (Epictetus)

Watch what you wear

To make a good impression, your clothes need to match the culture of your workplace. Make sure that what you wear is clean and in good repair. Follow the company's dress code as much as possible, and don't ever dress too casually.

A good rule to follow is: Don't dress for the job you have. Dress for the job you want.

Watch what you say and how you say it

The words you say will play a large part in the first impression you make. Be kind, respectful, and truthful when speaking. Don't participate in office gossip. Don't use slang or off-color phrases. Choose your words carefully, because everything you say will be judged.

> If you propose to speak, always ask yourself, is it true, is it necessary, is it kind. (Buddha)

20.2. CONNECTING WITH COWORKERS/ TELEPHONE ETIQUETTE

Have a reason for your call:

- Just calling to see how you're doing.
- Just calling to hear what's up.
- I haven't talked to you in a while.
- I was wondering what you've been up to.
- I was referred to you by Mr. Jones.

When the person answers the phone:

- Say hello.
- Ask for the person you are calling by name.
- Introduce yourself.
- Ask if they have time to talk.

When you want to end a call:

- Tell the person it was nice talking to them.
- Give a reason—for example:
  - I have to get going
  - I better let you go
  - I have to eat dinner.
- Tell the person you will talk to them or see them later.
- Say goodbye.

When leaving a voice mail:

- Make it quick—no longer than 30–45 seconds.
- Leave your name, phone number and the best time to reach you.
- Give a reason for why you are calling.
- Say goodbye.

The Two-Message Rule: Do not leave more than two messages in a row with no response.

The AWN Rule: If you would like to contact any professionals that you've met through the workshop, please coordinate with your instructor. Do not call or email any field trip hosts or guest speakers directly on your own.

20.3. CONNECTING WITH COWORKERS/ VOICE MAIL MANNERS

Why your voice mail greeting is important

Your voice mail greeting identifies who you are and includes instructions for the caller to leave a message. Especially if you are applying for a job, your employer may call to set up an interview.

Without a proper voice mail greeting, the employer may not know if they are calling the correct number. If the greeting is offensive, the employer may decide not to call you in for an interview.

Here are the basics of a good voice mail greeting:

- Your voice mail greeting should be brief and let the person know they've reached you.

- Record your greeting in a quiet place with no noise in the background.

- Your greeting should ask the caller to leave their name and number and ask them to speak clearly and slowly.

Sample voice mail greeting

Hello, you've reached John Smith. I can't come to the phone right now, but please leave your name and number and I will return your call as soon as possible. Please speak clearly and slowly. Thank you.

Why you should regularly check your voice mail messages

To make sure you don't miss any important information, you should get in the habit of checking every day for any missed calls and check your voice mail to see if the caller has left a message. It's also important to delete any old messages that you don't need any longer. Your voice mail will only hold a certain number of messages, and once you've reached the limit, callers will no longer be able to leave a message.

20.4. CONNECTING WITH COWORKERS/ CONVERSATION DOS AND DON'TS

CONVERSATION DOS
Great conversation starters—small talk tips and tricks
by Aaron Marino, I am Alpha M.
YouTube link: www.youtube.com/watch?v=5U3gWUuV1BI

- When you're not working, what do you like to do?
- How's your day going?
- Do you have any plans this weekend?
- Lead with a compliment but only about something the person is wearing:
  - For women: shoes, jewelry, accessories
  - For men: attire (if into fashion).

Ask about someone's interests (like our Interview Your Partner questions)

- **What** do you like to do...
- **Who** do you usually go with...
- **When** do you...
- **Where** do you like to...
- **Why** do you like to...
- **How** long have you been doing... **How** did you get started...

Ask about what the person likes (like our Icebreakers):

- Movies and TV
- Sports (especially if you discover the other person likes the same team as you)
- Vacations
- Restaurants
- Pets
- Weekend plans.

CONVERSATION DON'TS
Stay away from any controversial topics or anything where you might strongly disagree, for example:

- Politics or politicians
- Religion
- Gun rights or gun control
- Woman's reproductive rights.

21.1.1. LANDING A JOB/INFORMATIONAL INTERVIEWS: ESSENTIALS

What is an informational interview?

An informational interview is a process used to gather career information from professionals. Your goal is not to ask for a job, but rather to gain first-hand information about a specific occupation, job, or organization from someone with an insider's perspective.

Why conduct an informational interview?

An informational interview helps you accomplish several things:

- You make in-person connections with working professionals.

- You obtain a great deal of information about a career of interest and the types of skills you'll need to do the job effectively. All of this data is excellent information to include on a resume and use as the foundation of a social media profile.

- You gain insight into the hidden job market, employment opportunities that are found by referrals and are not advertised or posted.

- You gain confidence in talking with people.

What are the steps used in scheduling an informational interview?

- Identify a professional who is employed in your field of interest or at a company where you would like to work.

- Contact the person:

  - Explain why you are seeking personalized information about their field.

  - Ask if you can meet at their worksite for about 20–30 minutes.

- Send an email confirmation the day the interview is confirmed.

- Call your contact again no later than 24 hours before the start time of your meeting.

- Show up at least 15 minutes early.

- Take notes about important information that you discover during the interview.

21.1.2. LANDING A JOB/INFORMATIONAL INTERVIEWS: CONTACT LIST

List below the prospective professionals that you would like to meet. These can be people you know, referrals from friends, or professions that you found by browsing the internet.

Lead 1

Organization ....

Person's name/title ....

Business address ....

Phone number ....

Lead 2

Organization ....

Person's name/title ....

Business address ....

Phone number ....

Lead 3

Organization ....

Person's name/title ....

Business address ....

Phone number ....

Lead 4

Organization ....

Person's name/title ....

Business address ....

Phone number ....

Lead 5

Organization ....

Person's name/title ....

Business address ....

Phone number ....

21.1.3. LANDING A JOB/INFORMATIONAL INTERVIEWS: SCRIPTS AND CORRESPONDENCE

The best chance of success in scheduling an interview is with someone that you already know or have a personal referral for. You can also be successful in scheduling a meeting with someone with whom you don't have a connection, but you will need to prepare and practice your introduction before contacting them.

Below is a sample script that you can use to introduce yourself to someone you haven't met or don't have a referral for. The text in square brackets indicates where you can revise the script according to your own narrative.

SAMPLE TELEPHONE SCRIPT

[Ms. Jones],

My name is [George Michael], and I am enrolled in the Workplace Readiness Workshop with Autism Works Now. This program is helping me to learn the skills I need to get and keep a job. I have learned how to network as part of the program, and I am very interested in finding a job at a [movie theatre].

Because of your many years of experience as an executive with [Pacific Coast Cinemas], I would very much appreciate a chance to meet with you for career advice for someone like myself who is trying to find their first job. I know you are busy, but I only need 20 minutes out of your schedule.

Would you have time to meet with me soon to discuss the aspects of your job? When would be a convenient date and time to come by the theatre to talk with you?

Sample email script confirming your meeting

If you spoke over the phone, you'll need to send a very brief email to confirm the day and time of your meeting. Start your email by saying you appreciate their time and include your telephone number in the closing of your email to make it easy for the contact to get in touch with you. This should be sent no later than 24 hours after the meeting is confirmed.

EMAIL

Dear [Ms. Jones],

Thank you for taking time out of your busy schedule to speak to me over the phone this afternoon. I am confirming our meeting on [April 10 at 1:00pm at the Pacific Coast Theatre in Redondo Beach].

I look forward to meeting with you.
Sincerely,

[George Michael
310 555 1234]

✻

TELEPHONE SCRIPT

Contact: *This is Ms. Jones.*

You: *Hello Ms. Jones. This is George Michael. I am calling to confirm our appointment at 1:00pm tomorrow.*

Contact: *Hello George. Yes, we are confirmed for 1:00 tomorrow. Check in with the front desk when you arrive.*

You: *Thank you. I look forward to meeting with you.*

Contact: *Thank you. I'll see you tomorrow. Goodbye.*

You: *Goodbye.*

Telephone etiquette tips

When you call, remember to:

- practice what you are going to say so there are not a lot of 'ahhs', 'umms' and pauses
- smile so it will come through in your voice
- use appropriate language
- not talk too quickly, too slowly, too quietly, or too loudly
- not chew gum, eat, smoke, or drink during your conversation.

If you are leaving a message for a return call, make sure that:

- your voice mail message is professional and gives a favorable impression of who you are
- your voice mail isn't full and can receive messages
- if someone else is going to answer your phone, they know that you are expecting a call and they are pleasant and polite when they speak with the caller.

Tips for writing thank you notes

Your note should be short and friendly. It can be a card that you mail or send as an email. If you are mailing a card, choose one with a simple "Thank You" on the front on good quality notepaper with a matching envelope. This should go out no later than 24 hours after the meeting took place.

"Thank you" letter format

Date: *Date the note is being sent.*

Salutation: *Address as Mr. or Ms. with the person's last name unless you knew them before the interview.*

Paragraph 1: *Thank the individual for taking the time to meet with you.*

Paragraph 2: *Share something you gained from your meeting.*

Paragraph 3: *Thank the individual again and express interest in working in their field or with their organization in the future.*

Closing: *Use "Sincerely," or "Yours truly" and add your name.*

Sample "Thank you" on note
April 10, 2017

Dear [Ms. Jones],

Thank you for taking the time to discuss your job as [Manager of the Pacific Coast Theatre] and talk about your organization. It was a pleasure meeting you and [getting a behind-the-scenes look at a movie theatre].

The information you shared provided me with a new perspective of the position, a better understanding of the requirements of the job, and an increased interest in finding a job [in any capacity with a movie theatre].

Again, thank you for your time. I appreciate the information you shared with me and I look forward to the possibility of one day becoming an associate [at a movie theatre just like yours].

Sincerely,

[George Michael]

22.1.4. LANDING A JOB/INFORMATIONAL INTERVIEWS: WORKSHEET

Person interviewed: . . . .

Date of interview: . . . .

Person's title: . . . .

Organization: . . . .

Address: . . . .

Phone number: . . . .

Email: . . . .

Questions to ask

Why did you choose to become a . . . . ?

. . . .

. . . .

. . . .

What is a typical day like for you?

. . . .

. . . .

. . . .

What kind of skills would I need to be successful in this industry?

. . . .

. . . .

. . . .

What is a typical entry-level salary in this profession? How do the salaries progress in five years?

. . . .

. . . .

. . . .

What do you like most and least about your job?

....

....

....

What preparation would you suggest for someone interested in entering this field?

....

....

....

What do you wish you had known before you entered your career?

....

....

....

Can you recommend anyone that I can contact about job opportunities in this industry?

....

....

....

May I contact you in the future if I have any further questions?

....

....

....

Remember, at the end of the meeting, thank the person for their time and ask for a business card.

Questions to ask yourself after the interview

Is this a career I would be interested in? (*circle one*) YES NO

If yes, why?

....

....

....

If no, why not?

....
....
....

What action can I take now to prepare myself to achieve this goal?

Education: ....

Training: ....

Experience: ....

Community involvement: ....

Activities: ....

What action am I already taking to achieve my career goals in this field?

....
....
....

What skills were mentioned in the interview that I already possess and can be added to my resume?

....
....
....

21.2. LANDING A JOB/NETWORKING WORKSHEET

Referrals are the best source of job leads. Write down a list of people you know, along with their job title.

Teacher/Subject

....

....

Counselors

....

....

Parents, neighbors and family friends

....

....

Friends and acquaintances

....

....

Volunteering is a good way to gain work experience and expand your network of professional contacts. List five issues that you are most passionate about and organizations that are doing work in this area.

Causes I care about	Organization or non-profit
....	....
....	....
....	....
....	....
....	....

Internships provide excellent opportunities for entry-level jobs and ways to learn about the inner workings of the company. List five companies where you would like to work and the type of internship you would like.

Company	Type of internship
....	....
....	....
....	....
....	....
....	....

Job fairs and Chamber of Commerce mixers are excellent places to connect to professionals in your field of interest and business owners with companies that have jobs in your field of interest. Do a Google search for upcoming job fairs in your area and check the website of your local Chamber of Commerce to find the dates, times, and locations for their upcoming events.

Job fairs:

Organizer of fair	Date and time	Location
....	....	....
....	....	....
....	....	....
....	....	....
....	....	....

Chamber of Commerce mixers and events:

Event name	Date and time	Location
....	....	....
....	....	....
....	....	....
....	....	....
....	....	....

When attending a professional event, remember the following:

- Smile!
- Dress professionally matched to the culture of the companies at the event.
- When attending a job fair, bring at least 20 copies of your resume.

- When meeting recruiters, ask about job and career opportunities.

- Confidently recite your 30 or 60 second elevator pitch.

- Get a business card for everyone you meet; on the card, write down the date and the event where your meeting took place.

- At the end of a conversation, thank the person for their time.

- Write down important notes immediately after your meeting so you won't forget vital details and information.

- Follow up all meetings with a thank you note or email.

- For recruiters, send a short note every couple of weeks to check in and let them know that you are interested and available.

21.3.1. LANDING A JOB/VOLUNTEERING: HOW TO FIND A VOLUNTEER JOB

Start on step 1 and move up the ladder until you start volunteering!

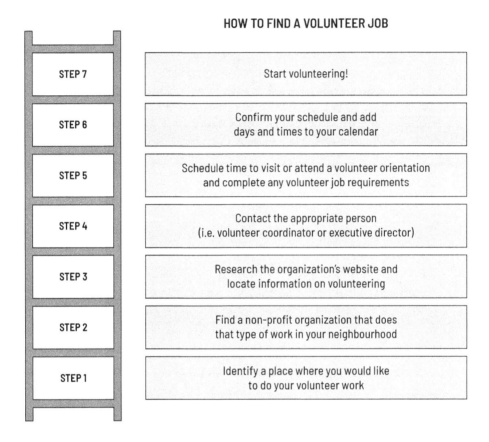

HOW TO FIND A VOLUNTEER JOB

STEP 7	Start volunteering!
STEP 6	Confirm your schedule and add days and times to your calendar
STEP 5	Schedule time to visit or attend a volunteer orientation and complete any volunteer job requirements
STEP 4	Contact the appropriate person (i.e. volunteer coordinator or executive director)
STEP 3	Research the organization's website and locate information on volunteering
STEP 2	Find a non-profit organization that does that type of work in your neighbourhood
STEP 1	Identify a place where you would like to do your volunteer work

21.3.2. LANDING A JOB/VOLUNTEERING: VOLUNTEER JOB WORKSHEET

1. List up to four causes you care about (from the section of the Networking Worksheet).

   ....

   ....

2. Do a Google search for an organization in your area doing this work.

3. List up to four organizations that focus on your cause and write down their contact information.

Organization	Website/Phone number	Address
A.		
B.		
C.		
D.		

Considerations:

- Will it be easy for you to get to this address?
- If you drive, is there available parking?
- If you take the bus, is there a route to and from your house?
- Can you do this job on your own or will you need support?

4. Write down the name of the volunteer coordinator or executive director.

Volunteer coordinator	Executive director
A.	....
B.	....
C.	....
D.	....

5. Search the website for volunteer requirements and write down your next steps.

A. ....

B. ....

C. ....

D. ....

6. Confirm your schedule, write it down in the space below and add it to your calendar with the address.

....

....

....

21.4. LANDING A JOB/COMPANIES THAT HIRE PEOPLE WITH SPECIAL NEEDS

COMPANY	LOCATION	WEBSITE
Acme	Various cities throughout the U.S.	www.acmemarkets.com
Bitty & Beau's Coffee	Various cities throughout the U.S.	www.bittyandbeauscoffee.com
Cameron's Coffee and Chocolates	Fairfax, Virginia	www.every1canwork.com/home
Chick-fil-A	Various cities throughout the U.S.	www.chick-fil-a.com
Cicis	Various cities throughout the U.S.	www.cicis.com
Delta Sonic Car Wash	Various cities in New York	https://deltasoniccarwash.com
Fazoli's	Various cities throughout the U.S.	https://fazolis.com
Furnace Hills Coffee Company	Rome, New York	www.furnacehillscoffee.com
Goodwill	Various cities throughout the U.S.	www.goodwill.org
H-E-B	Various cities in Texas	www.heb.com
Home Depot	Various cities throughout the U.S.	www.homedepot.com
Howdy Homemade	Dallas, Katy & Lubbock, Texas and Asheville, North Carolina	www.howdyhomemade.com
Hugs Cafe	McKinney, Texas	https://hugscafe.org
Ikea	Various cities worldwide	www.ikea.com
Jewel Osco	Nationwide	www.jewelosco.com
John's Crazy Socks	Farmingdale, New York	https://johnscrazysocks.com
Kroger	Various cities throughout the U.S.	www.kroger.com
Lifetime Fitness	Various cities throughout the U.S.	www.lifetime.life
Lowes	Various cities throughout the U.S.	www.lowes.com
Market Basket	Various cities in Maine, Massachusetts, New Hampshire and Rhode Island	https://marketbasketfoods.com
Market Street	Various cities in New Mexico and Texas	www.marketstreetunited.com
McDonald's	Various cities worldwide	www.mcdonalds.com

COMPANY	LOCATION	WEBSITE
Panera Bread	Various cities throughout the U.S.	www.panerabread.com
Park Cities Ford	Dallas, Texas	https://planetforddallas.com
Publix	Various cities in Alabama, Florida, Georgia, Kentucky, North and South Carolina, Tennessee, and Virginia	www.publix.com
Puzzles Bakery	Schnectady, New York	www.facebook.com/puzzlesbakery
Schnucks	Various cities in Illinois and Missouri	https://nourish.schnucks.com
Shaws	Various cities in Maine, Massachusetts, New Hampshire, Rhode Island, and Vermont	www.shaws.com
Stop & Shop	Various cities in Connecticut, Massachusetts, New Jersey, New York, and Rhode Island	https://stopandshop.com
Sunflower Bakery	Rockville and No Bethesda, Maryland	www.sunflowerbakery.org
SuperLo Foods	Memphis, Tennessee	www.superlofoods.com
Target	Various cities throughout the U.S.	www.target.com
Texadelphia	Various cities in Texas and Oklahoma City	https://texadelphia.com
The Chocolate Spectrum	Jupiter, Florida	https://thechocolatespectrum.com
The Kalahari Resort	Wisconsin Dells, Wisconsin	www.kalahariresorts.com/wisconsin
The Power Cafe	Watertown, Massachusetts	www.facebook.com/thepower cafe
Walgreens	Various cities throughout the U.S.	www.walgreens.com
Walmart	Various cities worldwide	www.walmart.com
Wegmans	Various cities in Delaware, Maryland, Massachusetts, New Jersey, New York, North Carolina, Pennsylvania, Virginia, and Washington DC	www.wegmans.com

21.5.1. LANDING A JOB/SOCIAL MEDIA: OVERVIEW

Your social media presence is not just a personal outlet. It is also your brand that identifies who you are, what you like to do, and the type of activities you like to participate in.

Reasons why you should have a social media profile

- Employers regularly screen the social media sites of prospective job candidates and some see it as a red flag if the person has no social media presence.

- It's a good way to promote your skills, talents, and abilities.

- It's a good way to highlight honor roll awards and competition medals.

- It's a good way to connect to coworkers outside the office.

- Many companies maintain a presence on many social media sites, so you should "like" the pages of any organizations where you'd like to work; checking these sites regularly is a good way to gather information about those organizations.

Foundation of a positive social media presence

- Because what you post on social media represents you, make sure that all of the information on your profile is accurate and current.

- Do not post anything that could be viewed negatively by a future employer because it could impact your ability to be hired.

- Use the privacy settings to limit what other people can post on your profile and to prevent you from being tagged in other people's posts and pictures.

- Review the profiles of professionals you respect to see how they format their profile and what information they include.

- Make sure your picture is recent, your hair was recently cut and is washed and combed. Men should be clean shaven.

Recommended social media sites
Facebook
This is one of the most popular social sites with over three billion active monthly users from around the world. When you become a friend with someone on Facebook, you can both view the post and share articles, photos, and videos on each other's page. In the "About" link on your profile page, you can list your education and employment information. Minimum age requirement: 13. www.facebook.com

X (formally Twitter)

This is a news and social networking service where users can post 140 character messages called "tweets." It has 250 million active users and is popular with many celebrities, politicians, and social activists. In addition to posting tweets, you can "follow" other users to view their tweets. Minimum age requirement: 12. www.twitter.com

Pinterest

This is photo-sharing website where users can upload, save, sort, and manage images, known as "pins," which can be organized in folders sorted by a central topic or theme. When you have a Pinterest page, you can follow the pages and browse the contents of the pages of other users. If you are creative or have a special talent or skill, a Pinterest profile can be used as an online portfolio to display your artwork and projects. Minimum age requirement: 13. www.pinterest.com

Instagram

This is a photo- and video-sharing social networking service that allows users to upload media that can be edited with filters and originated by hashtags. Posts can be shared publicly or with pre-approved followers. Users can browse other users' content, view trending content, and follow other users to add their content to a personal feed. With 2.4 billion active users, it ranks fourth among the biggest social media networks. Minimum age requirement: 13. www.instagram.com

Monster and CareerBuilder

These are two of the most visited employment websites in the United States and around the world. Both sites allow users to search their job listings and company profiles and post online resumes. They also allow users to sign up for their online, career-advice newsletter and offer free services like resume critiques. Minimum age requirement for both sites: 13. www.monster.com, www.careerbuilder.com

LinkedIn

This is a business- and employment-oriented social networking service with more than one billion members including more than 30 million students and recent graduates in over 200 countries and territories. LinkedIn users can search their job listings, post a professional profile, and view information about potential employers. LinkedIn also allows users to post updates about their activities, share information, articles, and join "groups" that are focused on specific interests and topics. Minimum age requirement: 18. www.linkedin.com

Indeed

This is a worldwide employment-related search engine of job listings that are aggregated from thousands of websites, job boards, staffing firms, associations, and company career pages. The site allows users to search their listings for available job openings and to post their resume online. Indeed also has a Career Guide which is an excellent resource for job-search related topics. Minimum age requirement: 14 but adult supervision is required for users under 18. Indeed Job Search: www.indeed.com; Indeed Career Guide: www.indeed.com/career-advice

21.5.2. LANDING A JOB/SOCIAL MEDIA: INVENTORY

Check off the sites where you currently have an account and profile

Social media

- ☐ Facebook
- ☐ Pinterest
- ☐ Instagram
- ☐ LinkedIn
- ☐ Other—list below

. . . .

. . . .

Professional websites

- ☐ Monster
- ☐ CareerBuilder
- ☐ Indeed
- ☐ Other—list below

. . . .

. . . .

21.6. LANDING A JOB/SO YOU WANT TO START YOUR OWN BUSINESS

Starting your own business has many benefits. As the owner, you get to set your own hours and are the ultimate decider on the direction of your company. But with the benefits come many responsibilities. Planning ahead and understanding the requirements of starting a small business helps you avoid missteps that could cost you time and money.

Answer these important questions

- What product will you be selling or service will you be providing?

- How will you find buyers for your products or services?

- If you are selling a product, who will be your vendors or suppliers of the items you need to make your product?

- What price do you need to sell your goods or services at to make a profit?

- Are any other businesses offering a similar product or service and what do they charge?

Ask questions

If you've identified a similar business or service, call the owner and ask to schedule an informational interview. The **Informational Interviews Worksheet** [21.1.4] will help you with scheduling an interview and what questions to ask.

What you'll need

Once you are ready to launch your business, this is what you'll need to get started:

- **Decide on your business structure:** There are four business structures: sole proprietorship, partnerships, limited liability corporations (LLC) and corporations. Most likely, your business will be a sole proprietor.

- **DBA:** This stands for 'doing business as' and allows a business to operate under a name different from the business owner. So, if John Smith's business is named "John Smith's Computer Repairs," he would not need a DBA. But if he named his company "Excellence in Computer Repair," he would. DBA requirements vary by state, county, city, and business structure. Filing fees vary as well. Some states also require a "public notice" to announce your business. Your local county clerk's office can help with paperwork and requirements to file a DBA.

- **Business license:** All businesses must have a business license if they are selling goods and services whether they make a profit or not. A business license can usually be purchased from the finance office at your local city hall where your company will be operating.

- **Financial transactions:** You'll need to decide how they'll accept payment for your products or services. Accepting payments online is easy using apps like Paypal, Venmo, or Zelle. The minimum age to open an account on these services is 18 years old and each one requires the user's account to be connected to a bank account.

- **Bookkeeping:** For tax purposes, all business transactions, both for incoming and outgoing expenses, need to be documented on paper or electronically. If the company has limited sales and a small amount of expenses, a simple *Excel* spreadsheet that shows credits for income and debits for outgoing expenses is sufficient.

- **Taxes:** According to the IRS, a sole proprietor or independent contractor is required to file an income tax return if their self-employment net earnings are $400 or more. State and local taxes would also be due on any income generated by the business and these rates vary by city and state. Small business owners also owe self-employment taxes based on their income. To cover both income and self-employment taxes, it is recommended that a small business owner set aside 30 percent of their income after business deductions to cover both federal and state income taxes. More information on independent contractors is provided in the worksheet **Labor Law Overview** [22.2].

- **Marketing your business:** To generate sales, you'll need to promote your business to find customers to buy your goods and services; here are some important considerations:

  - Pitch your business: Create an elevator pitch for your business; keep it to 20 seconds and make it interesting so people want to learn more.

  - Website: Establishing a website will require registering a domain name and hosting site. There are three companies that we recommend, and each provides services to register a domain name, web hosting, and website creation.

  - The easiest site to create a website is *Google Sites*, a free website creation app available from Google that allows users to create and edit files online. It is extremely user-friendly and utilizes the apps on Google to create content. The site is free to use, but users have to purchase a domain name for their website from an outside source. Companies that can help with registering a domain name, web hosting, and website creation include:

    > IONOS

    > iPage

    > GoDaddy™

  - Leverage social media: Create a page on Facebook and accounts on Instagram, Pinterest, TikTok, and Twitter and regularly post new content. Create a channel on YouTube and create a blog to promote your business.

- Get the word out: Hire brand ambassadors who can talk up your business—these can be friends and family who want to support you. Give them t-shirts with your company name—these are free walking billboards! Network at neighborhood events and Chamber of Commerce mixers—your elevator pitch will come in handy. Create a business listing on Yelp.com and Google. Both sites are free, and customers can post reviews of your products and services.

- Advertising: The rule of seven is based on a marketing principle that customers need to see your brand at least seven times before they commit to purchase. Purchasing adverts in local media is expensive, so stick to free resources using social media and attending networking events.

22.1. UNDERSTANDING THE WORKPLACE: WORKPLACE HIERARCHY CHART

Management Employees—Level 1

Chief Executive Officer

Chief Operating Officer

General Manager

Executive Employees—Level 2

President

Vice President

Executive Director

Chief Technical Officer

Chief Financial Officer

Community Relations Manager

Treasurer

Assistant Manager

Entry-Administrative Level Employees—Level 3

Administrative Assistant

Cashier

Sales Associate

Stock Clerk

Trainee

Intern

Non-Administrative Employees—Level 4

Security Guard

Custodian

Gardener

Foreman

Maintenance Worker

22.2. UNDERSTANDING THE WORKPLACE/ LABOR LAW OVERVIEW

Employment contract
This is a legally binding agreement between an employer and an employee regarding a term of employment. The agreement can be oral, written, or implied.

At will employment
An at-will employee can quit or be fired at any time for any reason that isn't illegal under state and federal laws. An employee cannot legally be fired for exercising their rights. If an employee is fired, it is up to the employer to show good cause for termination of the individual's employment.

Independent contractors
People who are self-employed in an independent trade, business, or profession in which they offer their services to the public are considered independent contractors. Independent contractors who earn more than $400 in a year must pay quarterly self-employment (SE) taxes based on their income. SE taxes are similar to the Social Security and Medicare taxes paid by employed workers.

Exempt vs non–exempt
Non-exempt employees are typically paid an hourly wage, have a set work schedule, and are covered under all FLSA regulations like minimum wage laws and overtime regulations. *Exempt* employees are excluded from all FLSA rules. These are typically employees in executive, supervisory, professional, and outside sales jobs who draw a set salary and have a work schedule with varying hours.

Federal income tax
Employers generally withhold federal income tax from an employee's wages. Upon being hired, a form W-4 is completed by the employee and this information is used to determine the amount of federal income tax that is withheld from each paycheck. Workers who make over $400 in a year must report their earnings to the Internal Revenue Service (commonly known as the IRS) each year by April 15.

State income tax
In all but ten states (Alaska, Florida, Nevada, New Hampshire, South Dakota, Tennessee, Texas, Washington, and Wyoming), workers are required to pay an annual state income tax that is due on April 15 of each year.

Social Security and Medicare taxes
Employers also deduct Social Security and Medicare taxes from each employee's paycheck.

Federal laws

In the United States, the United States Department of Labor administers and enforces federal laws covering workplace activities for about ten million employers and 125 million workers. These are listed below.

Wages and hours

The Fair Labor Standards Act (FLSA) sets the standard for wages and is administered by the Wage and Hour Division (WHD) of the U.S. Department of Labor. It establishes overtime pay of one-and-one-half times the regular rate of pay when an employee works over 40 hours in one week, but there are no overtime pay requirements for hours worked on weekends or holidays unless the employee has exceeded working 40 hours. FLSA establishes 14 years of age as the minimum age for employment, limits the number of hours that children under the age of 16 can work, and forbids the employment of children under the age of 18 for jobs deemed too dangerous. The Division also enforces the labor standard provisions of the Immigration and Nationality Act that applies to aliens working under certain immigrant visa programs. The current federal minimum wage standard is $7.25 an hour.

Family and Medical Leave Act (FMLA)

Administered by the Wage and Hour Division, the FMLA requires employers of 50 or more employees to give up to 12 weeks of unpaid, job-protected leave to eligible employees for the birth or adoption of a child or for the serious illness of the employee or a spouse, child, or parent.

Workplace safety and health

The Occupational Safety and Health (OSH) Act is administered by the Occupational Safety and Health Administration (OSHA). It covers safety and health conditions for most private sector and all public sector employees to guarantee employees are free from being exposed to recognized, serious hazards in the workplace.

Whistleblower and retaliation protections

OSHA administers the "whistleblower" protection provisions of 22 states. Under this law, an employee may file a complaint with OSHA if they believe that they have received dis-crimination or retaliation for exercising any right afforded by OSH. An employee must file a complaint about any health or safety issues within 30 days after the occurrence of the alleged violation.

Worker Adjustment and Retraining Notification Act

This federal law mandates that workers being laid off be given a written 60-day notice before the date of mass layoffs or plant closings. A worker who does not receive notice per the law may seek damages for back pay and benefits for up to 60 days depending on how many days of notice they received.

Harassment

Harassment in the workplace based on race, color, religion, sex, national origin, age, and disability in any form is prohibited by federal law. It becomes unlawful when the offensive conduct becomes a condition of continued employment or the conduct is severe or pervasive enough to create a work environment that a reasonable person would consider intimidating, hostile, or abusive. An employer is automatically held liable for harassment by a supervisor that results in a negative employment action such as termination, failure to promote, or be hired. An employer is also held liable if it was known or should have been known about the harassment and failed to take prompt and appropriate corrective action. The Equal Employment Opportunity Commission (EEOC) handles administration and enforcement of laws covering harassment.

Sexual harassment

Sexual harassment includes unwelcome sexual advances, requests for sexual favors, remarks about a person's sex, and other verbal or physical harassment of a sexual nature. The victim or abuser can be either a male or female and can be the victim's supervisor, supervisor in another area, a coworker, or non-employee.

State laws

State regulations vary from state to state. Below are the laws as they apply in the state of California:

State minimum wage rates

If the state rate is higher than the federal rate, the state rate would apply. In California, the minimum wage is $16.00.

Minimum rest periods

A paid ten-minute rest period is required for every four hours worked. This does not apply for employees who work fewer than three-and-a-half hours in a day.

Minimum meal periods

An employee is entitled to an unpaid half-hour meal period after five hours of work. If an employee works six hours or less, an employer and employee may consent to waive the meal period. For a work day of over ten hours, an employee is entitled to a second meal period of no less than 30 minutes.

Payday requirements

The minimum that an employee must be paid is at least twice during each calendar month, but there are variations on this law per the occupation. Some occupations that are excluded include executive, administrative, farm and labor contract workers, or an employee of a motor vehicle dealer who is paid on commission.

State unemployment insurance benefits

The Federal State Unemployment Insurance Program provides temporary financial benefits to unemployed workers. Each state administers their own program within guidelines established by federal law. The funding for the program in most states is provided by a tax imposed on employers. Benefits paid to recipients must be reported on a federal income tax return.

Worker's compensation

Workers' compensation (also known as workers' comp) is a state-mandated insurance program that provides financial benefits to employees who suffer job-related injuries and illnesses. The federal government administers the program, which provides replacement benefits, medical treatment, vocational rehabilitation, and other benefits, but each state establishes the rules and regulations for the workers' comp program in their state. In general, an employee with a work-related illness or injury can get workers' comp benefits regardless of who was at fault. In exchange for these guaranteed benefits, employees usually do not have the right to sue their employer in court for damages they've incurred due to their injuries.

Filing a grievance

- Wage and Hour Division: www.dol.gov/agencies/whd/contact/complaints

- Family and Medical Leave Act: Call 866 487 9243

- OSHA: www.osha.gov/workers/file_complaint.html or call 800 321 6742

22.3. UNDERSTANDING THE WORKPLACE/AMERICAN WITH DISABILITIES ACT (ADA) OVERVIEW

What is the Americans with Disabilities Act (ADA)?

- Civil rights law that prohibits discrimination against individuals with disabilities in all areas of public life.

- Its purpose is to make sure that people with disabilities have the same rights and opportunities as everyone else.

- Signed into law by President George H. W. Bush in 1990.

- Divided into five titles (or sections) that relate to different areas of public life:

    - Title I: Employment (we will only be discussing this)

    - Title II: State and Local Government

    - Title III Public Accommodations

    - Title IV: Telecommunications

    - Title V: Miscellaneous Provisions

Title I: Employment

- Designed to help people with disabilities access the same employment opportunities and benefits that are available to people without disabilities.

- Applies to employers with 15 or more employees.

- Requires employers to provide *reasonable accommodations* to qualified employees and applicants.

- *Reasonable accommodations* are changes in the workplace that accommodate employees with disabilities without causing the employer "undue hardship, too great a difficulty or expense."

- Regulated and enforced by the U.S. Equal Employment Opportunity Commission (EEOC).

- Enforced by the U.S. Department of Justice.

What is a disability under the ADA?

- An individual with a disability is someone who:

    - has physical or mental impairment that substantially limits one or more major life activities

    - must have documentation of a disability or impairment.

- There is no complete list of disabilities covered by the ADA, but the EEOC published documents that would easily be considered a disability within the meaning of the law. These include:
  - autism
  - intellectual disabilities
  - medical conditions: diabetes, cancer
  - mobility impairments requiring the use of a wheelchair
  - post-traumatic stress disorder
  - cerebral palsy
  - multiple sclerosis.

How does the ADA affect individuals in the workplace?

- Employers are required to provide reasonable accommodations for a job, work environment, or the way things are done so that individuals with disabilities can enjoy equal access to the workplace and the same benefits that are available to non-disabled individuals.
- "Reasonable accommodations" must be tailored to the needs of the individual and the requirements of the job.
- Accommodations must be agreed between the employer and the employee.

Questions to consider when deciding on accommodations for an individual with autism

- What limitations does the employee with ASD experience?
- How do these limitations affect the employee's job performance?
- What specific job tasks are a problem because of these limitations?
- What accommodations are available to reduce or eliminate these problems?
- Are all possible resources being used to determine the accommodations?
- Can the employee with ASD provide information on possible accommodation solutions?
- Do supervisory personnel and employees need training regarding ASD?
- Once accommodations are in place, would it be useful to meet with the employee to evaluate the effectiveness of the accommodations and to determine whether additional or alternative accommodations are needed?

Sample of supports that would be considered reasonable accommodations for most employers

Supports to assist with speaking and communicating

- Allow an employee to provide written responses instead of verbal responses.

- Allow an employee to bring an advocate to a performance review or disciplinary meeting.

Executive functioning/time management supports

- Divide large assignments into smaller tasks.

- Use a wall calendar to help emphasize dates.

- Develop a color-code system to organize files, projects, and activities.

- Use a job coach to teach/reinforce organization skills.

- Provide a "cheat sheet" of high-priority activities, projects, and people.

- Provide written instructions for tasks.

- Help an employee remember the faces of coworkers by providing a directory with pictures and providing coworkers with name tags.

- Provide written instructions of tasks and projects.

- Allow additional training time for learning new tasks.

Supports in working with supervisors

- Allow a supervisor to prioritize tasks.

- Provide a work buddy to help the employee "learn the ropes."

- Provide weekly or monthly meetings to reflect on the employee's performance, discuss any workplace issues, and target any areas that need improvement.

- When there is a change in the employee's supervisor, allow old and new supervisors to keep open their channels of communication to support the employee during the transition.

Sensory supports

- Allow an employee to use a hand-held squeeze ball.

- Provide noise-cancelling headphones to reduce noise and help the employee focus.

- Relocate an employee's office away from audible or visual distractions.

- Change fluorescent interior lighting.

- Allow telecommuting when possible.

Stress management

- Allow an employee to make telephone calls for support.
- Modify employee's work schedule.

On-the-job social skills supports

- Provide a job coach to help understand social cues.
- Help employee "learn the ropes" by providing a mentor.
- Use training videos to demonstrate appropriate social cues.
- Make attendance in social functions optional.

How do you negotiate for a reasonable accommodation?

- An employee is responsible for informing or disclosing their disability to their employer and requesting reasonable accommodations that they need to do their job.
- An employer and employee must engage in what the law calls a "flexible interactive process" to discuss and agree which accommodations are effective and practical.

What is an undue hardship exception?

- The ADA does not require employers to make accommodations that would be considered an undue hardship or any changes that would impose a significant cost or impact on the business.

Am I required to disclose that I have a disability?

- No, an employee is *not* required to disclose disability to their employee. However, to benefit from the protections provided under the ADA, the employee must disclose their disability. If there is no disclosure, there are no ADA protections.

How should I disclose my disability?

- Disclose a disability on a "need-to-know" basis.
- Provide details about the disability as it applies to your work-related accommodations.
- Disclose to an individual who has authority to grant requests.
- Inform your supervisor of your disability-related needs so they can provide the necessary supports and judge your job performance fairly.

Can an employer discriminate against an employee because of a disability?

- No. The ADA forbids discrimination when it comes to any aspect of employment, including:

  - hiring

  - firing

  - promotions

  - layoffs

  - pay or wages

  - job assignments

  - benefits

  - training.

What questions can and can't an employer ask in regard to an employee's disability?

- How the employee performs the job, with or without a reasonable accommodation.

- An employer can't ask a job applicant to answer medical questions or take a medical exam before extending a job offer.

- An employer can't ask if an applicant has a disability.

- After hiring the person, an employer can only ask medical questions or require a medical exam for documentation to support an employee's request for accommodations.

22.4.1. UNDERSTANDING THE WORKPLACE/ CONFLICT RESOLUTION ROLE-PLAYING TECHNIQUES: THOMAS-KILMANN (TKI) STRATEGY

Accommodate

This strategy is a form of "giving in" and letting the other person in the conflict have their way.

Pros: It quickly resolves the conflict.

Cons: The person that is doing the accommodating may become resentful.

Avoid

This strategy postpones resolving the conflict indefinitely.

Pros: Time may help the conflict resolve itself.

Cons: The conflict and bad feelings may increase the longer the conflict is left unresolved.

Collaborate

This strategy requires integrating multiple ideas to help resolve a conflict.

Pros: If effectively used, a solution will be reached that is acceptable to everyone.

Cons: It takes time and may be difficult to get all parties to agree.

Compromise

This strategy requires all parties to give up something in order to find a solution that is acceptable to all parties.

Pros: Once reached, the solution will seem fair to all parties.

Cons: It takes time and may be difficult to get each person to give up something.

Compete

This strategy pits coworkers against one another and has a definite winner and loser in the resolution of the conflict.

Pros: Works best in an emergency or crisis situation when time is of the essence in finding a solution.

Cons: It puts people against one another, and the loser will probably harbor resentment.

22.4.2. UNDERSTANDING THE WORKPLACE/ CONFLICT RESOLUTION ROLE-PLAYING TECHNIQUES: INTEREST-BASED RELATIONAL APPROACH

Ground rules

- Listen with empathy and see the conflict from each other's point of view.

- Explain issues clearly and concisely.

- Encourage people to use "I" rather than "you" statements so no one feels attacked.

- Be clear about their feelings.

- Remain flexible and adaptable.

Technique

STEP 1. MAKE SURE GOOD RELATIONSHIPS ARE A PRIORITY
Treat others with respect and acknowledge their viewpoint even if you don't agree. Be mindful during your discussion—stay calm, exercise acceptance, and be patient.

STEP 2. SEPARATE PEOPLE FROM PROBLEMS
Separate the issue from the person. Put personal feelings aside and address only the issue that is causing the conflict.

STEP 3. LISTEN CAREFULLY TO DIFFERENT INTERESTS
Keep the conversation courteous and don't place blame on the other person. Ask for the other person's perspective to identify the issue that the person thinks is causing the conflict.

STEP 4. LISTEN FIRST, TALK SECOND
Listen to other people's points of view without defending your own. Make sure that each person has finished talking before speaking. Identify what the person thinks is the issue and ask questions if you need clarification.

STEP 5. DETERMINE THE FACTS
Be fair and balanced in the gathering of information. Acknowledge the other person's feelings. Make sure the person feels listened to and has been a part of the discussion.

STEP 6. EXPLORE OPTIONS TOGETHER
By this point, the conflict may have already been resolved once everyone's views have been heard and understood, but it's important to be open to an alternate position. If needed, brainstorm ideas and be open to all suggestions to come to an agreement that will result in a satisfying outcome.

22.5. UNDERSTANDING THE WORKPLACE/
AWN RULES FOR DATING COWORKERS

Don't date your boss

Most employers have a policy that prohibits direct supervisors from dating their subordinates, and this is for good reason. If the relationship ends badly, a disgruntled employee could claim a hostile work environment and sue the company for harassment. A manager-subordinate romance can also create a perception of favoritism which can cause tension among coworkers who report to the same manager.

You can only ask your coworker out one time

If you want to ask out a coworker, you only have one chance. If you continually ask out a coworker after being told no the first time, the coworker could claim a hostile working environment and report the incident to HR. The consequence of these actions might get you a bad reputation at work or, if the incident is serious, result in you being fired from your job.

Avoid public displays of affection (PDAs)

If you are dating someone at work, it isn't considered professional to kiss or hug in front of your colleagues. These actions can make other people uncomfortable or possibly make others jealous.

Disclose to your company

It's best to disclose to your supervisor when you start dating a coworker. Letting your boss know about your relationship will keep you out of the workplace rumor mill and avoid the awkward situation when everyone at work finds out that you're a couple.

Set boundaries

Spending all your time with a boyfriend and girlfriend might not be good for your relationship. If you do start dating a coworker, it's okay to schedule time for yourself and with other friends to share in the hobbies and activities that you enjoy most.

Plan for the ending

Relationships do end, which can be a problem if the person you were seeing is someone that you also see every day at work. This could seriously impact your job, especially if the relationship ends very badly. Before you ask out a coworker, just remember that you're mixing business with pleasure. If the relationship works out, that's great, but if it doesn't, it could create a bad situation at work that might be impossible to fix.

23. WORKSHOP SUMMARY

Name: ....

Class and date: ....

Name three things we did in the Roundtable Discussion

1..

2. ....

3. ....

Name three things we did in Prepare and Practice

1..

2. ....

3. ....

Name some of our upcoming events and activities

1..

2. ....

3. ....

What do you need to do before the next workshop?

1..

2. ....

3. ....

List one thing you learned or know about someone else.

Candidate name	What we learned
....	....
....	....
....	....
....	....
....	....
....	....
....	....
....	....

25. WORKSHOP SYLLABUS

26. EXPECTED WORKSHOP BEHAVIOR CHART

1. Treat everyone with respect in words, action and thoughts.

2. Arrive on time and be ready to learn.

3. Phones should be turned off or silent during class.

4. Computers and phones to be used in class for instructional purposes only.

5. Remain in your seat until break or end of class.

6. Disruptive behaviors and off-topic conversations are not allowed.

7. Meals may not be eaten in class.

8. Snacks in moderation are okay—practice the two-cookie rule.

9. Mindful listening is mandatory.

10. Work collaboratively with peers.

27. WORKPLACE HABITS AND EXPECTATION

Courtesy of Miller Transition Center, Reseda, California

What you bring to the job

- Focus on greatness and believe in yourself. You can do it!
- Dress appropriately in clean clothes without holes, rips, or stains.
- Use proper hygiene: wash and comb your hair, clean your nails, shower and apply deodorant. Men should shave daily.
- Have a positive attitude—nothing is more important. *You are in charge of your attitude.*
- Be friendly, kind, courteous and customer service oriented!
- Take initiative, stay focused, stay busy and be responsible for your work.

What's expected of you

- Work is not what you see on television; work is not like school. Work is not like home; work is like...well work!
- Follow all equipment and workplace safety guidelines.
- Take constructive criticism in a professional manner.
- Follow the lead and instructions given to you by your supervisor.

Your expected behavior

- Advocate for yourself. If you don't know or are unsure, ask questions.
- Demonstrate respect to your coworkers and supervisors.
- Remember, you're at work and not on a date so act appropriately.
- Work is work and not social time. Break time is for social time.
- Interact productively with your coworkers in a positive manner. You're a team player!

Chapter 16: Instructor's Materials

Contents

Tips for Instructors

- Structuring a Class

- Sample Agenda

1. Forms

- Application and Candidate Information Sheet

- Expected Behavior Agreement

- Parent Permission Form

- Photo Release Form

2. Binder

- Cover

- Syllabus

- Field Trip/Guest Speaker Notes

3. Assessments

- Work Smarts

- Interests Inventory

4. Roundtable Discussion

- Icebreaker Questions

- Shout Out Count

5. Prepare and Practice

- Inspirational Quotes

6. Dress for Success

- Presentation: Can I Wear This to Work

7. Landing A Job

- Volunteer Spreadsheet

8. Understanding the Workplace

- Conflict Role-Playing Scenarios

- Work Situations

9. Recall and Review

- Quiz Questions

Links and Websites

TIPS FOR INSTRUCTORS/STRUCTURING A CLASS

Planning a class lesson plan

Each class consists of four parts:

1. Agenda and Introductions

2. Roundtable Discussion

3. Prepare and Practice

4. Recall and Review

Chapter 13, Classroom Meetings, goes into detail about topics and activities for each part of the workshop.

Agendas

- Creating an agenda is helpful because it lets candidates know what to expect and what is being covered.

- At least two days in advance, send a reminder email of any assignments that are due for the next class and attach the agenda.

Prepare and Practice

- It is helpful to assign reading from the book for the topic you will be covering so that candidates are familiar with the material when it's reviewed in class.

Recall and Review

- A list of questions compiled from five years of the original program are included at the end of this section.

TIPS FOR INSTRUCTORS/SAMPLE AGENDA

AUTISM WORKS NOW WORKPLACE READINESS WORKSHOP CLASS 7: 11/7/19
Roundtable Discussion

- Group check-in
- Candidate news
- Shout Outs! and Shout Out! Champion
- Stress Management:
  - MARC Guided Meditation
  - Stretching with Joan
- Gratitude Journal: review

Prepare and Practice

- Next fieldtrip: Arclight Theatre
  - Review website
  - Transportation Planning, Dress, Parking, Assign Questions
  - Input date, time and address on Calendar
- Dinner afterwards: Lucy's Restaurant

Dress for Success

- Presentation: Can I Wear This to Work?
  - Discussion: Variations on Attire
  - Activity: Measurement Worksheets

Review and Recall

- Class Review
- Class Quiz

Recommended assignments: Add to Google Tasks

- Preparation for field trip: practice question, select what you're wearing
- Complete: Finding a Volunteer Job Worksheet

Recommended daily assignments: What's your routine?

- Check email
- Meditate: three to five minutes, one or more times per day
- Write in your gratitude journal

1.1. FORMS/APPLICATION AND INFORMATION SHEET

**AUTISM WORKS NOW WORKSHOP APPLICATION/INFORMATION SHEET
YOUR INFORMATION**

Name ....

Email ....

Phone number ....

Emergency contact and relationship ....

Emergency contact phone number ....

List your work and volunteer experience		
Company and city	**Dates of employment**	**Position held**

How did you hear about the workshop? If you were referred, include their name and contact information so we can thank them.

....

....

....

What are your expectations? What are you looking to get out of the workshop?

....

....

....

Include any additional information you would like to share

....

....

....

1.2. FORMS/EXPECTED BEHAVIOR AGREEMENT

Notes on managing behaviors

It's always important to remember that workshop expected behaviors are the same behaviors that are expected at work. Any behavior that disrupts the class will also be disruptive at work.

As the instructor, you are in charge of the class, but candidates are in control of their own behavior. Your role is not to tell candidates what to do but to help them choose how to act or not to act.

The Expected Workshop Behaviors Chart is helpful in communicating to candidates what are acceptable behaviors to participate in the workshop. Revise as needed—if a candidate displays a behavior that disrupts the class and is not on the behavior chart, add that behavior to the chart.

The two-cookie rule is good to include if you provide snacks. Some candidates have challenges with moderation so communicating this rule upfront helps avoid any issues for overeating.

If the candidate has a history of aggressive or disruptive behaviors, it is recommended that the Expected Behavior Agreement be put in place prior to the start of the workshop. Revise the agreement as needed to include any behaviors that are problematic. The instructor, candidate and candidate's parents all sign the agreement, and each receives a fully signed copy. The candidate's copy should be filed in their binder in #26.

AWN EXPECTED BEHAVIOR AGREEMENT

Date: ....

Candidate name: ....

I understand that the expected behaviors in the Workplace Readiness Workshop are the same behaviors that are expected at work.

In order to participate in the Workplace Readiness Workshop, I will adhere to all of the following behaviors while in class, on field trips, and during AWN organized events.

1. I will treat everyone with respect in words, actions, and thoughts.

2. I will arrive on time and be ready to learn.

3. I will turn my phone off or to silent during class.

4. I will only use my computers and phone during class for instructional purposes.

5. I will remain in my seat until break or the end of class.

6. I will not disrupt class or have off-topic conversations.

7. I will not eat a meal in class.

8. I will eat snacks in class and practice the two-cookie rule.

9. I will mindfully listen at all times.

10. I will work collaboratively with my peers.

By signing below, I understand that if I don't follow the rules listed above, the consequence may be that I won't be allowed to participate in AWN workshop classes, field trips, or organized events.

Candidate signature   Parent/Guardian signature
                                        (*if Candidate is minor*)

. . . .

. . . .

. . . .

Instructor signature

. . . .

. . . .

. . . .

1.3. FORMS/PARENT PERMISSION FORM

In the topic, Understanding the Workplace, there is a discussion about harassment and sexual harassment. Some parents might be uncomfortable with this especially if their child is young. To avoid any issues or bad feelings, it is advised to let parents know prior to the lesson and get their written permission for their child to attend the class.

Autism Works Now: Parent Permission for Minor
Child to Participate in Class (*please print*)

Date ....

Parent or guardian's name ....

Child's name..

I give my permission for my child to participate in the following AWN class that will include a discussion on the following subject matter.

Date of class:

Subject matter:

☐ Harassment
☐ Sexual harassment
☐ Dating
☐ Other...

By signing below, the parent grants the instructor permission to include their child in the class discussion as indicated above.

PARENT

(*signature*) ....

(*print name*) ....

INSTRUCTOR

(*signature*) ....

(*print name*) ....

1.4. FORMS/PHOTO RELEASE FORM

LICENSE, ASSIGNMENT AND RELEASE

1. I, ... , **(the "Licensee") irrevocably grant to** (the "Producer") together with their employees, agents, licenses, successors, assignees, and those acting with the Producer's permission or on its authority (all of whom are referred to below as the "Licensed Parties") the absolute, exclusive and unrestricted right and permission to record, copy, reproduce, adapt, edit, summarize, copyright, publish, photograph, film, videotape, televise, exhibit, distribute, license, vend, rent, disseminate, display, perform, and otherwise exploit in any and all markets and media now known or hereafter devised (collectively "Use") my appearance, name, likeness, voice, documents, other property, views, performance, efforts, trademark or trade name, biography, artistry, recorded image and voice, and all other documents and artifacts provided to the Producer by me (collectively the "Materials"). This grant of rights is made without limitation on time, circumstances, location, market or medium of use, and includes without limitation all uses of the materials in and related to the production entirely entitled "Autism Works Now," and in all types of advertising and promotion of that program or any other factual or fictional film or program of the services of the Licensed Parties.

2. I hereby waive my right to inspect or approve the materials of Uses to which any Materials may be put, including without limitation, the completed program/spot or other film or program, and to related advertising and promotion of any film or program.

3. Recognizing the licensed parties' reliance on this agreement, I hereby irrevocably release, discharge and agree to indemnify and hold harmless the licensed parties and each of them from and against all actions, damages, costs, liabilities, claims, loses and expense of every type and description (including attorneys' fees and expenses) to which Licensed Parties or any of them may be subject as a result of or in any way related to any use of the materials by any of the Licensed Parties, including without limitation, any claim for violation, infringement or invasion of copyright, patent, trademark right, privacy or publicity right, defamation or any other fight whatsoever that I now have or may ever have resulting from or relating to any such use of the materials.

4. I agree that all audio and/or video recording of Materials or any of them as well as all descriptions or summaries of my personal history that are made and used by Licensed Party will be solely owned by Autism Works Now, the Producer, and that the Producers may copyright in this name and for its sole benefit any such audio or video recording containing any of the materials.

5. Nothing herein will constitute any obligations on the Licensed Party to make any use of the rights or Materials set forth above.

6. This License, Assignment and Release shall be governed by, and construed in accordance with, the laws of the State of California, applicable to contracts entered into and be fully performed therein.

7. The likeness of all materials provided by the party including all the above named, belong solely to Autism Works Now and the Producer, and may not be sold, released for all of the above markets, or distributed without prior consent from Autism Works Now or the Producer.

I have read this License, Assignment, and Release and I understand its contents.

Autism Works Now Representative   Licensee

Name . . . .   Name. . . . .

Signature . . . .   Signature . . . .

Date . . . .   Date . . . .

Is the Licensee signing for legal minor? Yes No

Name of minor: . . . .

2.1. BINDER/BINDER COVER

Workplace Readiness Workshop: Autism Works Now!™
Insert picture from program
Insert candidate name

Susan Osborne Director 3xx xxx-xxxx

Autism Movement Therapy

Autism Movement Therapy, Inc is a 501 c3 non-profit

2.2. BINDER/SYLLABUS

It is recommended that you create a syllabus for your program to provide your contact information and any important information you want to share with candidates, parents and caregivers. The syllabus is filed in #25 of the binder.

Include the dates when there is no instruction (e.g. holidays).

If there is a fee for the program, clearly explain how much notice you require for missed classes and what the refund policies are.

AUTISM WORKS NOW

Workplace Readiness Workshop Syllabus

Mission of the Workplace Readiness Workshop

To help individuals on the autism spectrum acquire the skills they need to get and keep a job.

Our beliefs

1. Individuals on the autism spectrum and related learning differences can develop essential employment skills.

2. Individuals with autism deserve meaningful jobs that contribute to the well-being of their communities and provide a living wage.

3. Employers will be motivated to hire individuals with autism when they experience first-hand the positive contributions that these individuals contribute to the workplace.

Instructors and contact information

| First name, | Last name | Phone number | Email address |
| First name, | Last name | Phone number | Email address |

Workshop address: . . . .

Workshop dates: . . . .

Workshop times: . . . .

Non-instructional days:

- The week of Thanksgiving
- Winter break
- Spring break

Candidate requirements

- **Candidates must have the ability to independently operate a computer.** If they need individualized computer support to participate in class, it is their responsibility to make arrangements to provide their own classroom aid.

- **Candidates are expected to complete assigned homework by the due date.** Work assigned outside class is designed to reinforce the concepts that are presented in class. To get as much as possible from the Workshop, candidates should complete all assignments by the due date.

Missed classes

There is no refund for a missed session. On request, candidates will be given access to copies of the materials that were distributed in class.

2.3. BINDER/FIELD TRIP/GUEST SPEAKER NOTES

Below is an example of notes taken for a field trip. The same format can be used for guest speakers.

26 Field Trip Recap with Manager, Brian Wilson
Best Buy Field Trip 11/10/2016

What are the various jobs at Best Buy?

- Seasonal cashier: this is how Brian started at Best Buy
- Customer assistance: checking receipts, check on safety
- Inventory: online and receiving merchandise from trucks
- Merchandising: creating look and feel of store
- Sales associates
- Administrative: accounting
- Geek squad

What are the traits that successful employees of Best Buy have in common?

- They enjoy what they do.
- They have passion for serving customers.
- They find satisfaction in solving problems.
- They strive to meet the expectations of customers.
- Advice: Customers are allowed to have a bad day. Employees aren't.

If I were going to apply for a job at Best Buy, what advice would you give me?

- Make sure that working at Best Buy is something you would enjoy.
- Don't be motivated to take a job for the paycheck.
- Money is a necessity but be motivated to work doing something you like to.

What is a typical day like at Best Buy?

- Ask questions to find out what the best solution is for the customer
  - What brings you into Best Buy? Are you replacing an item or is this the first time buying?
  - If you are replacing an item, how long since you last replaced it?
  - What will you use it for?

What types of jobs did you have before you worked at Best Buy?

- Best Buy was Brian's first job and he has worked there for eight years.

- He started at 17 as a seasonal cashier. Wanted to be a lawyer, so left to go to school.

- Returned when he finished school. He's been back for five years.

- Plans to return to school to finish his law degree.

Do you offer full and part time jobs at Best Buy?

- Yes. Also, seasonal and year-round.

Do you receive a company discount?

- Yes, and vendors also give employees discounts, sometimes better than store discounts. The reason is to have the employees use the merchandise and then promote it to customers.

3.1. ASSESSMENTS/WORK SMARTS

After candidates complete their Work Smart assessments, the results are tallied, color coded, and compiled on a Google sheet. The spreadsheet is then projected and shared with the group so everyone can see who has similar learning styles. To help identify similarities within the group, add a color for matches between candidates (i.e. all music interests are blue, all people are red).

The following is an example of a spreadsheet.

WORK SMARTS ASSESSMENT RESULTS

Cathy	Clark	Lucy	Parker	Steven	Wyatt
Music / 27	People / 25	Word / 27	Body / 30	Picture / 27	Body / 29
People / 24	Nature / 24	Body / 26	People / 30	Self / 24	Nature / 24
Body / 23	Picture / 24	People / 26	Music / 29	Body / 22	Picture / 24
Self / 22	Logic / 21	Picture / 26	Word / 29	Music / 22	Music / 21
Picture / 21	Self / 21	Nature / 26	Nature / 29	Word / 20	People / 21
Word / 20	Body / 20	Music / 22	Logic / 28	Logic / 19	Self / 20
Logic / 19	Music / 20	Self / 23	Picture / 28	People / 19	Logic / 16
Nature / 19	Word / 19	Logic / 21	Self / 26	Nature / 16	Word / 14

3.2. ASSESSMENTS/INTEREST INVENTORY ASSESSMENT

After candidates complete the Interests Inventory, the results are tallied and similar interests can be color coded. The information is compiled on a Google Sheet and it is projected
and shared with the group so that candidates can identify what interests they share with
other members of the group.

The following is an example spreadsheet.

	Cathy	Clark	Lucy	Parker	Steven	Wyatt
Do in free time	Talk to friends Browse Web Talk a walk	Music	Gaming Be with pets	Computer Movies Shop	Art Computer Write	Computer Music Cook
Favorite school subject	Art History Science	Art	Art Science History	Art Choir English	Band PE History	Math Language Arts
Favorite books	Manga Animals Fiction	Animals	Photography Architecture Travel	Hunger Games Harry Potter	Fairy Tales Disney	Disney Cooking Travel
Sports, hobbies	Drawing Cooking	Animals	Hiking Photography Painting	Collecting Soccer Running	Swimming Soccer Track & Field	Soccer Baseball Swimming
Internet	YouTube	YouTube	YouTube Google	YouTube Facebook	YouTube	YouTube Google
Do for long time	Movies Television	Travel Games	Computer Read	Movies Music	Disney Movies	Swim Run

4.1. ROUNDTABLE DISCUSSION/ICEBREAKER QUESTIONS

Icebreaker questions are used to help candidates get to know one another better and to help them learn information about members of the group. Icebreakers are also used in many work meetings. The best icebreaker topics are ones that are appropriate to discuss at work.
    This is just a partial list, so add new questions that are appropriate for your group.

- What pets do you have or would you like to have?
- What is your favorite vacation and why?
- What is your favorite type of food and favorite restaurant?
- Describe the best meal you ever ate.
- Is there any person living or dead that you would like to meet?
- Name three items that you would take with you if your house was burning down?
- What skill would you like to learn?
- If money was no object, what would you buy?
- If you had $10,000, what would you spend it on?
- If you could be granted a superpower, what would it be?
- What is your favorite movie?
- What is your favorite TV show?
- If you could choose an imaginary friend, who would you choose and why?
- If you were stranded on a desert island, what three things would you want to have with you?
- What is your favorite cartoon and why?
- If you had your own talk show, who would be your first three guests?

4.2. ROUNDTABLE DISCUSSION/SHOUT OUT COUNT

The Shout Out Count was created as a way to recognize candidate efforts and encourage candidate involvement in workshop activities. A point is awarded each time a candidate does something positive.

Here are a few examples of behaviors that would be awarded a Shout Out point:

- Responding within a day to an instructor's email.

- Completing an assignment and bringing it to class.

- Emailing the instructor a picture of themselves engaged in an activity, a picture of something they created or of a beloved pet.

The instructor records the candidate's effort on the day it occurs, then tallies points for the week. At the end of the month, points for all weeks are tallied, and the candidate with the most points for the month is the Shout Out Count Champ. We used to give the winner a small reward, like a $5 gift card. If a candidate won two months in a row, they would not be eligible to participate in the next month's Shout Out Count.

The chart is shared in each class at the start of the Roundtable Discussion, and the Shout Out Count Champ is announced at the beginning of the first class of the month.

If a candidate fails to be awarded any points like Lucy, it is suggested you have a private conference with them to find out why.

DATES	3/15–3/21	3/22–3/28	4/1–4//7	4/8–4/14	TOTAL
Cathy	3/14, 3/16, 3/18 (2): **4**	3/23, 3/26, 3/27: **3**	4/2, 4/5, 4/7 (2): **4**	4/8, 4/9, 4/10, 4/11: **4**	**15**
Clark	3/14, 3/18: **2**	3/27: **1**	4/7: **1**	4/14: **1**	**5**
Lucy					
Parker	3/14: **1**	3/27: **1**	4/7: **1**	4/14: **1**	**4**
Steven	3/16, 3/17, 3/18, 3/21: **4**	3/23, 3/25, 3/27: **3**	4/7: **1**	4/14: **1**	**9**
Shane	3/15, 3/17: **2**	3/25, 3/27, 3/28: **3**	4/5, 4/7: **2**	4/8, 4/10, 4/14A: **3**	**10**

5. PREPARE AND PRACTICE/INSPIRATIONAL QUOTES

Inspirational quotes are read at the beginning of class and there is discussion on how the statement applies to work. The goal is to convey important workplace information in short, easy statements so that candidates can remember what they've learned after they finish the workshop. There are a limitless number of inspirational quotes that are easy to find in a Google search. It's best to use a quote that relates to the topic being covered in Prepare and Practice.

Expected behaviors
This is especially relevant to #1 on the Expected Workshop Behavior Chart:

> Watch your thoughts, they become your words; watch your words, they become your actions; watch your actions, they become your habits; watch your habits, they become your character; watch your character, it becomes your destiny. (Lao Tzu)

How this relates to work: You are in control of your thoughts, actions, and feelings. Keeping your thoughts positive will help you keep a positive outlook, help you feel grateful, and help you maintain a positive self-image. This will help you make positive decisions which will help you get what you want out of life.

Connecting with coworkers

> I've learned that people will forget what you said, people will forget what you did, but people will never forget how you made them feel. (Maya Angelou)

How this is connected to work: Your coworkers will like you more if you have a positive attitude and are respectful at all times.

> Great minds discuss ideas; average minds discuss events; small minds discuss people. (Eleanor Roosevelt)

How this relates to work: Not everyone has a great mind like yours and coworkers won't always be as interested in your special interests as you are. Small minds gossip and talk about them when they aren't there and this isn't appreciated or respected by others. Show interest in what other people think and feel, but don't ask overly personal questions.

Dress for success

> You can do anything you want in life if you dress for it. (Edith Head)

How this relates to work: To get hired, it's important to dress to match the culture of the company or organization. To get promoted, you have to dress for the job you want.

Interview essentials: Perseverance

If you're trying to achieve, there will be roadblocks. I've had them; everybody has had them. But obstacles don't have to stop you. If you run into a wall, don't turn around and give up. Figure out how to climb it, go through it, or work around it. (Michael Jordan)

How this relates to work: Don't give up—it takes a lot of time and effort to find a job.

There are no mistakes in life. There are only learning opportunities. (Susan Osborne)

How this relates to work: If you make a mistake at work, don't be upset, learn from it so you can do better next time.

Perseverance is failing 19 times and succeeding on the 20th. (Julie Andrews)

How this relates to work: To get a job, you have to keep interviewing until you are hired.

Landing a job: Preparation

Success occurs when opportunity meets preparation. (Zig Zigler)

How this relates to work: To get a job, you need to prepare—do your research, prepare questions, and practice answers to commonly asked interview questions.

You can learn new things at any time in your life if you're willing to be a beginner. If you actually learn to like being a beginner, the whole world opens up to you. (Barbara Sher)

How this relates to work: You will need to be in your job for some time before you are good at it.

Understanding the workplace

The only way to do great work is to love what you do. If you haven't found it yet, keep looking. Don't settle. As with all matters of the heart, you'll know when you find it. (Steve Jobs)

How this relates to work: You need to feel a connection to the work that you do to have meaning in your life. If your job doesn't do that, keep looking until you do.

6. PREPARE AND PRACTICE/DRESS FOR SUCCESS

Presentation template: Can I Wear This to Work?

The attached presentation template was created on Google Slides and includes placeholders where pictures can be inserted. A Google search using "Images" provides easy access to pictures that can be used in your presentation. Under the Fair Use rule, you do not need to ask permission from an author or copyright holder when using copyrighted materials for educational purposes.

The month you are covering Dress for Success, add slides with men and women's attire that matches the culture of the company you will be visiting for your field trip. For example, the month you'll be using the presentation that you're scheduled to visit a pet supply store, the men's and women's slide should include people wearing polo shirts and khaki pants.

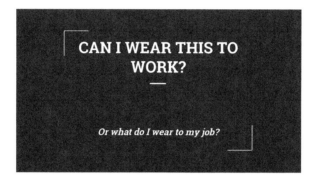

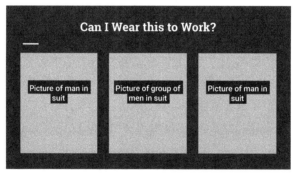

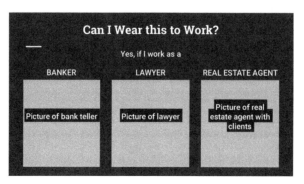

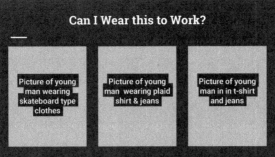

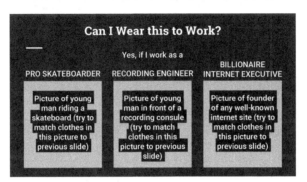

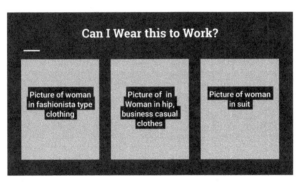

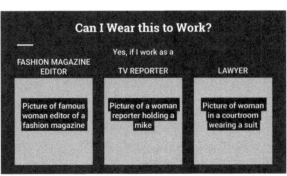

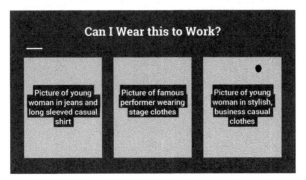

Can I Wear this to Work?

Yes, if I work as a

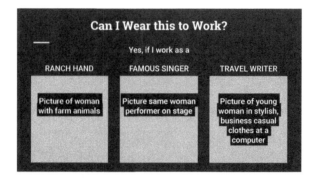

RANCH HAND	FAMOUS SINGER	TRAVEL WRITER
Picture of woman with farm animals	Picture same woman performer on stage	Picture of young woman in stylish, business casual clothes at a computer

Can I Wear this to Work?

Yes, if I work as a

DOCTOR OR NURSE

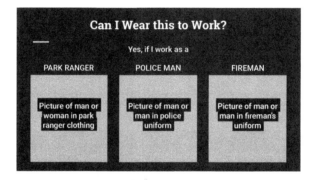

Pictures of men and women doctors & nurses

Can I Wear this to Work?

Yes, if I work as a

PARK RANGER	POLICE MAN	FIREMAN
Picture of man or woman in park ranger clothing	Picture of man or man in police uniform	Picture of man or man in fireman's uniform

ALWAYS REMEMBER ...

Wear clothes that fit properly - know your measurements.

Wear clothes to the job that match the workplace.

Dressing for success is dressing for the job that you want.

Keep your professional wardrobe clean and in good repair.

Volunteer spreadsheet

For the activity, Finding a Volunteer Job, each candidate's preferences are recorded on a spreadsheet like the one below which is shared with all candidates. You can add more columns and add notes to document each candidate's progress.

	Cause 1	Cause 2	Org 1	Org phone number	Org 2	Org 2 contact info
Cathy	Thrift Store	Animal Shelter	Woman's League Thrift Store	555 123 4567	WLA Animal Shelter	310 555 1345
Clark	Red Cross	Animal Shelter	Red Cross of LA	310 555 8888	WLA Animal Shelter	310 555 1345
Lucy	Art	YMCA	Artists Coop	213 888 9352	YMCA of LA	310 555 1345
Parker	Kids	Pets	Little Tykes Pre School	310 777 7777	Pets for Vets, Inc.	310 444 4444
Steven	Museum	Improv	LA County Museum	213 888 3333	Groundlings	213 565 6565
Wyatt	Healthcare	Animal Shelter	Motion Picture Hospital	310 555 9999	WLA Animal Shelter	310 555 1345

8.1. PREPARE AND PRACTICE/ UNDERSTANDING THE WORKPLACE

Conflict resolution role-playing scenarios

The goal of the exercise is to have candidates practice both the TKI and IBR conflict resolution strategies.

TKI Strategy

- Avoid
- Accommodate
- Complete
- Compromise
- Collaborate

Interest-Based Relational (IBR) Approach

- Step 1: Make sure good relationships are a priority
- Step 2: Separate people from problems
- Step 3: Listen carefully to different viewpoints
- Step 4: Listen first, talk second
- Step 5: Determine the facts
- Step 6: Explore options together

How to facilitate the activity

- Read through a scenario and discuss the options using both techniques.
- TKI: Discuss the pros and cons of each strategy.
- Choose the strategy that would end the conflict.
- ABI: Discuss how each step can be implemented.
- Decide on the best solution to end the conflict.

Scenarios

Below are some scenarios that can be used in conflict resolution role-playing activities using the TKI and IBR conflict resolution techniques. You can also create your own scenarios. Ask candidates for suggestions. If they feel comfortable, encourage them to share a conflict they experienced in their own life and use it as one of the scenarios. All of the scenarios included are related to work, but for a class of middle and high school students, they will most likely have very little experience as an employee. These students will find the activity more meaningful if it is related to a conflict they experienced at school, at home, or out in the community.

SCENARIO 1
You are working in an upscale music store. One of your coworkers makes fun of your clothes all the time. The coworker is not a very good dresser and you could easily make fun of the way the coworker dresses.

SCENARIO 2
Your coworker listens to music on his computer with headphones on. However, he often ends up going to sleep and snoring loudly, which irritates his coworkers.

SCENARIO 3
You work in an office and share a cubicle with Sally, who likes to talk a lot about politics. You do not share her opinions and find her political views to be extreme. You like Sally and want to get along with her, but her political beliefs are so far away from yours that you are starting to have a hard time stopping yourself from saying anything that opposes Sally's beliefs.

SCENARIO 4
You're waiting for your ride outside work when you observe two of the company security workers loading boxes of paper into a van and driving off. You've seen this happen more than once and suspect the guards may be stealing. They are quite large and tough looking.

SCENARIO 5
You are the secretary for a large bank, and the bank manager is in a meeting. You have been instructed to take messages for all of the manager's calls and tell the callers that he will return their call when he is out of his meeting. A customer calls and demands to talk with the bank manager, but you do as you are told and ask to take a message. The man gets angry and starts using abusive language towards you.

SCENARIO 6
You share an office with two other coworkers. One coworker, Jamal, likes to talk a lot about his family and his personal life. The other coworker, Blake, used to listen politely, but he is becoming increasingly annoyed every time Jamal starts to discuss his personal life. You find Jamal's monologues amusing, but you are also aware that Blake is slowly getting angrier and angrier. Jamal is also getting irritated with Blake. When he talks, he notices that Blake stares at the computer in an attempt to tune him out, and Jamal thinks this is very rude. You are sure that sooner or later your coworkers are going to have a major fight. You get along very well with both of your coworkers, but you don't want to get into the middle of anything.

8.2. PREPARE AND PRACTICE/
UNDERSTANDING THE WORKPLACE

Work situations

The purpose of the exercise is to have candidates come up with what they would do in each situation.

There are several ways to facilitate the activity:

- Assign the question to a group of two or three candidates and have them discuss and present their answer.

- Give the question as an assignment and candidates can share their answers in class.

- Ask the question to the class with three different solutions and call on candidates to choose which solution they like best.

You think you'd be a good fit to work at a company in your neighborhood. *What should you do?*

You submitted your resume and application online. *What should you do next?*

You've been called to schedule an interview. *What should you do while you are on the call?*

You just had an interview that you don't think went well. *What should you do to follow it up?*

You are taking the bus to an interview and the bus is running late. *What should you do?*

You were just hired. *What information will your new employer need from you?*

You're stocking shelves at Target and need to use the restroom. *What should you do?*

You're not feeling well and feel it's best to not go to work today. *What should you do?*

The funeral for a family member is happening the same day you are scheduled to work. *What should you do?*

The first day of your new job, one of your coworkers makes a negative comment about what you are wearing. *How should you respond?*

You've just had a negative performance review and you are upset. Your coworker notices you are upset and asks what's wrong. *What should you do?*

The dress code for your job requires you to have clean clothes and good hygiene. You come to work and your supervisor asks you to trim your nails before you begin work. *What should you do?*

It's the second time you've arrived late to work, and your boss made a comment. You're running late and it will be your third time. *What should you expect?*

You get into a disagreement with someone at work and she yells at you. *How should you respond?*

You and a coworker do not get along, but you find yourself in the lunch area together every work shift. *What are some possible options?*

You are a cashier at Ralphs, and your manager tells you that the cash in your register is $20 short for your shift. *What should you do?*

You think one of your coworkers is saying negative things about you. You don't have proof and you don't know who it is. *What should you do?*

You invite your friend to attend the company holiday party with you. He drinks too much and says something embarrassing to one of your coworkers. *What should you say to your coworker and your friend next time you see each of them?*

You are going to Starbucks and a coworker asks you to buy her a coffee, but she doesn't offer to reimburse you when you give it to her. At the end of the day, you mention it, and she says she'll pay you tomorrow but doesn't. *What should you do?*

You are caught by your boss watching YouTube while you are at work. *What should you do?*

Your coworker is obsessed with the show "Tiger King" and talks about it a lot. You don't watch the show, you aren't interested, and it's starting to annoy you. *What can you say to your coworker so they will stop bothering you?*

Your friend gives a presentation at work and asks your opinion, but you don't think she did a good job. *What should you say to your friend?*

You work as an administrative assistant and your boss asks you to organize a birthday party for his five-year-old son. This is a personal request and not in your job description. *What should you do and why?*

You brought your lunch to work and put it in the refrigerator. When you went to get it, it was not there. *What should you do?*

When you are on a lunch break with your friend, they tell you a joke that you think is offensive. *What should you do?*

A friend at work asks you to lunch but you've already made plans to pick something up from the grocery store during your lunch hour. *What should you do?*

You see someone at your job whom you don't know well but who is crying. *What should you do?*

Your workplace is having a potluck going away party for a coworker who is leaving the company. Everyone is expected to bring something. *What would you bring?*

You are stocking some shelves at work, and a coworker stops to talk. Your boss is standing nearby and can see you. *What should you do?*

Two friends from work invite you to have drinks at a loud and noisy bar, but you don't want to go. *What should you do?*

You and your friend are unloading boxes off a truck. Your friend stops working and starts texting, leaving you to do the work by yourself. *What should you do?*

Coworker 1 tells you a personal detail about themselves and asks you not to tell anyone. Coworker 2 is concerned about coworker 1 and asks you if you know why she's been acting differently. *Should you tell coworker 2 what you know about coworker 1? Why or why not?*

You go out for dinner after work with a coworker. She says she really likes you, but you aren't interested in a romantic relationship. *How should you respond to your coworker?*

You've finished your work and want to take a break surfing the internet on your work computer. *Is this okay and should you do it?*

You've been at your job at a hardware store stocking shelves for two years and you are starting to get bored. *What do you think you should do?*

You are working at Sprouts, and you don't think you'll be able to finish your work before the end of your shift. *What should you do?*

9. RECALL AND REVIEW/QUIZ QUESTIONS

Workshop classes end with the Recall and Review where candidates review what was learned. The Class Quiz is part of the review to let instructors assess how well candidates have grasped the key concepts and to gauge how much information they retained. Each workshop quiz is filed in #24 of the binder.

Creating your quiz

- You can use Google Forms to create the quiz.

- The best mix of questions for each quiz is one true/false and four multiple choice.

- After the candidates become acquainted, include a question on a fact about one of the candidates and list three candidate names as possible answers.

- For field trips scheduled or that have recently happened, you could include a question on a fact about the organization or the field trip host.

Introduction to workshop

True or False: Everything I'll be learning in the workshop will help me get and keep a job.

What should I do if I know I'm going to miss a workshop class?

- **Call or email the instructor to let the know**

- Have my mom or dad call the instructor

- Do nothing—the instructor will know I'm not there when I don't show up

How many cookies can I eat during class?

- 1

- **2**

- As many as I want

True or **False**: I am being mindful if I surf the web and participate in class at the same time.

Field trips

When preparing for an AWN field trip, what is good information to know?

- What the company does or produces

- The company's senior managers

- How long the company has been in business

- **All of the above**

What do I need to have for an AWN field trip?

- My elevator pitch
- Something appropriate to wear
- Knowledge of what the company does or manufactures
- **All of the above**

Mindfulness

True or False: Working in a friendly environment will reduce stress and help me feel happier at work.

True or False: Acknowledging and naming my fears can help me manage my emotions.

True or False: People who practice gratitude have better relationships with loved ones.

Which of the following is one of the seven things mindful people do?

- Show gratitude
- Get curious
- Accept change
- **All of the above**

What is a positive feature of mindfulness?

- It helps me not miss anything that's happening around me
- It helps me reduce stress
- It helps me have a more positive and less negative attitude
- **All of the above**

The M in MARC stands for:

- Meaningful
- **Mindfulness**
- Mighty

Stress management

On the 5-point scale, what level am I most calm?

- 5
- **1**
- 3

On the 5-point scale, at which level should I take a break, walk outside or meditate?

- 1
- **3**
- 5

On the 5-point scale, what levels are the best for work?

- **1 and 2**
- 2 and 3
- 4 and 5

When I'm at work and I feel as if I'm going to say or do something I shouldn't, it's time to...

- **Take a walk outside to clear my head**
- Force myself not to
- Yell out loudly because it's not good to hold in my feelings

When I'm feeling annoyed, stressed, or angry about something at work, I should:

- Tell my boss how I feel
- **Find a quiet place to sit down, close my eyes, and take deep breaths**
- Ignore my feelings and hope I feel better soon

How does my body react to stress?

- My face gets hot
- My heart beats faster
- My breathing becomes fast and shallow
- **All of the above**

When I'm at number 5 on the 5-point check-in scale, it means:

- I'm calm and don't need to do anything to manage my stress
- I'm starting to get stressed and need to use stress-reducing strategies to calm down
- **I'm so stressed I might have a meltdown**

When is the best time to use the Incredible 5-point scale?

- When I am already upset so I can calm down
- **As soon as I am starting to feel stressed**
- Never—I never get stressed

What should I do to relax when I feel stressed?

- Think about why I'm stressed
- Tell myself to stop feeling stressed
- **Take a deep breath, talk a walk outside or find a quiet place to sit**

According to Oprah Winfrey, when is the best time to write in a gratitude journal?

- **In the morning so I can reflect on my gratitude items throughout the day**
- At night so I can sleep on them
- She said I don't need to write in my gratitude journal

What are some benefits of meditation?

- Feeling less stress
- Being more creative
- Improvement in my immune system
- **All of the above**

Email

True or False: I should answer an email within 24 hours of receiving it.

Why should I check my email at least once per day?

- It's a good way to pass some time
- I've been told I should
- **If I don't, I could miss important information about a job or social**

How frequently should I check my email?

- **At least once a day**
- Twice a day: once in the morning and again at night
- Every couple of weeks

Workplace paperwork

True or **False:** It's okay to add information that isn't true, like work experience, to make it look better to the person reviewing it.

What information should be included on a job application?

- Current address
- Past employment history

- Education history
- **All of the above**

How long should my resume be?

- **1 page**
- 2 pages

What is the purpose of a resume?

- To summarize my work experience
- To list my skills and abilities
- To sell myself to an employer and show that I'm the best candidate for the job
- **All of the above**

Assessing yourself

True or False: The Work Smarts assessment will help me identify a job that will be a good match for me.

If I wanted to be a fashion designer, which Work Smart intelligence would score the highest?

- **Picture**
- Word
- Body

If I like working outdoors and working with animals, which Work Smarts intelligence would I score highest on?

- Music
- Logic
- **Nature**

Getting organized with Google

True or False: I can set a filter on Gmail to automatically assign a label to the emails I receive.

What is the best size font to use in Gmail?

- Small
- **Normal**
- Huge

Google Slides is like which Microsoft program?

- **PowerPoint**

Google Docs is like which Microsoft program?

- **Word**

Good Sheets is like which Microsoft program?

- **Excel**

What type of storage is Google Drive?

- **Cloud**
- Hard drive computer

What can I do on Google Maps?

- Find an address
- Find directions to and from an address
- Estimate time travel between two locations by car, on a bus, or on foot
- **All of the above**

Interview essentials

True or False: An elevator pitch summarizes who I am, what I can do, and how I can benefit a company.

True or **False**: An elevator pitch should always stay the same and never change.

True or False: A mock interview is a good way to practice interviewing skills.

True or False: A personal reference is someone who knows me and can vouch for my character.

True or False: A professional reference is someone who has knowledge of my work skills.

What are the reasons to have a job?

- To find meaning in our lives
- To make money to pay our bills and have fun
- To meet people
- **All of the above**

What is an elevator pitch?

- Something you throw when playing baseball in an elevator
- **A commercial about myself that tells who I am in a minute or less**
- Something that I use to bring attention to myself

How long should an elevator pitch last?

- 5 minutes
- 10 minutes
- **15, 30, or 60 seconds, depending on where it's being used**

How many times should I practice my elevator pitch?

- **Once per day**
- Once every couple of days
- I'm already good and don't need to practice

Which of the ten frequently asked questions should my elevator pitch answer?

- **Tell me about yourself**
- What are your greatest weaknesses
- A situation where you solved a problem

What is the most important question to prepare for in advance of an interview?

- How old are you?
- **Why should I hire you?**
- What did you eat for lunch?

What three things should you take to an interview?

- My resume
- Five to ten questions to ask
- My elevator pitch
- **All of the above**

How many minutes early should I arrive to an interview or any important meeting?

- 1 hour
- **15 minutes**
- 0 minutes—I should arrive at the exact time of my interview

Which of the following are good questions to ask during an interview?

- What is a typical day like in the office?
- What do successful employees at this company have in common?
- What do you like most about working at this company?
- **All of the above**

Within how many days should I send a thank you email after an interview?

- The same day
- **2 days**
- 1 week

What should I be mindful of during an interview?

- What I say
- What I do
- How I look
- **All of the above**

If I have held a paying or volunteer job, who would be the best person to ask for a professional reference?

- My mom or dad
- My aunt or uncle
- **A former employer**

If I don't have any work experience, who would be the best person to ask for a personal reference?

- My cousin
- **A teacher**
- My neighbor

If I don't have a lot of work experience, what are not good places to consider when applying for a job?

- Places where I shop
- Local companies or business that make or do something I like
- **A large motion picture studio**

Landing a job

True or False: An unpaid internship is a good way to make professional contacts.

True or False: I should always ask for a business card from a professional that I meet.

True or False: Hard skills are specific to the job and typically learned in college or training programs.

True or **False**: The purpose of an informational interview is to get a job offer.

True or **False**: I should ask for a job in an informational interview.

What is the best source of jobs?

- **Referrals from friends, family, and former coworkers**
- Online job boards
- Walking in off the street and asking for a job

What is an informational interview used for?

- Ask for a job
- Collect a business card
- **Seek leads and information regarding an industry, career path, or employer**

When identifying someone to contact for an informational interview, who is the best person to start with?

- Someone I found on LinkedIn
- Someone I just met
- **A friend or relative**

What are ways to increase my network of professional contacts?

- Ask friends and relatives for referrals
- Through volunteer jobs and internships
- Attending Chamber of Commerce events
- Attending a job fair
- Through informational interviews
- **All of the above**

When meeting a professional contact, what should I do?

- Use the entire time to talk about myself
- Take a selfie with the person and immediately post it on social media
- **Ask for the person's business card before the conversation is over**

Which of these social media sites is most appropriate for making professional contacts?

- Facebook
- Pinterest
- **LinkedIn**

My digital footprint is:

- Private if I post or tweet information anonymously
- **A public record of everything I've posted, tweeted, or liked**
- Not reviewed by employers when making hiring decisions

Connecting with coworkers

True or **False**: It's a good idea to date your boss so you can get to know them better.

Why is it important to remember something my coworkers tell me about themselves?

- It shows I'm interested in what they are saying
- It gives me something to talk about next time I see them
- I might find out we have something in common
- People like it when we remember something about them
- **All of the above**

Which of the following topics are good to bring up with my coworkers when I am at work?

- Religion
- Politics
- **Weekend plans**

What would not be a good topic for small talk at work?

- What movies have you seen?
- What did you do over the weekend?
- **Who did you vote for president in the last election?**

If I want to ask a coworker out on a date, how many times can I ask?

- **Once**
- Twice
- I should keep asking until the person says yes

Why is it a good idea to start a conversation with someone I just met about their hobbies and interests?

- People like to talk about things they like
- I might find a common interest with the person
- If I ask about their work, they may not like their job and won't want to talk about it
- **All of the above**

Which of these questions are good to use to make small talk?

- When you're not at work, what do you like to do?
- What is your favorite sports team?
- What movie are you going to see this weekend?
- **All of the above**

How many messages in a row can I leave for someone if they don't respond to my first message?

- 1
- **2**
- 3

Which of the following are good things to do while I am at work?

- Smile and keep a positive attitude
- Find a workplace "buddy"
- Say please when making a request and thank you when someone helps me
- **All of the above**

Why should I care about what other candidates like to do?

- Because my instructor told me to
- **I might find out we have something in common**
- I don't need to care about what other candidates like to do

What are effective ways to positively communicate at work?

- Dress to match the workplace
- Use appropriate body language
- Use good posture
- **All of the above**

What would be a good time to do something casual away from work?

- For breakfast before work
- **For lunch at a nearby cafe**
- For drinks at a loud nightclub

Who said, "If you proposed to speak, always ask if it's true, if it's necessary, is it kind?"

- Barack Obama
- **Buddha**
- Gandhi

Dress for success

True or False: Attire for a law firm is more formal (i.e. suit and tie), than it is for a job at an entertainment company.

True or False: Dressing for success is dressing for the job.

True or False: If I don't dress appropriately for an interview, I probably won't get the job.

True or False: To best fit in at work, my clothes need to match the company culture of the workplace.

How much time does it take for someone to make a first impression?

- **10 seconds**
- 1 minute
- 10 minutes

What would be appropriate to wear to work on casual Fridays:

- A suit and tie
- **A polo shirt and khakis**
- A t-shirt and shorts

Understanding the workplace

True or **False**: I am required to disclose my disability to my employer.

True or False: The ADA applies to employers with 15 or more employers.

True or **False**: It's okay not to bring anything to a potluck at work if I don't plan to eat anything.

Disclosing a disability to an employer should:

- Be done to a supervisor or someone in HR
- Be done on a "need-to-know basis"
- Be done when requesting an accommodation
- **All of the above**

Title 1 of the ADA applies to companies with at least how many employees?

- 2
- **15**
- 50

Under the ADA, when may an employer ask an employee if they have a disability?

- During an interview
- After the job offer is extended
- **Never. It is illegal for an employer to ask an applicant or employee if they have a disability**

When should an employee disclose their disability:

- During a job interview
- When the job is offered
- **An employee does not have to disclose their disability**

What would be a reasonable accommodation under the ADA?

- A job coach to help learn social cues
- Noise-cancelling headphones
- Written instructions on how to do a task
- A list of priorities of job duties
- A desk lamp to replace overhead fluorescent light
- **All of the above**

Which president signed the ADA into law in 1990?

- Barack Obama
- **George H. W. Bush**
- Bill Clinton

When disclosing a disability, what should an employee *not* do?

- Disclose on a need-to-know basis to a supervisor or HR manager
- Provide details about their disability as it applies to their work-related accommodation
- **Tell their coworkers the first time they meet**

What can an employer ask or do in regard to an employee's disability?

- The type of disability the person has
- **A medical question after a job offer has been extended**
- A medical question not related to the person's disability

LINKS AND WEBSITES

Chapter 2: The Workplace Readiness Workshop

- Susan Osborne Autism Advocate: www.pinterest.com/sosborneawn

Chapter 3: Matching the Job to the Individual

- California Career Resource Network: www.californiacareers.info
- California Career Zone: careerzone.org
- Occupational Outlook Handbook: www.bls.gov/ooh
- JIST: http://jist.encp.com/work-smarts.html

Chapter 5: Dress for Success

- Old Navy®: http://oldnavy.gap.com

Chapter 6: Interview Essentials

- Vistaprint®: www.vistaprint.com

Social media sites

- CareerBuilder: www.careerbuilder.com
- Craigslist: www.craigslist.org/about/sites
- Facebook: www.facebook.com
- Indeed: www.indeed.com
- Indeed Career Guide: www.indeed.com/career-advice
- Instagram: www.instragram.com
- LinkedIn: www.linkedin.com
- Monster: www.monster.com
- Pinterest: www.pinterest.com

Creating a website

- Google Sites: https://sites.google.com
- IONOS: www.ionos.com
- iPage: www.ipage.com
- GoDaddy™: www.godaddy.com

Chapter 7: Landing a Job

- YouTube: How to Make an Elevator Pitch: www.youtube.com/watch?v=Noowl0ydDvA. Video is 4:17.

- YouTube: Elevator Pitch Examples for Students: www.youtube.com/watch?v=aDt6cukCz7k&t=38s. Video is 4:19.

Chapter 8: Connecting with Coworkers

- YouTube: Oprah's Gratitude Journal Oprah Winfrey Network: www.youtube.com/watch?v=saZWjllwU8c&t=9s. Video is 3:34.

- YouTube: Gratitude is Good for You: John Templeton Foundation: www.youtube.com/watch?v=sCV-mEsASLA. Video is 1:30.

- "A Remarkable Gift of Forgiveness": www.pressreader.com/usa/los-angeles-times/20180107/281629600661327

- "On Christmas Eve, A Stolen Bicycle and A Lesson in Giving": www.npr.org/2017/12/15/570806606/on-christmas-eve-a-stolen-bicycle-and-a-lessonin-giving

- 4 Great Conversation Starters. Small Talk Tips and Tricks: www.youtube.com/watch?v=5U3gWUuV1BI&t=2s&ab_channel=alpham. Video is 4:09.

Chapter 9: Understanding the Workplace

- State Child Abuse and Neglect Reporting Numbers: www.childwelfare.gov/resources/states-territories-tribes

In Closing

I hope this book has provided you with the resources you need to start your own workshop or support a client, friend, or family member in their journey in securing meaningful employment.

Sadly, our beloved Joanne Lara passed away in June 2020, which brought an end to the original Workshop, the Glorious Pies food truck business that Joanne started to employ our candidates, and the non-profits, Autism Movement Therapy and Autism Works Now.

Joanne was a force of nature. She was a special education teacher, ABA therapist, and the Executive Director of both of her non-profits. She was also a powerful advocate for children, teens, and adults on the autism spectrum. She is greatly missed, but she lives on in the hearts of all who knew and loved her. She also lives on through your work as well, with inspiration from this book and the Autism Works Now program.

If you have any comments, questions or just want to say hi, I would love to hear from you.

Thank you for all that you do in support of individuals with autism. I wish you much success!

Susan Osborne
Susan@spectrumhelpservices.com

References

AARPRachelA. (2020, September 11). *7 Ways to Cope with Anxiety During the Coronavirus Pandemic*. AARP Online Community. Retrieved on May 1, 2023 from https://community.aarp.org/t5/Leave-a-Health-Tip/7-Ways-to-Cope-with-Anxiety-During-the-Coronavirus-Pandemic/m-p/2316966.

Alfano, C.A., Beidel, D.C., and Turner, S.M. (2006). "Cognitive correlates of social phobia among children and adolescents." *Journal of Abnormal Child Psychology*, 34, 2, 182–194.

American RadioWorks (2014). *The Troubled History of Vocational Education*. Retrieved on May 21, 2017 from www.apmreports.org/episode/2014/09/09/the-troubled-history-of-vocational-education.

Autism Speaks (2024). Autism Spectrum Disorder. Retrieved on May 26, 2024 from www.autismspeaks.org/what-autism.

Bar, M., Neta, M., and Linz, H. (2006). "Very first impressions." *Emotion*, 6, 269–278.

Baron-Cohen, S. (1997). *Mindblindness: An Essay on Autism and Theory of Mind*. Cambridge, MA: MIT Press.

Billstedt, E., Gillberg, C., and Gillberg, C. (2005). "Autism after adolescence: Population-based 13-to 22-year follow-up study of 120 individuals with autism diagnosed in childhood." *Journal of Autism and Developmental Disorders*, 35, 3, 351–360.

Biswal, R. (2022). *Top 20 Most Popular Google Products and Services*. Retrieved on May 21, 2024 from www.ecloudbuzz.com/most-popular-google-products-services.

Blair, I.V., Judd, C.M., and Chapleau, K.M. (2004). "The influence of Afrocentric facial features in criminal sentencing." *Psychological Science*, 15, 674–679.

Bloomberg (2024). *Bloomberg Billionaire's Index*. Retrieved on May 28, 2024 from www.bloomberg.com/billionaires/profiles/warren-e-buffett.

Bock, M.A. (2001). "SODA Strategy: Enhancing the social interaction skills of youngsters with Asperger Syndrome." *Intervention in School and Clinic*, 36, 272–278.

Broadwater, L. (2018, January 7). "A Remarkable Gift of Forgiveness." *Los Angeles Times*.

Brown, M., Setren, E., and Topa, G. (2016) "Do informal referrals lead to better matches? Evidence from a firm's employee referral system." *Journal of Labor Economics*, 34, 1, 161–209.

Buron, K.D. and Curtis, M. (2003). *The Incredible 5-Point Scale: Assisting Students with Autism Spectrum Disorders in Understanding Social Interactions and Controlling Their Emotional Responses*. Shawnee Mission, KS: Autism Asperger Publishing Company.

California Department of Education (n.d.a). *Career Technical Education*. Retrieved on May 15, 2023 from www.cde.ca.gov/ci/ct.

California Department of Education (n.d.b). *The California Career Zone*. Retrieved on May 15, 2023 from www.cacareerzone.org.

California Department of Education (2023). *California Career Resource Network*. Retrieved on May 15, 2023 from www.californiacareers.info.

CareerBuilder (2014). *Number of Employers Passing on Applicants Due to Social Media Posts Continues to Rise, According to New CareerBuilder Survey*. Retrieved on March 8, 2017 from www.careerbuilder.com/share/aboutus/pressreleasesdetail.aspx?sd=6%2F26%2F2014&id=pr829&ed=12%2F31%2F2014.

Chery, K. (2024, January 22). *How to Practice Gratitude?* Verywellmind. Retrieved on February 13, 2024 from www.verywellmind.com/what-is-gratitude-5206817.

Devine, G. (2015). *10 Reasons to Dress for Success*. Retrieved on March 8, 2017 from www.linkedin.com/pulse/10-reasons-dress-success-gerard-devine.

Doyle, A. (2021a, January 13). *Who to Ask for a Job Reference?* Retrieved on May 15, 2023 from www.thebalancemoney.com/who-to-ask-for-job-reference-2060802.

Doyle, A. (2021b, June 9). *What is a Professional Reference?* Retrieved on May 15, 2023 from www.thebalancemoney.com/what-is-a-professional-reference-2062823.

Doyle, A. (2021c, June 9). *What is a Personal Reference?* Retrieved on May 15, 2021 from www.thebalancemoney.com/what-is-a-personal-reference-2062060.

Duffy, C. and O'Sulllivan, D. (2022, October 28). *Twitter confirms completion of Elon Musk's $44 billion acquisition deal*. Retrieved August 16, 2024 from https://www.cnn.com/2022/10/28/tech/elon-musk-twitter-deal-close/index.html.

Eberhardt, J.L., Davies, P.G., Purdie-Vaughns, V.J., and Johnson, S.L. (2006). "Looking deathworthy: Perceived stereotypicality of Black defendants predicts capital-sentencing outcomes." *Psychological Science*, 17, 383–386.

Esty-Kendell and Dorbin, I. (2017, December 15). *On Christmas Eve, a Stolen Bicycle and a Lesson in Giving*. NPR Story, Corp. Retrieved on May 15, 2023 from www.npr.org/2017/12/15/570806606/on-christmas-eve-a-stolen-bicycle-and-a-lesson-in-giving.

Fisher, R., Ury, W.L., and Patton, B. (2011). *Getting to Yes: Negotiating Agreement Without Giving In*. New York: Penguin.

Founder, J. (n.d.). *How to Create a Memorable Student Business Card*. Retrieved on May 1, 2023 from www.theintern-hustle.com/create-memorable-student-business-card.

Gardner, H. (1991). *The Unschooled Mind: How Children Think and How Schools Should Teach*. New York: Basic Books.

Giffords Courage to Fight Gun Violence (2023). *Gabby's Story*. Retrieved on May 15, 2023 from https://giffords.org/about/gabbys-story.

Google. (2006, October 9). *Google to Acquire YouTube for $1.65 in Stock*. Retrieved August 17, 2024 from https://www.sec.gov/Archives/edgar/data/1288776/000119312506206884/dex991.htm.

Guerin, L. (2017a). *Employment at Will: What Does it Mean?* Retrieved on March 8, 2017 from www.nolo.com/legal-encyclopedia/employment-at-will-definition-30022.html.

Guerin, L. (2017b). *Types of Employment Contracts*. Retrieved on March 8, 2017 from www.nolo.com/legal-encyclopedia/types-employment-contracts.html.

HG.org (2017). *What Is Employment Law?* Retrieved on March 8, 2017 from www.hg.org/employ.html.

Hierarchy Structure (n.d.). *Company Employee Hierarchy*. Retrieved on March 8, 2017 from www.hierarchystructure.com/company-employee-hierarchy.

Home at 30. (2019a, May 13). *How to Make an Elevator Pitch*. [Video]. YouTube. Retrieved on June 1, 2023 from https://youtube.com/watch?v=Noowl0ydDvA.

Home at 30. (2019b, May 13). *Elevator Pitch Examples for Students*. [Video]. YouTube. Retrieved on June 1, 2023 from https://youtube.com/watch?v=aDt6cukCz7k&t=38s.

House, J.S., Landis, K.R., and Umberson, D. (1988). "Social relationships and health." *Science*, 241, 4865, 540–545.

Hughes, M. (2023, June 15). *How to find your ikigai*. Retrieved on October 1, 2023 from https://mindtoolsbusiness.com/resources/blog/what-is-your-ikigai.

Ingram, D. (2016). *Why Is Organizational Structure Important?* Retrieved on March 8, 2017 from http://smallbusiness.chron.com/organizational-structure-important-3793.html.

John Templeton Foundation. (2015, November 18). *Gratitude Is Good for You*. [Video]. YouTube. Retrieved on June 1, 2023 from www.youtube.com/watch?v=sCV-mEsASLA.

Kahneman, D. and Deaton, A. (2010). "High income improves evaluation of life but not emotional well-being." *Proceedings of the National Academy of Sciences*, 107, 38, 16489–16493.

Kerpen, D. (2020, June 18). *9 Moments to Appreciate Every Day if You Truly Want to Be Happy*. Retrieved on May 1, 2023 from www.themuse.com/advice/9-moments-appreciate-every-day-be-truly-happy.

Kilmann, R.H. and Thomas, K.W. (1975). "Interpersonal conflict-handling behavior as reflections of Jungian personality dimensions." *Psychological Reports*, 37, 3, 971–980.

Lancaster, V. (2023, March 8). *Why Kindness Matters*. Psychology Today. Retrieved on May 15, 2023 from www.psychologytoday.com/us/blog/everyday-resilience/202303/the-remarkable-power-of-kindness-and-why-it-matters#:~:text=Key%20points,in%20the%20world%20of%20another.m.

Lara, J. (2015). *Autism Movement Therapy® Method: Waking Up the Brain!* London: Jessica Kingsley Publishers.

LaSalle Network (2015). *LaSalle Network Explores Top Job Interview Trends*. Retrieved on March 8, 2017 from https://thelasallenetwork.com/newsroom/new-lasalle-network-explores-top-jobinterview-trends.

Liptak, J. and Allen, P. (2009). *Work Smarts: Using Multiple Intelligences to Make Better Career Choices*. St. Paul, MN: Jist Publishing.

Little, A.C., Burriss, R.P., Jones, B.C., and Roberts, S.C. (2007). "Facial appearance affects voting decisions." *Evolution and Human Behavior*, 28, 18–27.

Marino, A. [iamalpham]. (2015, April 11). *4 Great Conversation Starters. Small Talk Tips and Tricks*. [Video]. YouTube. Retrieved on May 15, 2023 from www.youtube.com/watch?v=5U3gWUuV1BI&t=2s&ab_channel=alpham.

Mavi, M. (2018, May 7). *10 Rules for Building a Stronger, More Positive Self Image*. Retrieved May 15, 2023 from www.atriumstaff.com/10-rules-for-building-stronger-positive-self-image.

McKnight, P.E. and Kashdan, T.B. (2009). "Purpose in life as a system that creates and sustains health and well-being: An integrative, testable theory." *Review of General Psychology*, 13, 3, 242–251.

MindTools (2011). *Conflict resolution: Using the interest-based relational approach*. Retrieved on March 8, 2017 from www.mindtools.com/pages/article/newLDR_81.htm.

Monster (2017). *What's the difference between exempt and nonexempt employees?* Retrieved on March 8, 2017 from www.monster.com/career-advice/article/whats-the-difference-between-exempt.

Montepare, J.M. and Zebrowitz, L.A. (1998). "Person perception comes of age: The salience and significance of age in social judgments." *Advances in Experimental Social Psychology*, 30, 93–161.

Moore Norman Technology Center Employment Guide. (n.d.). Retrieved December 30, 2016 from https://career-connection.mntc.edu/sites/default/files/public/mntcemploymentguidefy142.pdf.

Moraine, P. (2015). *Autism and Everyday Executive Function: A Strengths-Based Approach for Improving Attention, Memory, Organization, and Flexibility*. London: Jessica Kingsley Publishers.

Nationwide (n.d.). *How Much Do Small Businesses Pay in Taxes?* Retrieved on May 15, 2023 from www.nationwide.com/business/solutions-center/finances/how-much-small-businesses-pay-taxes#:~:text=Income%20tax%3A%20Small%20business%20.

Prakash, P. (2022, March 31). *DBA (Doing Business As): What Is It and How Do I Register*. Retrieved on May 15, 2023 from www.nerdwallet.com/article/small-business/dba-doing-business-as.

Pritchett, E. (2018, January 23). *Small Business Marketing 101*. Retrieved on May 23, 2023 from www.forbes.com/sites/forbesbusinessdevelopmentcouncil/2018/01/23/small-business-marketing-101/?sh=3b40e51d45ff.

Reference.com (2017). *What Is the Purpose of a Human Resources Department?* Retrieved on March 8, 2017 from www.reference.com/business-finance/purpose-human-resources-department-82c1cc6e20b894b?qo=contentSimilar Questions.

Rosenthal, M., Wallace, G.L., Lawson, R., Wills, M.C., *et al.* (2013). "Impairments in real-world executive function increase from childhood to adolescence in autism spectrum disorders." *Neuropsychology*, 27, 1, 13.

Smith. R. (2016, January 13). *46 Companies that Hire People with Special Needs*. Retrieved on May 15, 2023 from https://noahsdad.com/special-need-employers.

Steger. M.F. (2009, June 9). *Meaningful Work: What Makes Work Meaningful?* (Psychology Today blog). Retrieved on March 13, 2017 from www.psychologytoday.com/blog/the-meaning-inlife/200906/meaningful-work.

Stoeffel, K. (2015, April). *How to Date (Responsibly) at Work*. Retrieved on January 16, 2017 from www.glamour.com/story/dating-at-work-rules-for-dating-coworkers-tips-advice.

The Global Eagles. (2013, October 26). *Oprah's Gratitude Journal. Oprah's Lifeclass Oprah Winfrey Network* [Video]. YouTube. Retrieved on June 1, 2023 from www.youtube.com/watch?v=saZWjIlwU8c.

The North Dakota Statewide Developmental Disabilities Staff Training Program. Minot State University Center of Excellence. (2018, April). *Positive Behavior Support*. Retrieved on November 1, 2023 from https://ndcpd.org/wp-content/uploads/sites/16/2021/06/MOD-.51-Positive-Behavior-Supports-4-18.pdf.

UCLA Mindful Awareness Research Center (n.d.). *Guided Mediations*. Retrieved on November 1, 2023 from www.uclahealth.org/programs/marc/free-guided-meditations/guided-meditations.

United States Department of Labor (n.d.a). *Employment Law Guide: Laws, Regulations, and Technical Assistance Services*. Retrieved on March 13, 2017 from http://webapps.dol.gov/elaws/elg/minwage.htm.

United States Department of Labor (n.d.b). *Minimum Wage*. Retrieved on August 16, 2024 from https://www.dol.gov/agencies/whd/minimum-wage.

United States Department of Labor (n.d.c). *Workers' Compensation*. Retrieved August 17, 2024 from https://www.dol.gov/general/topic/workcomp.

United States Department of Labor, Wage and Hour Division. (n.d.d.) *Family and Medical Leave Act*. Retrieved August 16, 2024 from https://www.dol.gov/agencies/whd/fmla.

United States Department of Labor, Bureau of Labor Statistics (2016a). Table A-6. *Employment Status of the Civilian Population by Sex, Age, and Disability Status, not Seasonally Adjusted*. Retrieved on March 13, 2017 from www.bls.gov/news.release/empsit.t06.htm.

United States Department of Labor, Bureau of Labor Statistics (2016b). *American Time Use Survey*. Retrieved on October 25, 2016 from www.bls.gov/tus/charts.

United States Department of Labor, Bureau of Labor Statistics. (2017, May). Table A-6. *Employment Status of the Civilian Population by Sex, Age, and Disability Status, not Seasonally Adjusted*. Retrieved on January 15, 2017 from www.bls.gov/news.release/empsit.t06.htm.

United States Department of Labor, Bureau of Labor Statistics (2023, February). *Persons with a Disability: Labor Force Characteristics—2022*. Retrieved May 15, 2023 from www.bls.gov/news.release/pdf/disabl.pdf.

United States Department of Labor, Employment and Training Administration, Fact Sheet. (1989, February). *The Worker Adjustment and Retraining Notification Act*. Retrieved on March 13, 2107 from www.dol.gov/agencies/eta/layoffs/warn.

United States Department of Labor, Occupational Safety and Health Administration (n.d.). *How to File a Safety Complaint*. Retrieved on March 13, 2017 from www.osha.gov/workers/file_complaint.html.

United States Department of Labor, Office of Disability Employment Policy (2013). *Job Accommodation Network. Employees with Autism Spectrum Disorder*. Retrieved on May 21, 2017 from https://uniquelyabledproject.org/wp-content/uploads/JANs-Accommodation-and-Compliance-Series-Employees-with-Autism-Spectrum-Disorder.pdf.

United States Internal Revenue Service (2016). *Independent Contractor Defined*. Retrieved on March 13, 2017 from www.irs.gov/businesses/small-businesses-self-employed/independent-contractor-defined.

United States Internal Revenue Service (2024). *Estimated Taxes*. Retrieved on May 26, 2024 from www.irs.gov/businesses/small-businesses-self-employed/estimated-taxes.

University of California Berkeley, Career Center. (2016). *Informational Interviews*. Retrieved on March 13, 2017 from https://career.berkeley.edu/start-exploring/informational-interviews.

U.S. Equal Employment Opportunity Commission (n.d.a). *Fact Sheet: Disability Discrimination*. Retrieved on March 13, 2017 from www.eeoc.gov/eeoc/publications/fs-ada.cfm.

U.S. Equal Employment Opportunity Commission (n.d.b). *Harassment*. Retrieved on March 13, 2017 from www.eeoc.gov/laws/types/harassment.cfm.

U.S. Equal Employment Opportunity Commission (n.d.c). *Sexual Harassment*. Retrieved on March 13, 2017 from www.eeoc.gov/laws/types/sexual_harassment.cfm.

U.S Equal Employment Opportunity Commission. (2002, October). *Enforcement Guidance: Reasonable Accommodation and Undue Hardship Under the Americans with Disabilities Act*. Retrieved on March 13, 2017 from www.eeoc.gov/policy/docs/accommodation.html.

U.S. Equal Employment Opportunity Commission. (2017, February). *United States Department of Justice, Civil Rights Division. Americans with Disabilities Act, Questions and Answers*. Retrieved on March 13, 2017 from www.ada.gov/archive/q&aeng02.htm.

Wellbeing People. (n.d.). *The Importance of an Engaging Community*. Retrieved on December 3, 2023 from https://wellbeingpeople.com/workplace-wellbeing/the-importance-of-an-engaging-community/2023.

Willis, J. and Todorov, A. (2006). "First impressions: Making up your mind after a 100-ms exposure to a face." *Psychological Science*, 17, 7, 592–598.

Wright, S. (2009). *Three Components of Meaningful Work*. Retrieved on March 13, 2017 from www.new.meaningandhappiness.com/meaningful-work/360.

Yager, J. (1999). *Friendships: The Power of Friendship and How it Shapes our Lives*. Stamford, CT: Hannacroix Creek Books.

Zebrowitz, L.A. and McDonald, S.M. (1991). "The impact of litigants' baby-facedness and attractiveness on adjudications in small claims courts." *Law and Behavior*, 15, 6, 603–662.